I WAS
ELVIS PRESLEY'S
BASTARD LOVE-CHILD

&

other stories of
Rock'n'Roll excess

by ANDREW DARLINGTON

CRITICAL VISION
an imprint of **HEADPRESS**

A Critical Vision Book
Published in 2001
by Headpress

Critical Vision
PO Box 26
Manchester
M26 1PQ
Great Britain
email: info.headpress@telinco.co.uk
www.headpress.com/

I Was Elvis Presley's Bastard Love-Child

British Library Cataloguing in Publication Data
A catalogue record for this book is available from the British Library.

ISBN 1 900486 17 2

For Catherine for her patient and long-suffering indulgence through the years these features were written.

With thanks to HOT PRESS *for a twenty year association, to* ROCK'N'REEL, JAMMING, ZIG ZAG, TERMINAL, IT (INTERNATIONAL TIMES) *and other publications in which the original versions of some of these interviews first appeared, and for creating the opportunities for me to do them in the first place.*

Although all interviews have been extensively revised and rewritten, I have left unaltered the contemporaneous sense of time and place.

Ingredients

Andy has been a persistent seeker after the Ether since about the age of ten when he would walk the full nine miles to the library at Beverley and back to get a fix of Rosemary Sutcliffe or Henry Treece. One day, on the way, he asked a gang of construction workers what they were building. They replied that it was the launch-pad for a spaceship project. Since then, whenever he has passed that site he has seen not an Auto-showroom but a "giant spacecraft straining against the undertow of gravity, like the power of dreams and myth straining against this drabness."

Fractured Art
Splintered Stories

Andy is a poet, but he is also an intrepid pioneer at the edges of all things creative and life-affirming: editor, publisher, journalist, writer of fiction, promoter/entrepreneur, Poet for Sale, often simultaneously. Rocketing around the country to bring back the next interview for *Hot Press*, *The Edge*, *Zig Zag*, *Knave*, *Jamming* or *Rock'n'Reel*, writing the legendary 'Lost Book' on Martin Fry, or riding through the night from club to pub, gig to cabaret, often finding that the gig in question, difficult to get to and not cheap on an artist's wage, despite being well publicised has just a few drunks as audience. Un-

Foreword by
Michael Butterworth

daunted — Andy takes advantage of the deserted stage to practise his microphone techniques. Arriving at a gig before an audience of deaf drunken students once, on the same bill as Richard Mason and Henry Normal, he discovered they had been promoted as 'Three Comedians' and — darn it — found that he was clean out of mother-in-law jokes. "Why the fuck do we do it?" he asked me. "I'll tell you why we do it," he answered before I could reply, "… 'cos it gets the adrenaline *roaring*."

Andy and I are kind of epistolary soul mates who go back thirty years to when we edited small press magazines and cross-pollinated each other's periodicals. We have only occasionally met. We were both born in 1947, and I am the elder — by a couple of months. We also have this in common: as kids we both listened to Jet Morgan's weekly *Journey into Space* on the radio and watched the first episodes of *Quatermass* on black-and-white TV. For all I know, we also played Boris ('Boris') Pickett and the Crypt-Kickers, stayed up nights to watch the moonlandings, knew exactly where we were when we read that Jimi Hendrix had died, and took our first acid on a sugar cube.

The magazine Andy was editing when he contacted me as long ago as 1971 was called *Ludd's Mill*, a community alternative which he and fellow poet Steve Sneyd rescued from obscurity. They were using it as a vehicle for articles on the likes of Mark Mothersbaugh, William Burroughs, Bix Beiderbecke, Jack Kerouac, ———, ———… tab in who you want. The Right People. Ever since, we have exchanged images and words, the latest being Andy's *Euroshima Mon Amour*, a selection of his poems from the last twenty-five years.

To get these interviews with Rock's baddest, saddest and maddest, Andy has braved penury, alcoholic nirvana and physical harm. He brings a consistent curiosity and freshness to his subjects, and everyone should read them. If I've one gripe about this majestic Headpress book it's that there is no room in it for the rest of Andy's interviews to complete the picture — Patrick Moore, Jack Dee, Prince Naseem's trainer Brendan Ingle, M John Harrison, Carolyn Cassady, William Burroughs, Kurt Vonnegut, E C Tubb and others, which together show the rich variety of the gestalt of this uncanonised saint of Rock'n'Roll, SF and literature of North Humberside and West Yorks.

As Andy once told me: "Man's true environment is the mind… I concede no limitations, or no barriers in art. It all, after analysis, must stem from the same universal source… the poetry of Philip Lamantia, the art of Dali's *Premonitions of Civil War* period, the music of Stockhausen's 'Mixtur' or the images of Strindberg's plays… In the same way that The Who repaints Peter Blake in musical terms. The difference is surely only one of language."

The musical form is not the sole port of entry, or the music subject the sole muse of the sublime.

When I eventually teamed up with David Britton, Andy set his energy and knowledge to paying obeisance to the Black Flag, first writing about us for *International Times* in an article called 'Doin' That Savoy Shuffle', then, more recently, penning the sleeve notes for the *Savoy Wars* CD.

There is one other thing you should know about Andy. He is constantly asking for more sex in our comics. Hardly a letter goes by without a request for more cocksucking and general debauchery. Apart from this he would make very good company at the dinner table of Francis Bacon and Lord Horror.

It is an honour to know the man.

Bo Diddley!

Darlington photo manipulation: Neil Taylor

I WAS ELVIS PRESLEY'S
BASTARD
LOVE-CHILD

It's a quarter of a century after his death at Graceland, but some of us are still goofin' on Elvis. Perhaps it's genetic? Perhaps it's autobiography, something to do with the way records wrap themselves around whatever emotion you happen to be hooked into when you first hear them? Or perhaps it's recognition of a purely animalistic genius that comes totally untainted by intellect? Whatever, this is a personal orbit around my real father, and a quest to discover exactly what it is we are supposed to respect about Elvis.

 y biological father died on Sunday, November 28, 1993, after falling downstairs drunk and never regaining consciousness.

My real father was discovered on the bathroom floor of Graceland, August 16, 1977, and was pronounced dead at 3:30pm having never regained consciousness.

I first met my biological father when I was sixteen. By then it was too late. I already had the albums. Lacking a male parental role model I'd already decoded sexual mores by studying Elvis. Specifically the texts of the movies. I was Presley's Bastard Love-Child. He taught me all I need to know.

Barbara Stanwyck is in *Roustabout* in which Elvis is Charlie Rogers, a scrupulously clean soft-option *Easy Rider*-lite drifter-on-a-(Japanese)-motorcycle. Barbara Stanwyck is now a Nun, but has a son who claims to be a Presley Love-Child. It could well be true. I must have thousands of bastard siblings out there with the same hereditary ghost of a lip-curling sneer, the same slicked-back hair. In the movie Elvis shows lingering traces of his earlier mean surliness and sexually

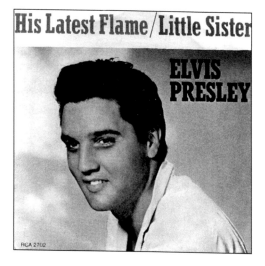

His Latest Flame / Little Sister
ELVIS PRESLEY
RCA 2702

charged predatory behaviour. "You never quit, do you?" she accuses. "No, I never quit" agrees Elvis. "You must get your face slapped a lot." "About fifty-fifty" he concedes. This is part of my education in seduction technique.

When an artist dies, the relationship we have with their work goes through instant transformations. Michael Stipe looks me straight in the eye and sings 'Andy, have you heard about this one… / Andy, are you goofin' on Elvis, hey Baby?' Well, yes, Michael, it's 2001 and I'm still goofin' on

Elvis.

Elvis was born in a two-room plank house raised off the ground on concrete and brick struts. There was a porch, three windows, and a pointed roof. In *Loving You* he is Deke Rivers. A poor-white orphan who chose his name from a tombstone. It's left to Susan (Dolores Hart) to detect the hurt and vulnerability that lurks beneath the impenetrably cool veneer of the Presley sneer. She wants to soothe this angry tenderness. At sixteen I identify with and mimic those same careful profiles of rejection through my acne and NHS spectacles. Without the same seismic female response. In life, and in *Loving You*, Elvis re-constructs himself from small-town squalor to Rock'n'Roll stardom. According to another, much later movie, it was a kid called Forrest Gump who first taught Elvis to twitch his hips. But no, Elvis was a natural. If God hadn't intended Elvis to be King he wouldn't have invented the 45rpm vinyl seven-inch single.

I'm an atheist, anti-monarchist, predominantly heterosexual male. But (to paraphrase Pete Townshend) Elvis inspired in me the closest I ever came to religious feeling. I know Elvis was the only king that mattered. I was there at his investiture. And since his death there's been nothing but a republic. In the movie *True Romance* Christian Slater says "If I had to fuck a guy, I'd fuck Elvis". Me too. To surrender up my anal virginity to a thrusting Big Hunk O' Presley pelvis would be an epiphany. An act of reverence.

"Gee Vince" says the Groupie in *Jailhouse Rock*, "when you sing it's really Gonesville." She's not wrong. Still.

A HUNKA HUNKA BURNIN' LOVE

1964 is monochrome. The blacks blacker and the whites whiter than they are now. I'm sixteen and already fucked-up. I measure time in issues of comics. And hit records. A Big Hunk O' Love, I Need Your Love Tonight, A Mess Of Blues, His Latest Flame. English culture is dead. I can't rationalise it. But I can feel it. I read Stan Barstow and Alan Sillitoe, recognise their Working Class unease and their depiction of being trapped in claustrophobic Northern drabness. They help define my dissatisfaction. But they can't show me escape. Elvis is napalm. He alone understands my sexuality.

I first meet my biological father this same year. But he can't measure up. By then it is too late. Elvis has already taught me all I need to know. In *Jailhouse Rock* he is Vince Everett, an ex-con on the make. In the brooding intense monochrome in which blacks are blacker and whites whiter he abruptly and without warning kisses Peggy (Judy Tyler). "How dare you think such cheap tactics would work with me?" she protests indignantly. Elvis knows his James Dean. In full magnificently sensual drawl he retorts "That ain't tactics, Honey. That's just the beast in me." That's lesson two.

But wait — let's analyse this properly. When I argue against monarchy, which I frequently do, what is it, I suggest, that we are expected to respect? I respect creativity. Writers, musicians, artists. People who produce work that is inventive, innovative, exciting. I respect that. But what exactly have royalty *done*, beyond genetic accident, to deserve respect? But turn that one around. What did *ELVIS* create? To Jerry Lee Lewis (in the book, *Killer*, by Charlie White) Elvis is "King Kong, the world's biggest trained monkey".

I read an interview with Jordanaire Gordon Stoker. He had what he considered to be an amusing anecdote illustrating Elvis' relationship with huckster manager Colonel Tom Parker. It goes like this. Elvis has an appointment with the Colonel. He goes into the Colonel's office. The

Colonel tells him what he's going to do, the next shit movie he must shoot, the sub-standard soundtrack recording schedule he must follow. Elvis goes "Yessir Mr Parker, Yessir Mr Parker" at intervals as required. Then Elvis leaves the office. Later, goofin' and spoofing with the boys, they snigger, imitate and send-up the interview like schoolkids who've just been to the headmaster's office. This, from the world's biggest star! Think about it. John Lennon tolerates Brian Epstein's commercial strategies until he outgrows their usefulness. The Rolling Stones allow Andrew Loog Oldham to manage their career growth for as long as it is convenient for them. And Michael Jackson? Just to pose the question is to answer it. But Elvis' career is dragged into the deepest pits of commercial and musical disrepute by the ineptitude and petty-minded grubbiness of his management, and he has neither the will nor the artistic vision to stand out against that process.

There's evidence that during the early studio work he exercised a kind of tireless perfection. Subsequently released session out-takes confirm this. Hound Dog was selected from thirty-one gruelling takes as Elvis sought to transfer to vinyl the sound he heard in his head. Even later when he felt his status was under threat, he could reconnect with that 'beast in me'. His come-back album following his army years — *Elvis Is Back,* is among the most powerful work he ever committed to disc. Its range and depth goes from the most perfect Pop ever recorded (Girl Of My Best Friend, Dirty Dirty Feeling), to Presleyised standards (Fever, Such A Night) and his finest Blues covers (Reconsider Baby, Like A Baby). When he felt under pressure he could produce work of genius. It was the very devotional uncritical loyalty of us, his fans, that worked against him. No matter what dross he recorded we'd buy it by the millions. He didn't have to try. And because he didn't *have* to try, he didn't.

The perfectionist fine-tuning of material that once resulted in those thirty-one takes for Hound Dog seems to have later resurfaced only on the sacred albums, where Elvis personally arranged traditional gospel and spiritual songs such as In My Father's House, Swing Down Sweet Chariot and Farther Along. It sometimes seems that beneath the gold lamé exterior, Elvis, an early champion of close-harmony vocal groups such as the Inkspots, felt most at ease working in that group context. Which is why he chose to record with the Jordanaires in the first place. The gospel albums *His Hand In Mine* and *How Great Thou Art* bear this out. Lynn Segal (professor of gender studies at Middlesex University) says that, towards the end of his life, Elvis always came on stage "bejewelled and bewigged, essentially in drag" (*Changing Masculinities, Changing Men,* Virago). But even then, as late as the 1970 road-movie *Elvis: That's The Way It Is,* away from the tacky grandeur of that stage persona-in-virtual-drag, the sequence he seems most emotionally involved with is an impromptu group vocal jam of gospel songs in a rehearsal studio around a piano.

So, beyond offering a role model to a sexually awkward and fucked-up adolescent, what is it in Elvis that we respect? He didn't write. He gets co-writer credits on All Shook Up and Don't Be Cruel shared with prolific R&B writer Otis Blackwell. But Presley's contribution to the songs, beyond minor lyric alterations during recording, is open to question. He also supposedly co-wrote the four songs that he sings in his first movie. Perhaps he did. The other composer-name bracketed on the *Love Me Tender* EP label with Elvis is Vera Matson, wife of musical director Ken Darby. But, Mick Farren suggests (in *Elvis: The Complete Illustrated Record*), it was that self-same Ken Darby "who was solely responsible for the soundtrack score. The reason for such contortions was strictly a question of finance". There was a technique used by jobbing Pop writers in the 1950s as an inducement to get stars to record their work and hence guarantee royalties. That technique was to offer the bribe of part-writing credits. This, according to Farren, is the real story.

Some years later — 1962 — a further credit turns up on the *Pot Luck* album, written apparently with Bobby 'Red' West of the 'Memphis Mafia'. That's Someone You Never Forget is a ponderously slow ballad reportedly intended as a tribute to Presley's recently deceased Mother. Then there's You'll Be Gone — a B-side recorded March 18, 1962, with the classic line-up of guitarist Scotty Moore, pianist Floyd Cramer, drummer DJ Fontana, and saxist Boots Randolph. It supposedly began as a florid Italianate attempt to replicate the Begin The Beguine format, and is also the product of a Presley/West hook-up. There were to be no further writing credits. And even among these dubiously authorised by-lines there's little of lasting worth. You'll Be Gone, incidentally, was finally issued in 1964, flipped under a movie song called Do The Clam — which, in turn, was co-written by Dolores Fuller, a former actress and 'Superstar' in several Ed Wood Jr films!

MYSTERY (S)TRAIN

Well, it's a one for the money!
Two for the money!!
Three for the money, now go cat go!

When an artist dies, they leave a persistent shadow that continues for an intense period after they've gone. Their songs have a way of wrapping themselves around whatever emotions you happen to be hooked into when you first hear them. I am Elvis Presley's Bastard Love-Child. It's hard to be objective. To Albert Goldman Elvis was "good and evil in more or less equal parts". He could sing gospel with a sincerity pure enough to touch the soul of the most atheistic cynic. And he sang Rock'n'Roll like napalm, through that 'beast in me'.

In *Roustabout* 'Charlie' riles college kids by taunting them over their 'panty raids', and gets riled himself over their retaliatory taunts about his rootless lack of parentage. Pace Deke. Pace me. "You mean there's a real me?" enquires the movie-Elvis existentially. "You ought to know. You fight with him enough" she parries. But it's wrong to read too much into such filmic repartee. As an actor Elvis initially tries his best. Memorises his own lines, and those of the rest of the cast too. Studies James Dean and carefully reproduces his rebel angst at its most charismatic in *King Creole*. But essentially the films are extended promotional videos.

Between March 25, 1961, (Pearl Harbour, Hawaii benefit) and July 26, 1969, (Las Vegas International Hotel) Elvis does not play a single live date. Neither does he appear on TV from May 12, 1960, (*The Frank Sinatra Timex Show*) to December 1968 (*Elvis NBC-TV Special*). This seems incredible now when selling an album is a two-year project involving a strategic sequence of spin-off singles — each with its concept video, and a tie-in high-profile world tour. But during a period in which Elvis scored twelve straight UK No 1 hits, including It's Now Or Never, Are You Lonesome Tonight, She's Not You, and Return To Sender, there is no promotional activity whatever. Not only does he not tour Britain, but he doesn't tour *anywhere!* The inept three-a-year movies tour in their stead. As cinematic works they may be cringeworthy garbage, but that is to miss the point. They exist solely as vehicles to carry the Presley image to the world.

And on video, fast-forwarding through the junk dialogue, fake fights, and phoney glamour, it's still possible to glimpse something of what Elvis *did* create. To the sophisticated BeBop Jazzers and the precise interpretative phrasing of Sinatra who preceded him, Presley was an eruption of illiteracy, a musical mindlessness. They were right. Even when he covered Blues or R&B, the Presley versions are more crude, raw, and spontaneous than the often sly and knowing Black originals he lifted from. Elvis might not have understood it himself. His genius comes unfiltered by thought. Untainted by intellect. What he has comes naturally. The most perfect physicality of any recording artist, ever. He was incapable of rationalising it. He just felt it, on a deeply primitive, almost cellular level. When he lost it he didn't know what he'd lost or how to go about recapturing it.

He only had the voice. And yes, even bejewelled and bewigged, that could still be pretty damn good. Even to the end. As his Bastard Love-Child, it still gets me every time. Never fails. No biological father could ever measure up to that.

ALL SHOOK UP

Now it's the next century. And it's Prodigy live at Temple Newsam Park, Leeds. It rips your head. Trying to sleep afterwards, the flashbacks continue strobing inside your skull. You see Keith Flint drooling and leering, spitting fire and smoke, sucking blood and devouring human flesh. A grotesque exaggerated cartoon, Charles Laughton's Quasimodo gone wrong, everyone's nightmare scary nutter sat next to you on the last bus to Hades, feral and damned. Is Keith dangerous? on overload? or just a roll of Andrex to Liam Howlett's Labrador puppy? Whatever, Prodigy is an unnatural phenomenon with a zero-tolerance boredom threshold. And they exist in the forbidden zone where (what Americans call) Digi-Rock meets Chernobyl.

And then there's Beck, a giant Rubik Cube of all-over dead-pan humour and angular riffs, coming on for his umpteenth encore dragged up in full Rhinestone Cowboy gear as his band prance in horses heads, and DJ Small impossibly scratches out Smoke On The Water with just two turntables and a microphone. An OD is stretchered off while his delighted girlfriend takes Family Album photos of it all for posterity. And there's an Auto-Geddon sculpture of impacted VW Camper Vans with painted-on Dinosaurian ribcage structures Dub-Henged into a mystic techno-collage you can walk through. While Bluetones, harder than last time we saw them, but still kitten-soft, do Heartbreak Hotel, their tribute to the portly drugs'n'burger-meister who (allegedly) returned home twenty years ago this day. "Hope you're not one of the cynical ones who believe he's dead" demands Mark Morriss earnestly. And just for once, I suspend disbelief.

And then Prodigy stomp all over everything. They ignite on maximum, with Smack My Bitch Up (or, as Chumbawamba prefer, "Smack My Keith Up"), working on up through the psychotic toyshop of Fat Of The Land plussed out with Voodoo People and Poison, enhanced by Gizz Butts (aka Janus Stark) of English Dogs, and it's a study in dementia that not even a sudden ten-minute halt to prevent excess front-line crushing and the high body-count extraction of cracked-rib casualties etc, can impede. It's otherwise seamless. It rates 10,000rpm and Digging it Yeah on the Weird-Shit-O-Meter. Noise is its native language, and its only laws are the 140bpm sonic cosh, sound waves so intense, so dense that they curdle your cerebral fluid. "I'm on peak" announces Maxim, "performing 100 per cent proof," his head cricking like it's disconnected. An alien biohazard resulting from some forbidden neural atrocity. It's beyond dispute. Prodigy are vicious, disgusting, and beautifully drawn, their Not-Quite-Right-In-The-Brain card on permanent display. It rips your head. Prodigy is awesome. The end of history. The culmination of the hundred-year evolution adrenaline rush of helter-skelter musical momentum. This is what Presley died on the crapper for. This is what Charlie 'Bird' Parker accelerated Jazz through quantum heroin-hell for. This legitimises Dylan's Motor-Psycho Nightmare. This is what Joe Meek blew his own head off for. What Peter Green crucified himself on. It's the vomit Hendrix choked on, the smell of napalm in the morning. It justifies Lennon's assassination, and the Cuba crisis, Sid & Nancy's diseased love, Charlie Manson's ritual slaughter, Cobain's pain, and Lou Reed's im-maculate fix. It's all in here, from Punk to Metal through maximum voltage and back out again. Beyond this there can be nothing but regression. The culmination of a millennium is here and now, and it's stunning.

Sometimes truth comes in strange disguises. Today it comes midpoint in this mutant notion of Love and Peace, paved in regurgitated pizza and veggie noodles. The noise-soundtrack of my life makes your ears sore and your arse so numb it's like it belongs to someone else. You're going to throw up any minute. It tastes raw, post-ironic and distressed. What it lacks in taste it makes up for in pace and in your face. It says Cake? Let them eat *drugs…!* But it's the greatest legal high on Earth. And trying to sleep afterwards, the flashbacks begin strobing inside your skull all over again.

© Dogger

LEFTFIELD IN MOTION
LET'S GET ELECTRIFIED!

If Pop is sexy, then Dance is its most erogenous zone. And while rhythm is a dancer, it's as serious as cancer. This is Neil Barnes. He is fifty per cent of **LEFTFIELD**. *Cut him, and his blood pulses dance rhythms. "This could have been any city..." to quote Leftfield's contribution to the* SHALLOW GRAVE *movie soundtrack. But this isn't any city. This is London. Ladbroke Grove. And I'm here for a gab-fest with an Electro-Dance ikon. From Kings Cross I decide on a literary/Rock'n'Roll homage tour, foot-slogging all the locations between, through Wardour and Goodge Street, Soho, through the Waterloo Sunset, along Holloway Road, Islington past the location of Joe Meek's original studios, and out under the Westway and all the sunblasted points beyond, dodging tourists,* BIG ISSUE *sellers with psycho-grins and aggressive street-sleepers, my* HEAD *bag with banana strap containing* ITT *cassette recorder. I arrive early. I heft my bag onto a record company table. The table is collaged with promo mug-shots,* CDs *and fax-printouts. It's then I find that en route my* ITT *has pureed my banana, and like some vile* DNA-*splicing experiment from David Cronenberg's* THE FLY *the two objects have become merged on a near-cellular level. So while contriving a cool pro journo-mode I'm splattering the room with shattered fruit-sludge, and throughout the interview my cassette spits and squishes banana-particles as it squelch-spirals onto tape. All parties pretend not to notice. But I can tell they're not impressed.*

utside, it's raining. A black deluge of rain. The 'a real rain will come and wash all this scum off the streets' kind of rain that Robert DeNiro monologues about in *Taxi Driver*.

Neil Barnes stabs a finger out through the rain and out over Portobello Street Market where the stall canopies sag and drizzle onto hunched-up browsers. Dub Vendor, he coolly enthuses, is down just *there*. Fine selection of Reggae, Augustus Pablo, Dub, Peter Tosh, Reggae, right through to Busta Rhymes. Then there's a trade-in emporium over *there* for twelve-inch Rare Grooves and Collector's cut-out picture discs. While Rough Trade is a block or so in *that* direction. You know Rough Trade, of course?

I could be wrong, but I get the impression Neil's probably no Party Animal. But he knows his music. Dance. Dub. Electro. DJ Culture. House. And all the acerbic rhythm japery and weirdness beyond. With Paul Daley he's one half of Leftfield. They sold over 220,000 copies of their CD, enough to shove *Leftism* up there with contemporaries like Blur's *The Great Escape*, Pulp's *Different Class*, and Oasis' *(What's The*

Story) Morning Glory, and if their faces aren't as tabloidly soundbitten as such company would suggest, that's deliberate. Neil doesn't wanna compete or talk street, street, street.

Leftfield are no fire-breathing Pop behemoths, no rampant teen sex gods. They're an (even more) Radical Dance Faction. And that's enough. "The whole industry is geared towards guitar bands. Rock is an easier thing to market" he explains agreeably. "The three-minute single is what it all revolves around. There was something familiar about the music of Oasis. It's the harmonies of the Beatles and all that, which is such a part of our culture. It's that simple." But while the likes of Oasis got rapidly absorbed into the cross-generational Pop mainstream, Dance retains that outlaw element. "That's right. Anything that questions, anything that isn't familiar, is never going to be as big in the mainstream. Perhaps in ten years time when *everything* sounds like the Prodigy it'll be different. But in the meantime, it's amazing how we still keep coming back to guitar bands."

Perhaps it's just that Oasis began by deliberately offering themselves up as Pop Stars? "Yes. They're not frightened of it." Whereas Dance in general, and Leftfield in particular, are determinedly anti-Star. "Yes. Yes. But I mean, it's easier for guitar bands to do that, because they've got a vocalist who's out front. They are the whole Rock'n'Roll thing. While Dance comes from a darker area. It is a thing that comes out of the clubs. And there's an attitude that, I suppose, we and the Prodigy share. We don't *want* to behave like that. We don't *want* to see ourselves all over the place. We're just not that type of person. Also, face facts, the press aren't really interested in bands like us. Two guys. When we were in the chart with Open Up (their incendiary coalition with John Lydon), the NME put us on the cover. But they cut the photograph of me and Paul in half to put John Lydon between us. This is it. *He* was the focal point. Not us. So in a way, you're denied it even if you want it. It's more like an attitude thing. It's just an image that the press want, and people seem to like it 'cos it's what they associate with Rock Stardom. It's the lifestyle that comes with the environment. But to me it's all very unimportant anyway."

Doesn't that Rock Star lifestyle appeal to you at all? "No. I don't know what a Rock Star lifestyle is. Take a lot of drugs and die young, isn't

it? I don't think either Paul or me are into that." There are advantages though, surely? Women, Models, Starlets, Celebrity Girlfriends. Even Liam Gallagher got Patsy Kensit *and* Nicole Appleton. "I'm a family man. So is Paul, really. We're both in long-term committed relationships. So we're not interested in that either." Which firmly curtails that sleazy line of enquiry. So tell me, O Well-Vibed One, would you happen to have any illegal substances on you?

The pressure's gotta stop
the future's gotta rock
... are you ready for the New Age?
　　　　—Africa Shox, from *Rhythm and Stealth*

Dance. If you understand it, you've missed the point.

A tube train shuttles and mumbles past the window, where the Underground briefly goes overground on its way to Ladbroke Grove station. Neil's eyes switch behind his shades. Watching the graffiti'd slug of London's enfeebled transport infrastructure as it wades through tides of black rain. As he's distracted I'm thinking: on TV they have flashbacks. And when they show archive film-clips they illustrate them with historic hits representative of the period. For blurry 1950s Cold War News Shots they add, say, the Tornadoes' Telstar. For Swinging Sixties miniskirt Carnaby Street London it's the Kinks' Dedicated Follower Of Fashion. Then it's the Gary Glitter thump-thump double-drumming stomp of the 1970s, and Duran Duran for the Yuppie eighties. So what will future programmers select to represent the 1990s? In terms of ideology, recording technique, and song structure, I'd hazard a guess at Dance. Prodigy, Orbital, or Leftfield. Unlike the timeless Trad-Rockery of Brit-Pop, they could *only* operate in the 1990s, both technically and attitude-wise.

"Yes. I think so. Dance is the most radical music around at the moment, in terms of popular music. Obviously there are more extreme specialist styles of things that are truly amazing. But in popular terms, what bands like Orbital and Prodigy are trying to do is very valid. I mean, *everybody* likes Firestarter — even if it *does* sound like John Lydon. It's a wicked record. It's extreme. It's the *hardest* record that's got to No 1 in years. Nothing can compete with it. But in terms of what's happening in Dance it's not where it's at. It's not on the cutting edge *by any means*. It's a Pop record. Even though they might not go on *Top Of The Pops* it's still a Pop record. It's got this element to it which is about mass sales. So what's most representative of the 1990s? That's tricky." He pauses. Scruffs his hand through his short spiky disarray of hair. Then "it'll be Celine Dion, probably," with a leer and a nasal South London drawl.

The seeds of progress, them dun get sown,
the choice is, there is no choice but to pursue it,
... against the grain, we shall remain
　　　　　　　　—Dusted, from *Rhythm and Stealth*

So the future might not necessarily be orange. But we know what its soundtrack will be. Leftfield is Dance of a different hue, where BPMs have more fun. It could *only* be happening *now*, and finding a dull moment on a Leftfield record is as unlikely as finding Mother Theresa at Stringfellows.

Neil's partner Paul Daley is not here. Does that mean we can slag him off behind his back? "Yeah, we can really have a go!" So tell me, O Dance Activist Supremo, do you have points of contention, group in-fights and conflict? "Yeee-ah. There's bound to be points of contention when you're working on tracks together. You argue about what should go on it — 'what're you do-ing *that* for? That chord's *really* strange. Really mad. Why're ya *doing* that? That don't *work!*' Arguments like that are all part of the creative process. We *always* discuss things. Should we do this? Should we do that? Too much exposure. Not enough exposure. But we generally sort it out. We're not just in this because we're a partnership, y'know? The most exciting thing for us is actually writing music together. That's more exciting than anything. And normally, because we've been working together for so long, we trust the other person to know what they're doing — even if, initially, we can't always get our heads around it. At least... that's the way I like to think about it."

Paul divided his growing up years between Ramsgate and Margate, where he drummed with Punk bands The Rivals and Johnny & The Haters, before switching to club DJ-ing, spinning early Electro while moonlighting from his daytime hairdressing job. Meanwhile, Neil, from Kentish Town, already had a prototype Leftfield underway with a Rhythm King deal (the label that brought you Bomb The Bass and The Beatmasters), and a blueprint for Not Forgotten even as Paul was moving on and up, and touring America with the Brand New Heavies crew. But the alchemaical fusion of the two diverse elements was probably preordained.

Since the cross-Atlantic innovations of Hip-Hop and House, Electro-Dance has been through a period of remarkably creative vigour. And Paul and Neil were in on it from the beginning. "More or less, I suppose so, yes" he concedes. "Since the start of the Alternative Dance Scene anyway. In the early nineties there wasn't much going on, apart from perhaps Nirvana. So Dance kept things going. Before that there was Kraftwerk. They influenced Electro with their repetitive beats. And their synth sounds were so modern. That's originally where it all came from.

Kraftwerk took ideas from the 1960s San Francisco bands, turned it into a form of early Dance Music, and then it went back to America. To New York and Detroit where the Electro-type thing developed. And out of that, really, came House."

And out of House, came Leftfield. Delivering only four well-spaced but awesome singles spread across the years from Not Forgotten (1990) — a seismic dancefloor crush siamesing Low Riding samples from 1970s Funksters War, to Pakistani singer Fati Ala Khan — followed by Release The Pressure ('... we *always* wanted to make a Reggae-based record like that'), then nine minutes of what *i-D* magazine called the 'glacial digital elegance' of Song Of Life in November 1992, and, of course, the charting Open Up — a pyrotechnical No 13 a year later. Someone tagged them 'Progressive House', and tacked on terms like Dance Provocateurs to explain Leftfield's cool excursions into Trance, Hardcore hybrid, deep Dub remixology and Global Trip-Hopping from Cabaret Voltaire to Frankie Knuckles.

But the fact that mixes of three of those singles appear on *Leftism* says less about their productive rate than it does about the mitigating circumstances of their working methods. Taking Dance remix restructuring further into the Technosphere than just about anyone else, where ideas fly so fast your thoughts fry in your brain.

"Well, it's like writing your first book, isn't it? It's a free-flowing thing. Like doing a painting or a sculpture. Nothing is ever final. I mean, I wrote the idea for Open Up three years before John Lydon came in and did it. We worked on instrumental versions at different stages, changing it, remodelling it. But I knew his voice would work with it, so we sent him a demo and he liked it. We got him in the studio and basically he sang over the demo. He supplied the lyrics, but I knew what the chorus was going to be because he'd already sung it to me — well, actually he *screamed* it to me down the 'phone! I've still got that original untreated Lydon demo on cassette, and it's really exciting. It's one long incredible jam. But that's not our style. We like organisation. And that's what the technology frees you up to do. So we actually sampled up all of his vocals. Everything he did. So that all of the bits we wanted were in the sampler. I mean — it's John. It's no different to live vocals. It just means that as far as the arrangement went we could actually put John anywhere we wanted him. Rather than getting him back in and saying 'look, here's the new arrangement, can you sing that bit there, that bit there, and that bit there'. It's a bit more complicated, but you end up with something quite different. Because then we realised that the backing track wasn't good enough. So we rewrote the backing track. Not completely. But a lot of the finer elements of it were rewritten. John didn't recognise the finished track."

It's a process of continual remix. Just as they've turned down offers from Pulp, Paul McCartney, and U2, there are Leftfield remixes of Pressure Drop, Stereo MC's (Step It Up), Inner City, and... David Bowie's Jump They Say. "Yeah. We did that some time ago. Didn't get to meet him though" he adds ruefully. "At the time Bowie was going through a very lean period. But we were big fans, particularly of albums like *Low*. So you've *got* to listen to a Bowie record if it's offered to you. We listened. And we liked it. It had a lot of Brian Eno string sounds on it. And we thought 'yeah, we can do this one. There's something in it that we can get our hands around'. Later on Bowie 'phoned us up to say how much he liked what we'd done. Though again... I didn't actually get to speak to him."

So what do you look for in a good remix? "When we first started doing it, in about 1990/91, it was interesting doing a Dance remix of a

Rock record. I thought that was good. I thought that sort of added a twist. So perhaps you look for a bit of a twist. It's not about money. You look for something that you can add to, really. A bad remix is when you take absolutely everything off and make it into your own record. For me, that's not a remix. That's just extending your own reputation. We've never tried to do that."

With *Leftism* "we left off on tracks like Inspection (Check One) and Storm 3000. And my favourite track, Melt. That's where we left off, so that's the point where we started from with the material for the second album, *Rhythm And Stealth* (1999). But album three is where you're expected to go all experimental, isn't it? Playing pots and pans and stuff like that. We're writing new material now... *as we speak*! And it'll be an advancement, hopefully, on what we've already done. So it will be different, but it won't be too much of a leap. We're not going to suddenly become a three-piece Rock band halfway through..."

And after David Bowie, John Lydon, and Curve's Toni Halliday, are there other vocalists you'd like to work with? "I'm really into Christy Moore as a vocalist" he admits. "Perhaps if I say

it in enough interviews he might get to hear about it. He's got a great voice. Love his voice. And, of course, his lyrics. I've been very much into him. I used to go down and see him play in an Irish Club in Stockwell. Just him and his guitar. I really do like slow Irish music in particular. I've listened to it since I was really young. I can hear similarities between Christy Moore, John Lydon, and Fati Ala Khan. Different styles, but you can hear the same kind of keening Folk thing which seems to cross the barriers of countries and cultures. I love voices like that. I love that quality of vocals. I can hear it fitting into so many different contexts. So he's someone we'd love to do something with. But whether it'll ever happen... I don't know."

Add *this* to life's long list of magnificent improbabilities.

Let's get electrified, Let's get electrified
The World is on fire... gonna take you HIGHER!
　　　　　—Africa Shox, from *Rhythm and Stealth*

Is there life beyond the Rave?

On the wall above us there's a gold CD for the *Trainspotting* soundtrack. Outside it's still raining a black deluge of rain. And Neil Barnes shuffles a ten-pack of Berkeley Red on the table between us, his eyes impenetrable behind his shades. He's wearing a T-shirt that says 'SENSI'. "It's a joke on 'PEPSI'" he explains unnecessarily. In June 1996 Leftfield went out live for the first time. Playing a thunderous multi-rhythmic sonic fusion that could *only* be happening at that particular intersection of the space-time continuum. Theirs is no Trad guitar Rock. It will never achieve the mainstream Pop acceptance of a Pulp or an Oasis. But when future TV programmers select the music that most crucially defines the time, they'll choose something very like Leftfield.

It's already happening. If there's one movie

that catches the darkly narcotic flavour of living at the dying end of John Major's Britain, then it's got to be *Trainspotting*. The Irvine Welsh story of bad haircuts, first degree sartorial abuse, and drug-ingesting holidays in hell. Leftfield are there on its massively unit-shifting soundtrack. And "it's gone gold!, even though our track on there wasn't really intended to be an album track. It's meant to go in the film. It wasn't *written* for anything else but the film, and it doesn't work outside that setting. They gave us the scene for us to work on, and it's fun because you're working in a visual environment. It's just a different challenge entirely, although it's actually easier in a way than writing for an album. Because you already have an inkling of the mood that the track has to work around. But sometimes surprising things work with film. Like when they show really violent scenes, yet use stately classical music! — I love that mad contrast. And the sound quality in cinemas is so much higher than anything you're ever going to hear at home. It really brings out the track. We did *Shallow Grave* too, and for that we just saw the opening five or ten minutes of it. We wrote a piece of music very roughly around

it and then they edited it in. It worked very well. So Danny [Boyle, director] asked us to do *Trainspotting*, but this time they had a more specific idea. We actually had it time coded. So we worked completely around the dialogue on it. Which is why our contribution to the movie is quite mellow compared with some of the other stuff. Like the Underworld track. We do the bit where the characters try out their big hit of heroin, and it goes all wobbly. That's the start of our piece. Then they go down to London on the coach, and we're there in the background. There's actual dialogue all over the bits we do, so you can't have a banging House track over that."

Neil pauses thoughtfully. His eyes switch behind his shades, out through the rain and out over Portobello Market towards Ladbroke Grove where the black deluge is washing all the scum off the streets. "I think we'd like to do a whole soundtrack next. If the right offer comes along, we'd love to do it" he resumes. "Who knows, we might get the chance to do the next Danny Boyle project… but you never know."

© Dogger

JOE MEEK
DEATH OF THE
TELSTAR MAN

So where did Indie Brit-Electro begin? **JOE MEEK** *was fascinated by the crude potential of his primitive home-made technology, and used his 'stars' to voice-over his own electro-drenched production ideas. But although his career began as Britain's first Indie record pioneer and gay maverick, it ended up with gunshot murder and suicide. He died on February 3, 1967. I was there... almost.*

'm stood outside 304 Holloway Road, Islington. Beyond my cold reflection in the plate glass window of the Cycle Logical store there are the skeletal frames of Mountain Bikes and Racers, Sports Cycles and Speedsters. Beyond them are the fainter traces of even older ghosts.

Squeeze your eyes tight to narrow slits. Concentrate hard. It's possible to time-warp back to a previous, more monochrome world. Listen. There are the fading echoes of gunshots. The one that murdered Mrs Violet Shenton. Then, after a pause, a second sharp precise retort, a hint of electronic distortion phasing the detonation that — over thirty years ago — blasted the wild life and career of Joe 'The Telstar Man' Meek to oblivion.

By all Rock'n'Roll logics none of this should matter. Meek was wilful and petulant, a spectacularly self-destructive eccentric who believed that the spirit of the dead Buddy Holly was writing songs through him. He was a pill-popping loner haunted by mysticism and the occult, who made records in his bathroom to get exactly the right level of weird spacey echo. He was a gay man at a time when homosexuality was wishful sinful, a shameful deviation punishable by long-

FB 67

Tragic death of Joe Meek

RECORD producer and songwriter Joe Meek was found shot dead last Friday at his London studio where he once turned out hits by the Honeycombs, the Tornados and Heinz.

Meek, in his thirties, had apparently been worried for some time about his business.

He came to London from his home near Gloucester in 1956 and after a spell as a television engineer, turned to recording and opened a small studio.

In 1962 he wrote and produced the Tornados' hit "Telstar" which topped the NME Chart for five weeks and is now estimated to have sold more than five million.

The following year a member of the Tornados, Heinz Burt, left the group to pursue a solo career and his first two solo discs "Just Like Eddie" and "Country Boy" were also Joe Meek productions.

Meek's small studio flat in Holloway Road was known as the Bathroom but he always refused to move anywhere else. "This old dump has been lucky for me," he once said.

The Honeycombs' chart-topping "Have I The Right" was another of his productions. It was also his last really big success.

"I'm a fairly rich man," said Meek just over a year ago, "and I want to become a millionaire but this is an uncertain business." N.D.

term prison sentences. But the plaque halfway up the wall, between the first storey old-style sash windows, calls him 'pioneer of sound recording technology', and that's true too.

The wind coming down from the Archway Tavern and tube station has an edge of ice.

Although Meek has been dead thirty years, his presence persists. His cult is probably now bigger than at any other time since the early six-ties. CD compilations carefully salvage even his most obscure material, preserving it for record buyers not yet born when those gunshots took his life, and the life of his unfortunate landlady. Andy Warhol wrote that "the Record Producer really makes the sound, the composer just gives him something to work with" (probably referencing his own 'production' credits for Velvet Underground). But Warhol's epithet is never more true than it was for Joe Meek. More so than it is for Trevor Horn, Stephen Street, Flood, Stock Aitken Waterman, or just about anyone else. Meek is often referred to as 'Britain's Phil Spector'. But that's inadequate too. He recorded the Tornadoes (Telstar), John Leyton (Johnny Remember Me), the Honeycombs (Have I The Right?), Tom Jones, Freddie Starr, Heinz, and Screaming Lord Sutch. But you buy Meek records because they contain the 'Joe Meek Sound'. The artist name on the label is incidental.

RECORDS MADE FOR THE HIT PARADE

Joe Meek was born in 1929 in rural Newent, by Gloucester's Forest of Dean, carrying its softly burring accent all his life. He's bitten early by the Electro-Bug, a 1950s techno-dweeb in the days before there is a name for it, to the extent that he's able to endure his compulsory National Service stint as a Radio Technician, acquiring experience there which sets him up to score work as a studio engineer at IBC in London on his release in 1953. But the record industry is different then from now. Virtually unrecognisable. It is the Dark Age of British Pop in which a massive monopoly of a few inflexibly conservative labels dominates a bland 78rpm record market, and independent recording studios are rare. But IBC gives him the opportunity of engineering for

some of the leading pre-Rock'n'Roll names of the day: Frankie Vaughan (the original version of Shakin' Stevens' hit Green Door), Denis Lotis, Shirley Bassey, Petula Clark, Lita Roza, Anne Shelton and Goon Harry Secombe. Then in 1956 he up-twitches to the greater freedom of Denis Preston's Lansdowne Studios where he records jazz with Humphrey Lyttelton and Chris Barber, and where a slightly more hands-on position enables him to cut tracks for Lonnie Donegan (Cumberland Gap and Don't You Rock Me Daddy-O) and to get his own songwriting onto disc. Tommy Steele has a minor hit with Meek's Put A Ring On Her Finger, its royalties financing his next, and most decisive move.

Joe Meek is usually pictured in the kind of sharp suits and slicked-back quiff you expect from Laurence Harvey-style Room At The Top business-heads, or the Kray twins, but that's deceiving. He was an anti-organisation man who seldom fitted. He was angry, bored and frustrated by the claustrophobically repressive conventions rigidly enforced by the stultifyingly smug music industry. And he had ambition. So, in 1960, after a fiery row, he quit to launch his own studio, and his own label. Relocating to 304 Holloway Road with £3000-worth of scrounged pre-owned electronic equipment he sets about converting the flat above what was then a leather shop (AH Shenton — Travel Goods, Handbags, Leather & Grindery) into RGM Sound, the home of Triumph Records. Announced in the press as 'Records Made For The Hit Parade' it was a brave monster-busting venture, but one that immediately yielded a chart hit! Angela Jones by Liverpool-born Michael Cox is a limp song about a teen-age schoolboy crush. Its sound is as fresh as your first pubic hair. But this sweetly adolescent dutna-da-doo slow rocker enters the Top Ten, and peaks at a high of No7. Alarmed by its success the system hits back, ensuring that such

MEEKSVILLE HITS LTD.

Joe Meek, Terry O'Neill and the artistes would like to thank everyone for the plays given these records, especially the Radio London DJs, Radio Caroline, the B.B.C., Luxembourg DJs.

21
IN THE
RADIO
CHARTS

GLENDA COLLINS

'THOU SHALT NOT STEAL'

The disc with the fantastic MOD BEAT The 'B' side is just as great

'Been Invited To A Party'

THE SYNDICATES

'ON THE HORIZON'

of the Hit Parade but is going right to the top.

23 IN THE RADIO LONDON CHARTS

---

mavericks won't happen again in a hurry. At least not until the brief flourish of Andrew Loog Oldham's Immediate — part-financed by Rolling Stones' revenue — and then not again until Punk unleashes Stiff, Rough Trade, Factory and the rest.

Denied the commercial lifeline of market distribution Joe Meek reschemes new strategies. From now on he'll use RGM to create taped masters, then lease them to majors through a network of devious and often one-off deals. And

again the results are instantly astounding. John Leyton hits No 1 and No 2 in the August and October of 1961, while sides credited to Mike Berry, the Flee Rekkers and the Outlaws, all chart beneath him, all of them united by the macabre Meekatronic imprint of eerie low-budget futuristic stomp and cheap electronic echo. Then Mike Berry — later camp actor John Inman's sit-com stooge in TV's *Are You Being Served?*, becomes the first to commit Meek's dead Rock Star fixation to vinyl with the *Tribute To Buddy Holly* EP, as Heinz will do with Just Like Eddie [Cochran]. And John Leyton's Johnny Remember Me remains a classic Goth flesh-crawler of from-beyond-the-grave necro-kitsch; 'when the mist is rising and the rain is falling and the wind is blowing cold across the moor / I hear the voice of my Darling, the girl I loved and lost a year ago.' Mystic Meek was morbidly paranormal long before it was X-Filed.

Leyton was a bit-part actor whose previous career high-point was playing 'Ginger' in ATV's *Biggles* kids series. But when he's offered the role of a Pop singer (called 'Johnny St Cyr', pronounced sin-cere!) in TV's dire *Harpers West One* department store soap, Meek not only manages to wangle the deal to supply the episode soundtrack, but also uses it to levitate his own career, and to cross-over the television Pop fiction into real life. During their association John Leyton becomes a legit Pop Star with full fan-mag celebrity. A fame that lasts — significantly — until he quits Meek and signs to HMV, after which he never achieves another hit record. Meanwhile, Johnny Remember Me, the macabre minor-key lament created by Meek and song-writing colleague Geoff Goddard, fares better. It returns to the Top Ten in 1985 as part of a Bronski Beat/Marc Almond collaboration.

But already Meek has bigger and more urgent concerns — the American Space Flight programme is about to intervene in his career! Predicted by sci-fi guru Arthur C Clarke in an article for *Wireless World* as early as October 1945, the world's first-ever communication satellite — precursor of all things B-SKY-B and beyond — beams its debut cross-Atlantic TV simulcast on July 11, 1962. The jerky-blurry monochrome test transmissions become a huge international event which so excites Meek's tacky sci-fi sensibilities that he creates a single named in its honour virtually overnight: Telstar. The vehicle he

uses, the Tornadoes, are merely the regular session crew he's already used on Leyton's hits, a group who also double as Billy Fury's stage back-up band. But with Meek at the faders they become a huge B-movie Bug-Eyed-Monster phenomenon in their own right, one that — like the orbital space-junk their record is named for — hits all the right hot buttons and crosses continents to top charts across the world; anticipating psychedelia in ways that the rest of Rock will not catch up with until at least *Revolver*. The record fades in through a blizzard of effects more radioactive than a cloud of Chernobyl fallout, until the piercingly strong naggingly infectious up-tempo organ breaks through — with Meek's trademark hoofbeat rhythms powering it massively until it dissolves into a mayhem of intergalactic electronic static.

While the Beatles were still working sleazy Hamburg strip-joints and a full two years before the so-called 'English Invasion' of the American charts, the Tornadoes knock Elvis' She's Not You off the British top slot (October 4), then make the American No 1 the third week of November. Again, industry politics intervenes to prevent a tie-in US tour and subsequent American hits, but closer to home four more instrumental titles follow Telstar into the charts, and for a while the Tornadoes even challenged the Shadows' twangy-guitar Pop domination.

THE WHAM OF THAT TELSTAR MAN

Joe Meek is dead. It is no longer possible to acquire the unique flavour of *being* there at the creation of his hits. Except by proxy. So in a recent interview, Noddy Holder — former full-frontal frontman with seventies Glam-Rockers Slade — confides to me *his* impressions of working at RGM Sound. "Everybody recorded with Meek at some time in those early days" he recalls. "And with Steve Brett & The Mavericks, a band I had many years before Slade, I had experience of recording in the set-up he had there in his bathroom. I mean, he's this legendary figure — when the BBC showed Neil Armstrong landing on the Moon, Telstar was the song they used as a soundtrack. But when we actually went to record there it wasn't how we'd imagined it to be at all. It wasn't a professional set-up by any means. The particular sound-rooms that he had were very, very stuck together with spit-and-sawdust. Basically, he had a studio up in his bathroom for the echo effects and that was where he made all his hits. We had imagined that this notorious bathroom would be filled with state-of-the-art equipment, but in fact he had one shoddy little bathroom where all the amps were set up — and artists had to piss as well as play in there. We couldn't believe our eyes. He was this big name and he worked in a dump. But he got great sounds out of the studio. They were totally over the top."

And Joe as a person? "He was very quiet, and very unassuming, really. A portly bloke, much older than us, with slicked-back hair. We got in his studio and he just told us the sort of thing he wanted. We all stood out on the landing, playing our instruments, while Joe was in his control box, mixing. He did the technical side of it. Y'know, he just got on with the job in hand. He didn't really talk that much. We didn't really have any personal relationship with him whatsoever... there was no sort of personal rapport there at all. He was very, very... shy, I suppose. He was with us, anyway. Maybe he was a bit nervous of us — we'd just come down from the Midlands! But you need those sort of characters in the business. Phil Spector was the same in America. Nobody actually knew how he did it. He just had the ears to be able to do it and build up those fabulous sounds. That is the greatness of a good

producer, to be able to have their own mark on production. Unfortunately we never had anything released that Joe Meek produced."

In fact, despite a subsequent Slade odds-and-ends CD collector-compilation which includes a version of Buddy Holly's Take Your Time recorded by the pre-Slade Vendors, the Meek tapes remain missing.

In spite of his shyness, Joe Meek was always impatient with the essential passivity of the role the music industry expected from the engineer/ producer, which was simply to mic up the studio and control sound levels to ensure as clean as possible a reproduction of the artist's live performance. At IBC or Lansdowne Studios the producer did not innovate or participate in the creative process. In Memphis there was Sam Philips of Sun Records who shared something of Joe's vision. And, as Noddy Holder points out, there was Phil Spector. While later, among Meek's immediate contemporaries, there was George Martin who had the full 1960s state of the art EMI studios to play with — while Joe had his wired-up third-floor flat above a leather shop! But Joe Meek had always seen the studio's potential to be as pro-active as the artists and musicians themselves. And, much to his landlady's distress, he contrived an entire boffin's romper room of DIY electronics that overflowed into the toilet, onto the stairs, and down into the floor beneath, all inadequately insulated by primitive egg-box soundproofing. Operating from Holloway Road he was able to fully indulge his obsession with Martian Hop extraterrestrial effects by accelerating tapes, adding layers of echo and compression, varying tape speed by finger-pressure applied to the revolving spools, and adding a quantum jump of other 'secret' techniques he'd devised himself, including a home-made reverb unit, plus additional found-sounds that might involve tapping an ash-tray with a

JOE MEEK: RECORDING WIZARD

r3 64

Joe Meek, man behind the mammoth - selling "Telstar" and many other hits, who was found dead with shotgun wounds in his Holloway, London, flat on Friday, always believed his sounds would succeed again in the chart—although he had been hitless for more than a year.

Keith Goodwin, who handled record producer Meek's publicity, said it was only a question of time before Joe came roaring back with another succession of hits. He believed strongly in his sounds.

Honey Lantree, whose Honeycombs group gave Joe his last hit, "That's The Way," said: "He was such a brilliant man. It was tragic. If you lacked confidence, you could be sure he'd put it into you. It was the mark of a great recording manager."

Meek also recorded Cliff Bennett in his early days. "He was a great help and friend to us when we started out in the business," recalled Cliff this week.

Meek's major triumph was "Telstar" by the Tornados, a world-wide No. 1 in 1962. Among the other hits associated with him were Frankie Vaughan's "Green Door," Anne Shelton's "Lay Down Your Arms," Lonnie Donegan and John Leyton hits and, more recently, the Honeycombs' successes.

screwdriver, or just thumping heavily on the correct area of bathroom floor. He was also able to draw on a pool of very able musicians, who were by now immune and well-used to his temperament, his unorthodox recording techniques and his high-voltage extra-sensory flimflam. These included Ritchie Blackmore of the Outlaws (later Deep Purple), and Tornadoes' Clem Cattini and Alan Caddy (both ex-Johnny Kidd's Pirates).

By this point the Music Industry distrusted everything about the tortured Pep-Pill popping maverick with his Heath-Robinson studio, his spiritualism, and his occasionally tinny treble-drenched records. But his ratio of hits was proving impossible to ignore. As well as records, the Holloway Road crew soon found itself working together on soundtracking two Pop-trash movies (*Farewell Performance* and *Just For Fun*) using Heinz as front-man, and then contributing to another (*Live It Up*) which gave Joe the opportunity to get Gene Vincent to record one of his songs (Temptation Baby). But it is always Meek in total control. And it's here that the Phil Spector analogy falls down.

Both Meek and Spector were unique in their approach to production. Both were innovative and years ahead of their time. And Spector was a similarly motivated conceptual record producer who demanded an identical degree of absolute control over his product. But *he* was confident enough of his genius to work with equally powerful vocalist collaborators, including Tina Turner, the Righteous Brothers, Darlene Love, and even John Lennon. Whereas it often seems that Meek makes it a deliberate policy to select artistic non-entities to 'front' his discs — as though the challenge is to purposefully create Pop hits from the least promising material. A kind of 'cash from crud' approach. Far from being fashion conscious, half the time Meek's 'artists' seem lucky to be considered semi-conscious! John Leyton was an actor before and after his brief Meek-fuelled Pop fame. His singing voice, to be generous, has severe limitations. Sleepy-eyed sleepy-voiced Mike Berry is equally blandly anonymous and similarly vocally challenged, often sounding like little more than the ghost of Buddy Holly conjured up at one of Joe's seances, yet Meek feeds him more hits, including a Top Five Don't You Think It's Time and a cover of the Shirelles tentatively sexually-charged Will You Still Love Me Tomorrow (tellingly gender-inverting its 'will-you-respect-me-in-the-morning' dilemma). There are persistent stories about Meek's early sessions with Tom Jones, which result in some failed pre-It's Not Unusual singles. And there's endless what-if speculations about hypothetical sessions with the Beatles. Meek was apparently on Brian Epstein's list of industry contacts during the period he was attempting to nail down a deal for his protégés following the failure of their Decca audition. But neither association *could* have worked out. Meek purposefully avoided artists who were opinionated enough to answer back, or talented enough

or detract attention from his own essential input. Nothing could be permitted to interfere with that.

A symptom of ego paranoia. But of insecurity, too.

Being gay in the early sixties, as Brian Epstein knew, as Joe Meek knew, was a subworld of guilty tainted love, furtive meetings haunted by the fear of queer-bashing, potential blackmail, and the even greater fear of exposure. Such a concentrated weight of social prejudice has ways of seeping in beneath the skin to poison your own self-image, and hence devour your most intimate relationships. Although he had a long-term live-in 'friend' called Lionel, Joe had already been persecuted for 'cottaging' by the out-dated Sexual Offences Laws. He was arrested (in November 1963) for 'Importuning for Immoral Purposes' outside a Madras Place public toilet. A conviction that led to a £15 fine, but more significantly involved public humiliation in the press. Homosexuals were seen as degenerates, deviant outsiders. And Meek was always the outsider. By turn he could appear headstrong or uncertain, arrogant or vulnerable. It's as though, un-

THE MEEK THAT SHALL NOT INHERIT...
JOE MEEK'S TOP TEN SECOND BEST RECORDS

1 ANGELA JONES by Michael Cox (Triumph RGM 1011) Who is Michael Cox? It doesn't matter, Meek chose him at an *Oh Boy* TV show audition, then chose a hit from the American charts by Johnny Ferguson for him, mildly Anglicising it for what was Britain's first-ever Indie hit single.

2 WILD WIND by John Leyton (Top Rank JAR 585) Leyton was

a young thespian managed by a struggling young Australian promoter called Robert Stigwood. He was destined for roles in *The Great Escape* (1963) alongside Charles Bronson, Steve McQueen and James Garner, then *Von Ryan's Express* (1965) and *Krakatoa* (1968). But with this Geoff Goddard-penned banshee-wailing wind-tunnel weirdo he hits

No 2 (October 26, 1961), a bare month after Johnny Remember Me had quit the top slot! It's also one of the first singles I ever bought.

3 ROBOT c/w LIFE ON VENUS by The Tornadoes (Decca F 11606) This No 17 hit from April 18, 1963, clones Telstar's sci-fi continuum with its robotic effects book-ending an up-tempo organ-domi-

able to come out of the closet, he decided to stay in it and make hit records there instead. As a kid in Gloucester he'd flounced and cross-dressed to entertain his confused, amused, and decidedly non-camp brothers. Now, like Brian Epstein's eternally unconsummated crush on John Lennon, Meek becomes infatuated by the Rough Trade charms of the Tornadoes bass-player, Heinz Burt. But, born in Hargin, West Germany, now living in Sheffield and still a regular on the Rock revival circuit, Heinz insists to this day that there was 'no sex', despite Meek's gifts and amorous advances.

To make matters worse, Joe also finds himself out of step with the Beat Boom groups who exploded across Pop the following year. To Joe, groups are too self-contained, too resistant to moulding, too resistant to producer manipulation. He prefers more docile pretty-boy solo 'Stars' who can be left to get on with the necessary TV and fan-mag duties while Meek concentrates on the more important function of actu-ally fabricating their hits. Grafting their often inept vocals onto the session almost as an afterthought, expertly masking their inadequacies with a spatchcock of studio effects. So Meek's response to Beatlemania — prompted as much by sexual attraction as by artistic considerations — is directed at the Tornadoes' bass-player. Given an Aryan blonde peroxide bleach-job and an abbreviation to the more easily memorable Heinz, the inevitable hits soon came. And then, when Meek finally succumbs to the inexorable logics of the group format the results are even more spectacular. The Honeycombs' Have I The Right? gives him yet another No 1 (August 27, 1964) squeezed in between Manfred Mann and the Kinks (You Really Got Me) — which goes on to return him to the American Top Five that same October. Ideally suited to Meek's requirements, the Honeys are bland and totally lacking any trace of character. They are ciphers, but they do have the marketable gimmick of an ex-hair-dresser girl drummer called 'Honey' Lantree,

nated instrumental. But the Tornadoes — George Bellamy (rhythm guitar), Heinz Burt (bass), Alan Caddy (lead guitar), Clem Cattini (drums) and Roger Laverne Jackson (keyboards) — are probably the purest expression of the Joe Meek vision, uncompli-cated by the irritating necessity of a singer. They were the RGM house band who also play on records by John Leyton, Don Charles, and Billy Fury (the live We Want Billy LP), before providing the TV theme for Gerry Anderson's Stingray puppet series. Cattini goes on to become an in-demand session musician and was last heard of touring with The Rocky Horror Show.

4 THAT'S THE WAY by The Honeycombs (Pye 7N 15890) It hits No 12 on September 23, 1965, blending Ann 'Honey' Lantree's beehive-hairdo voice with Dennis D'Ell's lead vocals to create a pleasant little rocker Joe Meek-ed into ethereal strangeness. The Honey's were also early recipients of songs by Ken Howard and Alan Blaikley who later requisitioned Meek's electro-stomp to mastermind the Dave Dee Dozy Beaky Mick & Tich hit machine (and Flaming Youth — Phil Collins' vinyl debut!)

5 PLEASE STAY by The Cryin' Shames (Decca F 12340) Joe Meek's last hit, peaking at No 26 on May 5, 1966, a slow pleading Soul cover of a Drifters original.

6 WHO TOLD YOU c/w PETER GUNN LOCOMOTION by

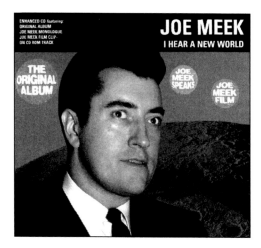

Bennett & The Rebelrousers, and the Buzz. But the Honeycombs will be Meek's last huge chart hurrah. The two-minute single with a six-week maximum shelf-life is supreme. You are only as good as your last hit. And then the hits finally stop coming.

From now on the Beat route will lead directly to that February 3 murder and suicide. But Meek's reputation is harder to kill. As early as 1977, Decca issue a *The Joe Meek Story*, a double album initiating a process of rediscovery accelerated a few years later by John Repsch's fine biography *The Legendary Joe Meek*. Soon CD re-issues are rescuing even his most obscure B-sides and out-takes from the archives. Sequel's forty-eight track double CD, *The Joe Meek Story*, includes tracks by the Honeycombs as well as previously lost items by Jess Conrad, Peter Cook and the Riot Squad. *Joe Meek: Work In Progress— The Triumph Years* collects John Leyton alongside the Fabulous Flee Rekkers, Yolanda and Eve Boswell, while an ambitious ten volume series

and that's enough of a novelty in those dark pre-Feminist days to guarantee TV exposure and press column inches. The records are pure Joe Meek, however, the curiously compelling beat punched out by formulaic electro-quivers of cleanest Meekesqueness.

There will be more highly collectable work to emerge from names like the Riot Squad, Cliff

---

Freddie Starr & The Midnighters (Decca F 11663) Yes, that's Freddie of hamster-eating notoriety in his previous life as a failed Merseybeat Starr... Another of Joe Meek's near brushes with megastardom happened when he auditioned North London group the Raiders in a local church hall. He liked them enough to rename them and give them a chart single — on condition they exclude their singer, a sixteen-year-old urchin called Rod Stewart! As The Moontrekkers they

reached No 50 with the instrumental Night Of The Vampire (Parlophone R 4814).

7 I'M A HOG FOR YOU c/w **MONSTER IN BLACK TIGHTS** by Screaming Lord Sutch & The Savages (Decca F 11747) One of the things that *really* annoyed Meek's landlady, Mrs Violet Shenton, was this future Parliamentary candidate arriving outside 304 Holloway Road in his hearse. Led Zeppelin's Jimmy Page was once one of Sutch's

Savages, as was Ritchie (Deep Purple) Blackmore.

8 IN MY WAY by Davy Kaye (Decca F 12073) Following Meek's tributes to Buddy Holly and Eddie Cochran came this fan-club sponsored nod to Elvis, with a puke-inducing spoken word dedication leading into a song originally axed from the soundtrack of Presley's *Wild In The Country* movie. An item much sought-after by both Meek completists and collectors of Elvis memorabilia, it sounds

kicks off in 1992 with (yet another) *The Joe Meek Story Vol 1: 1960*, followed by *304 Holloway Road: Joe Meek—The Pye Years Vol 2*.

His cult survives. By all Rock'n'Roll logics, none of this should matter. So why was he — why *is* he — important?

He was fiercely independent. Against all the odds, he always made his own way — even when he was wrong. At the end of his career his neuroses would fill a psychiatrist's filing cabinet. He even believed his flat was being bugged by jealous music industry rivals. But he took on impossible giants, and, for a while, he gobbled them up.

That means a lot. Still.

MEEKSVILLE: HITS UK

But now I'm stood outside 304 Holloway Road, Islington. It's February 3, 1967. Mid-morning. The shopfront reads: AH Shenton — Travel Goods, Handbags, Leather & Grindery.

Mrs Violet Shenton is climbing the stairs towards Meek's flat, determined to 'have it out once and for all' with her troublesome tenant. For her, it's unfortunate timing. Joe's just heard that EMI have rejected his latest batch of tapes. The Telstar royalties, long locked in litigation, will not be resolved for at least another year. And it's the exact anniversary of Buddy Holly's plane-crash death: February 3, 1959. Joe has always been a better record producer than he is accountant, and now, as his personal problems and tangled financial affairs worsen, his mixed-up delusions intensify.

Lips tight with paranoia, eyes harshly shadowed, depressed and in a state of pill-heightened panic, he seizes Heinz' shotgun and empties it into her. Then he calmly reloads. Puts the barrel up against the roof of his mouth, and blows the top off his own head too. He is thirty-eight-years-old.

But I swear that sometimes, when the mist is rising and the rain is falling and the wind is blowing cold across the moor, I still hear the sound of his records.

like a failed Alvin Stardust doing an inept Freddie Starr impression of Elvis.

9 **LITTLE LONELY ONE** c/w **THAT'S WHAT WE'LL DO** by Tom Jones (Columbia DB 7566) He turns up at Meek's studio as Tommy Scott & The Senators, and records these sides long before It's Not Unusual. A subsequent EP called *Tom Jones* (Columbia SEG 8464) collects four Meek-produced tracks in time to cash-in on Jones' later chart success.

10 **I HEAR A NEW WORLD** by Joe Meek's Blue Men (LP) (CD-RPM 103) An album archaeologically reconstructed by Meek archivist Roger Dopson, after the fashion of the Beach Boys' *Smile* sessions, and issued in 1992 (and again in 2001) with full facsimile Triumph label logo and documentation. Meek's peak, and a Holy Grail to obsessives, this on-going instrumental sci-fi magnum opus of strange Meekian echo-filled visions of other worlds was originally issued as a series of incredibly rare white label off-beat stereo EPs which have been known to change hands for around £400 each! To writer Alan Clayson, tracks like Disc Dance Of The Globbots, Valley Of The Saroos, and Dribcot's Space Boat are "much the same as Marty McFly's futuristic rampage through Johnny B Goode at a 1954 High School Hop in *Back To The Future*" (quoted from his book *Beat Merchants*).

© Dogger

THE KINKS
DAVE DAVIES THE KINK THAT TIME FORGOT

I de-coach at Victoria. Take a stroll across Waterloo Bridge to Waterloo Station. Locations redolent of Kinks imagery. Song strands ripple in the wind as I walk. It's by way of my own personal tribute to the Davies brothers — Ray and Dave, and their insidious influence on my life across years, and decades. Kinks songs get inside skins. Some say Rock'n'Roll arrests your character development into an eternal adolescence. And it does if you do it right. While Ray sat at home and wrote about it, Dave was out there doing it. Making his autobiography a Rock'n'Roll horror story that shapes three decades of music history. Expelled from school at fifteen, and No 1 in the charts two years later; his hedonistic lifestyle of drugs, sleaze, paternity suits, paranoia, fashion subversion, a host of sexual contradictions, and a stream of classic hits defines all that the 1960s are best remembered for. And that's before he discovered UFOs! For **THE KINKS** *there was never a formulaic groove. And they never ran out of that initial seam of inspiration. Once the sixties were gone the scene shifted downgear a little, and the focus of attention moved slightly elsewhere, but the Kinks never went away. Never stopped touring. Never stopped producing fine albums full of perfectly crafted Pop. I first saw the Kinks in 1965, a misty Yorkshire night when they played Bridlington Spa.* **DAVE DAVIES** *doesn't remember. But I do. And to me, meeting him now is a big deal. Even though he's probably been over all this a thousand times. "Not really," he concedes generously, "no." And over the next hour-and-a-half we talk through the entire Kinks escapade...*

*KINK (Kink) n (4) a flaw or idiosyncrasy of
personality, quirk (5) Brit, informal, a sexual
deviation (6) US, a clever or unusual idea*
—Collins English Dictionary

ay. Let's get that over with right away. Dave is the *other* Kink sibling. Not the one who writes Waterloo Sunset, Lola, Well Respected Man, Come Dancing and the rest. But the one who invented the granite-hewn fractured proto-Grunge You Really Got Me guitar riff, and so patented all of Heavy Metal. He's the one whose flamboyant gender-bent sartorial style supposedly inspired the 'frilly nylon panties right up tight' line in Dedicated Follower Of Fashion. He's the Kink in the early group photos with the flying-V guitar, the centre-parting and thigh-high Cavalier boots. The *other* Davies brother who had one-and-a-half solo hits in 1967, three solo albums in the first half of the 1980s... and now *Kink*, the autobiography.

Is the reading Pop public being fed another dodgy beefburger? Well yes, and no. The Kinks are a sitcom set in Hell. A band that not only stand at the very G-Spot of the Sixties, but go clear round its S-Bend too. By 1964 Dave has not only hit the charts, but been hit by his first paternity suit too. Aged seventeen. And it's all here. The Sex. The Drugs. The Hits. The UFOs. The Blow-Jobs. The Sibling Ribaldry. To now.

When the Kinks songs and the Kinks legacy is out there surfing the tired old new waves of guitar Pop in newly extreme states of mind, techno-tweaked and shot through with darkly black-humorous lyrics. And it's an appallingly fascinating documentary trip through Rock'n'Roll weirdness. Dave goes tour crazy in a hotel and urinates "in the drawers and in the wardrobe, and in my final act of crazed triumph I defecated in the handbasin. To my manic delight and surprise it was a formidable-sized piece of excrement."

Then again, he hangs out with Eddie Thornton, West Indian horn player with the Georgie Fame Band, a guy "who was able to score the best dope in town". And with Kim, who manages the trendy Biba's boutique in Chelsea. After a night's wild clubbing they wind down narcotically in Eddie's flat. "I smiled at Eddie with Chinese eyes and a Cheshire Cat grin as Kim licked my chest and eased her tongue down onto my stomach and then on to my penis. She eased her mouth on to it so delicately. As she continued, I started to feel dizzy. Uncontrollably, and without warning, I was overcome with terrible nausea. Suddenly I threw up all over poor Kim who was so far into her act that it was downright tragic."

But today, this Kink could not be a more open or engaging creature. "It's strange, 'cos when I was first commissioned to write the book I thought 'I don't think I can handle this'. Apart from the fact that I couldn't *remember* stuff, I was scared of stirring up all the emotions which it takes to do something like this. But it was quite a..." he pauses for a very long time, "y'know, quite a cleansing experience really. Getting rid of a lot of the emotional garbage that you carry around with you. It's kinda good to get it off your chest."

The Kinks are myth fast-breeders. Always have been. Stories abound of internal conflict, jealousies, hatred and deviance. Most of them are true. Dave's book explodes a few, but generates a lot more. Kim Deal of the mighty Breeders told me this one: she's watching a Kinks American concert, and during the show a violent on-stage fist fight breaks out between Ray and Dave. She goes 'Oh wow, I'm seeing Rock'n'Roll history happening live!' But later she goes to a further show on the same tour. And at exactly the same point in the set exactly the same fight develops.

"And she thought it was a set-up?" Dave cracks up. "That's *really* funny, that is. And it's quite possible, yes. We used to play around for our audience quite a lot. We were doing a lot of tours in the early seventies and we used to get bored playing some nights. So Ray and I might deliberately wind each other up just to get a bit of energy happening. Know what I mean? One night we started the show with Victoria, and we actually played it *backwards*, you know — going 'SHEEEE OOOO SHEEEE OOOO!, SLEE SLURP SLURP SLURP!! NYA NYA NYEE!' while walking and playing backwards. It was real fun. The audience must have thought we were....", he dissolves into incoherent laughter. "It's all a bit daft. But sometimes you have to do things like that to keep your spirits up. It can be quite miserable sitting in a shitty hotel when everybody really just wants to go home, and you're looking at cold pizza from last night with only a bottle of Heineken for company. And all the things that surround you come together when you get on that stage. But when things are great it's worth the effort."

The Breeders, of course, famously included sisters Kim and Kelly. "Yes. I wonder how *they* get on?" And the Oasis legend is built around the same problems. Do you have any advice for the Gallagher brothers? "I don't know to what degree... how do they get on? What's the general thing with them?" Similar to you and Ray. A loving contradiction. A loyal rivalry. "That's really strange" he muses abstractly. Already lost in his own analysis of Rock'n'Roll brothers-in-arms. "You know, it's like, I was talking to someone the other day and they were saying this thing that I say in the book about Ray, about how... how he abused me. But it's a relationship *built* on abuse! Really. Maybe it's because of it that the work we've done is so good. Y'know, if it had been all sort of lovey-dovey and 'dahn the pub together', then the music would have been different. Not as good. Maybe..."

THE KINK KRONIKLES
THE KINKS KONTROVERSY

My girlfriend packed her bags
and moved to another town,
she couldn't stand the boredom
when the video broke down

—The Kinks, State Of Confusion

I look up.

Outside the air-conditioned hum of the boardroom, Dave Davies arrives. He's kissing Sarah effusively, she's Boxtree Book's bright PR. As I watch for a moment, side face, he looks uncannily a lot like Ray. It's true. Brothers tend to grow increasingly alike as they get older. The same long dark hair, streaked with paler brown, and brushed straight back. Long black coat. Soft slip-on shoes. I think of a Leeds Kinks concert I saw with horror novelist Simon Clark last year. Or was it five years ago? Ray on the Town & Country stage inverting the old Elvis disclaimer: "I think the Kinks have arrived in the building now."

And here, as we shake hands, I'm thinking of the line in his book about 'cynical pressmen with treacherous grins'. And the bit about "doing interviews for the first time, you can say anything and people will think it interesting or at least newsworthy, and if you can't think of anything then you just make it up". In appropriate tabloid-speak, he's with a curvelicious babe he introduces as Kate. She's dressed smartly in pale orange, with Lethal Weapon legs and immaculately painted nails. Can she sit in? Sure she can. Every now and then he turns to her — "how am I doing?" Then slyly to me "She'll hit me over the head if I go too far!" She sometimes picks him up on factual errors. "We'd played the Empire the night before." "No, you'd played Ireland the night before." "Yes... that's right, we'd come across from Ireland."

At one point he breaks off an extended anecdote, turns to Kate, and says "nice orange upholstery in here, innit? You're colour co-ordinated." He's like that. Dave doesn't speak in neat soundbites either. His is more a slow laconic meandering, punctuated by ers and erms, which he uses as pauses for thought. But to err is human, and there's plenty of highly biteable material on offer.

I watch them on stage in Leeds last year, or perhaps the year before last. They do a song called Phobia. Ray describes it as "a serious Rock'n'Roll message song", then proceeds to climb up onto the speaker cabinets behind the band. Adding "I'm into psychology. I don't know why," as he prowls down the front gesticulating inanely behind the bouncer's heads. The song's chorus goes "everybody got phobia / What you got? — PHOBIA!"

And it's easy to probe phobias and try some cheap psychology to explain the Davies brothers. A large warm Muswell Hill family in the late 1940s. Six sisters. Then Ray, and finally... Dave. DIY psychology says, initially, that Ray — as the firstborn son — received all that gushing female attention. Until Dave, younger and cuter, came along and 'stole a bit of his space in the limelight'. Resentments and jealousies are not always rational, and they can go deep. Secondly, Dave — as subsequent recipient of all that female nurturing — grows to take female pampering and compliance for granted. He adores women ("I loved to sneak a peek at my sisters dressing and undressing..."), and knows exactly how to exploit their affections. Sexual mores, and addictions also go deep. On stage in Leeds Dave sings his solo hit Death Of A Clown, and his writing contribution to the Kinks Words Of Mouth album — Living On The Thin Line. He plays a Fender guitar that has Seaside Postcard girlie legs climbing all the way up the strap.

"As I reflect back on this crazy life, I'm still trying to figure out what happened between us then, and what continues to go on between us now. Maybe I'll never know." As kids Ray and Dave shared a bed, and invented their own private gibberish language. And the Kinks sound was accidentally — and almost fatally — invented during a rainy afternoon in the Davies front room. By now, Dave is sixteen. He wires his guitar through a series of cheap cannibalised amps... and blows himself across the room when the super-charged first chord short-circuits.

But as the 1960s begin there are a number of separate cells of musical activity happening around the country, all attuned to the same R&B vibe, but all initially unaware of each other. The Beatles in Liverpool. The Yardbirds, Fleetwood Mac and the Rolling Stones in Richmond and Croydon. The Animals in Newcastle. The embryonic Kinks in Muswell Hill...? "Yes, I mean, I always say, the Animals were a very similar kind of band to us. Not musically. But their background. Newcastle was a Working Class town, a provincial Northern town, wasn't it? And yet they were getting a lot of their influences from Blues music, in the same way that we were in the South. And when you think about it, a similar thing happened in America. Rock'n'Roll came up through poverty. The music was basically Blues, and it grew out of oppression, slavery, and all kinds of deprivation. That's *obviously* where the Blues came from. It, in turn, triggered off Elvis, Buddy Holly, and all these people. It was really curious. I come from a big family. I grew up listening to a lot of different types of music. But it was really only Blues, and people like Eddie Cochran, who said to me 'there's something different happening here. I want to be a part of it. I want to do that. I want to be like that'. It was saying something that I wanted to find out about, or express. I couldn't articulate it at the time. [he laughs] I'm probably not doing a very good job of it now either! But — erm — yes, the Blues was very important. It kinda struck a chord. Think of the movies that were going around at the time, the Arts generally, fashion too. They were all changing. Art *was* fashion. Kids were rebelling *through* their clothes. Just see the clothes that *we* were wearing! Out of bravado, really. We just wanted to be noticed by wearing the silliest clothes we could find. But it grew and became fashion. That was a really interesting aspect of the sixties. There was this unconscious expression happening... it was kinda like a coded message going round the planet."

Teenage code-decrypter Dave Davies idolises Eddie Cochran, and sees guitarist Duane Eddy live at the Finsbury Park Empire in 1963 ("my devotion to Duane Eddy was not misplaced"). His own first band — the Ramrods — ends in a brawl at a US Air Base backing a black body-building contortionist on a bill that also includes a couple of over-the-hill strippers. The band gets renamed The Ravens after a Vincent Price horror movie, then the Bo-Weevils after the title of an Eddie Cochran B-side. Then a singer called Robert Wace wangles them some society dates on condition that he can sing with the group. One night he comes on, gets as far as the first chorus of Buddy Holly's Rave On, trips up and accidentally smashes his front teeth out on the mic. Ray steps up to take over vocals — and never quite gets to stand down. But Wace sticks around long enough to contribute the group's next name change. The Kinks. "I thought the idea of being called the Kinks was silly, but it was a saucy name for the time. The Profumo Affair was all over the news then, establishing the names of Christine Keeler and Mandy Rice-Davies, and phrases like 'Kinky Sex' were starting to appear in the tabloids."

Brian Epstein comes to watch them. Promises he'll call. Never does. Instead they follow their first failed single (a surprisingly restrained jog-along reading of Little Richard's Long Tall Sally c/w the Beat-Boom harmonies and harmonica-led Davies original I Took My Baby Home, issued February 7, 1964) with a riff-heavy You Really Got Me — a sound so raw it bleeds. And suddenly this 'scruffy inexperienced bunch of kids' are No 1 on the chart, and the madness begins.

"A lot of the girls I met were quite young, but very willing. Young girls were prepared to do *anything* to be with their adored stars. By March 1964 when we went out on our first package tour with the Dave Clark Five, I was already quite experienced with women — at the ripe age of seventeen."

When Right Wing politicians fulminate about the root causes of sexual permissiveness, the break-up of the family and the break-down of social discipline — all, they claim, the product of the 1960s — they're attacking all the things that the Kinks at their finest, most perfectly represent. In hits that still sound almost virally infectious. And the hits continued, with each subsequent single and album charting their increasing lyrical and structural sophistication — from

the raucous All Day And All Of The Night (No 2; November 19, 1964), through Tired Of Waiting For You (their second No 1, February 18, 1965), the stridently infectious Carnaby Street anthem Dedicated Follower Of Fashion (No 4; March 31, 1966), Sunny Afternoon (a third No 1, July 7, 1966), the satiric Well Respected Man (an America No 15 in February 1966), into the wistful melancholia of Waterloo Sunset (No 2; May 25, 1967) where 'Terry meets Julie, Waterloo Station, every Friday night'. In myth it image-freezes Terence Stamp and Julie Christie. In reality, the song becomes a perfect elegy for the sixties London dream.

"Those first two or three years (1964 to 1967) were unbelievable. A roller coaster ride. The amount of work we did! And the recordings. The record companies expected us to churn out singles every other week virtually. Which we did.

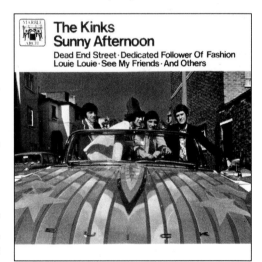

And I mean... Oasis recorded their first album in three weeks. Which is good. That's hard going in this day and age. But we had less than a week to record our first album!" Recorded during a week in August 1964 and issued on October 2, that first album is a strange cauldron of raw regulation Chuck'n'Bo Brit-R&B fare (the Berryesque Beautiful Delilah, Too Much Monkey Business, and Diddley's Cadillac), plus two songs foisted on them by American genius-producer Shel Talmy (the up-tempo instrumental Revenge — a wordless version of Things Are Getting Better done later on their *Kinksize Session* EP — and Bald Headed Woman with Jimmy Page's twelve-string guitar and Jon Lord's Hammond organ sessioning), alongside early examples of Ray's songwriting expertise — So Mystifying, Just Can't Go To Sleep (with Page's guitar string-bending), and Stop Your Sobbin' (many years later destined to be a Top Ten hit for The Pretenders). Songs which already show tantalising hints of what is to come.

"There was just so much pressure, but we were on a roll. You get on a roll don't you? And it was just coming out. New music was just pouring out. Almost as if it was on automatic. And there was no real structure or method to it. It just kind of happened. I don't mind the Kinks being called a Garage band. Because when we started that's all we were. We're probably still like that even now, if we set up in here, that's what we'd sound like today. All of us were very aggressive. It was very much 'Okay, I want to do it *now*. And if that don't work out go on and do the next thing'. Very much like that. I was very impulsive as well, which isn't always good. And I think that generated

around the band. And of course, Ray was still only really feeling his way as a writer. Pulling ideas out of everywhere, this way, that way, and the other. He was kind of more in the background. I was out there sort of sifting through everything. And Ray was learning his craft really, over those first two years. Which is amazing when you think about it. It was a job that none of us had been trained for. Only sort of accomplished to a certain degree musically, do you know what I mean?

"We could do anything. It was like one night we were last-minute booked to do a *Top Of The Pops*. This was when the show was done live in Manchester. We went to the airport, but there were no seats left on the plane. So they immediately took ten people off the plane so they could put us and our entourage on the plane to fly us to Manchester to do the show! You could do literally anything you liked. It was only when it got to around about 1968 or '69, when we *weren't* achieving the same levels of success, and we were having problems in America, that we kinda started to realise what we were doing. Well, I did. I started to realise that we were actually doing this thing for a living. That it was an occupation. A vocation. Other than just being one long party…"

Party? Guests are name-dropped with alarming frequency. John Lennon, for example. "When I wasn't too stoned to know whether or not he was there, we managed to find our way into some disagreements. Once during a conversation he suddenly got up from the table and left. His parting words were, 'YOU'RE PROBABLY ONE OF THE MOST OBNOXIOUS PEOPLE I'VE EVER MET!' I suppose in retrospect I should have regarded that as a compliment. Yes, I *was* arrogant and obnoxious."

Then there's Hendrix drummer Mitch Mitchell, who seemed even more obnoxious. Dave kicked him out of his flat for keeping pigeons under the bed ("his drumming style irritated me too… Hendrix probably didn't care anyway, or even hear him half the time"). And Marianne Faithful ("constantly prick-teasing everyone"). The Kinks toured on bills with most of the major sixties bands. "I got on really well with the Yardbirds, all except Eric Clapton, who was a very quiet, shy sort who always seemed to keep to himself." Manfred Mann was "a self-styled intellectual, cynical, grumpy, hyper-critical and very funny — at least to us." Animals' vocalist Eric Burdon was "usually too pissed to talk." While Searchers' drummer Chris Curtis' night-clubbing "hung out until the end, to catch the male staff before they went home. He had a fetish about what he called 'ugly waiters'."

Honourable mentions, however, do go to Viv Prince who — despite passing up an audition for the Kinks drum-chair due to a drugs overload — later drummed heroically for the Pretty Things. He "understood the true art of self-abuse, and had the stamina to be permanently stoned." And, oddly enough, Gerry Marsden of Gerry & The Pacemakers gets the thumbs-up for being "outrageous, silly and funny." Together, he and Dave smash up the bar of the Grand Hotel, Taunton, with a medieval axe.

There's even a Close Encounter of the Erotic Kind with Rolling Stone Brian Jones. Dave is having gymnastic sex in Paris with Su-Su, a girl 'remarkably experienced in the ways of love-making'. It emerges that she is also a sometime recipient of the Brian Jones penis too. A *ménage à trois* is discussed with all three potential participants enthusiastic about it. But, "the timing was never quite right." Dave did, however, have other 'rather more real encounters with men', including a heavy-petting snog-session with Long John Baldry, a long-term sexual relationship with a designer called Allen, and an affair with camp *Ready Steady Go* TV show host Michael Aldred. 'There is a tender side to a man-to-man relationship that is often sadly forgotten and definitely misunderstood,' he explains in his book, *Kink*. But 'my sexual relationships with men were not nearly as satisfying to me as my liaisons with women.'

He grins wickedly as I probe. His eyes widen and narrow. "It seemed that all of a sudden we were in a business where it was quite normal for people to be bisexual. And homosexual. And when you consider that homosexuality wasn't even *legal* until 1967, it was quite... [pause]... amazing. So we used to have a tongue-in-cheek laugh just to shock people, y'know. I mean Pete [Quaife, Kink bassist] and I were always camping it up. He was a big instigator. We used to get on really well, but not in that bisexuality way. Pete and I would walk down Carnaby Street and develop a little feminine sort of lilt to our walk. The hand would go... Mmmmmm," he mimes campily, minces, puckers and flounces, "just to tease and provoke people."

Long before Ray wrote the 'boys will be girls and girls will be boys' line in Lola, Dave was already immersed in sleazoid sexual oddness. "While I was out carousing and living it up, Ray was content to observe. I did the partying, he wrote about it." It's an intriguing exercise in Rock literary detection to compare and contrast passages in Ray's fictionalised autobiography *X-Ray* (Viking, 1994) with coverage of the same events in Dave's *Kink*. Particularly the bizarro deviancy that lies within the dark origins of David Watts — Ray's Kinksong from the 1967 album *Something Else*, which later became a singles chart hit for The Jam. By now their initially raw unsettling two-and-a-half-minute vinyl-bites have evolved into stories originating in the virtual reality of Ray's head, dressed in Dave's hard-sell riffology, and emerging as preposterously joyful documents full of the trade secrets of 1960s strangeness. But beneath the barcoded surface of consumer lives there are shrewd perceptions,

and surreal journeys twisting through a magic kinkdom of lazy old-world nostalgias commuting through fashion and uncertain sexualities towards the unfamiliar brand-named futures of an ad-mad world. With the compassion, humour, and wistfully yearning laments often camply layered in the symbolism of innuendo and sexual repression. David Watts is a case in point. For he was real. He had a house, a very big house in the country. He promoted a Kinks concert in Rutland, and a post-gig party which rapidly decayed into something of a gay extravaganza during which David propositioned Dave. Compare and contrast texts.

"Yes, the David Watts incident just got a bit out of hand," he understates breathtakingly. In *Kink* he recalls

'...our night at David Watts' was turning into a wonderfully amusing party. The gay police strutted their stuff with total abandon in scenes that could have been right out of Monty Python. Without the least provocation Mick [Avory, Kinks drummer] started to strip his clothes off. As Mick displayed his wares to the delight of the assembled company like some screaming gay truck driver on acid, David took me aside to a quiet corner for a chat. He was extremely drunk. He leered lustfully at me... I seized the opportunity like a true prick-teaser. Now I understood how women felt when being leched at by some perverse and dirty old man.'*

"Pete and I were dancing like this," he resumes, acting it out in grotesquely flamboyant caricature. "We were camping it up. And they took all the messages seriously, as if behind closed doors we really *were* naughty little schoolboys in need of a good spanking. Probably we did. So this incident just kinda got a little out of hand." He smiles dourly. It later turns out that Ray has arranged Dave's seduction all along. Pimping him, trading him for use of the house, the very big house in the country. "Yes, Ray made it a lot worse by trying to flog me for a piece of architecture." Suddenly, the humour is gone. And the story trails off into what looks remarkably like an expression of confused hurt.

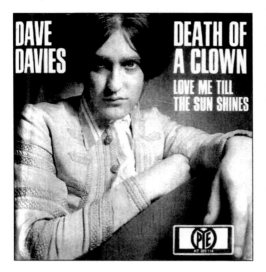

RAY'S A LAUGH
KWYET KINKS

Whisky or gin, that's all right,
there's nothing in her bed at night.
She sleeps with the covers down
hoping somebody gets in,
it doesn't matter what she does,
she knows that she can't win

—Dave Davies, Suzanah's Still Alive

Ray. Let's get that over with right away. For the Kinks are not an Equal Opportunities employer. And one of the submerged sub-themes of *Kink* is hurt. Beneath its rampaging picaresque surface is a long drawn-out howl of anguish against the unfairness of it all. The unequal genetic lottery that divides genius from mere talent. The neglected credit for riffs, song ideas, and unac-

knowledged collaborations. And the devious cruelties deliberately or unfeelingly inflicted by Ray, the arch Kinkster himself.

He balances a lager bottle on his head — Ray that is, live during their most recent tour. Then he feigns harmonica until he gets bored with that. So he stops and addresses the audience direct. "How're ya doin' Chief?" He side-glances at brother Dave with an exaggerated cartoon nod. "I worry 'bout this boy". And all the while the riff roars. They're doing The Informer from the *Phobia* album — but written, according to Ray, ten years earlier. Influenced by living in Ireland. It's slow paced with acoustic overtones. The lyrics go: 'a couple of losers / putting the world to rights.' And I think of Dave writing 'I believe Rock can change the world, and nobody does it better than the Kinks'. Theirs is a relationship built on abuse, maybe, but there's a fierce mutual pride there as well.

Another recurring theme of the book is Sue. Dave is thirteen. Sue is a year older, 'pretty, clever, tall, with large breasts and beautiful long legs'. It's inevitable, says Dave, "that we would wind up losing our virginity to each other." Sitting on a kitchen chair "she straddled herself across my lap after hitching up her delightfully pleated skirt, and I entered her". She becomes pregnant. He's expelled from school. Then their parents collude in splitting them up. And it leaves a scar. Throughout the book, whenever things go wrong or relationships crack up, whenever he feels down or depressed, he thinks of Sue. And their child. And he wonders. Eventually they're briefly reunited, and he's reconciled with the daughter he never knew. It's an oddly touching moment.

"I think Ray's book [X-Ray] was... erm... interesting" he admits. "But it was written in the third person. It was sort of like, in a maze, and it didn't really cover a lot of areas that I thought he could have." Dave's book, by contrast, is less devious. More direct and anecdotal. Ray's tapers off around 1973. Dave's continues through the years beyond. The huge bleak tours. The women. The contentious RCA and Arista albums which eventually break the Kinks big on the American market. The women. The relationship bust-ups and the late flowering of 1983 hits like Come Dancing. Chrissie Hynde. And more women.

But even as the sixties begins to nose-dive into extinction, Dave scores a run of solo hits: Death Of A Clown, Suzannah's Still Alive, and Lincoln County. And he takes a debauched promo trip to do German TV, which starts out with booze and a Diana Dors low-down ('her mirrored bedroom ceiling, her lust for men, and general sexual antics'). Then the soundcheck, drugs and complimentary whores in the hotel...

'This voluptuous woman began to give me a massage... my mouth was so dry I could barely speak and my head was reeling, but I felt wonderful. She moved her hand down to my stomach and stroked and kissed my abdomen with the gentle and sensual ease of a consummate artist. I felt her mouth on my penis, it felt as if her tongue was inside my head, touching and stimulating every nerve ending and sensory centre in my brain.'

For the actual telecast, he's so blobbed out of it he's unable to stand, and has to go through the motions of miming to his hit sitting on a stool.

There are no Black Holes in Muswell Hill. But Dave is creating his own. It was "as if I were being devoured by a dark psychic swamp that was dragging me into its secret world in all its subtle and insidious power." People he'd clubbed with — Keith Moon and Brian Jones — didn't make it through. Yet Dave survives the nightmare of what he calls his 'psychic death'. He gives up meat, drugs and excess. And tunes into a Loony-Tune

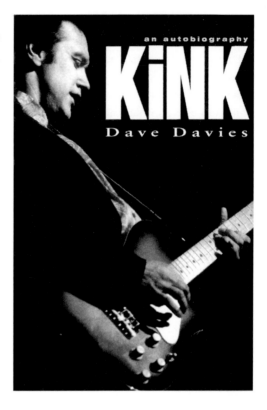

New Age consciousness wide enough to include UFO-chasing openness to X-Filed millennial possibilities, and which he even ties in with the current TV sci-fi boom. "It's not by accident that all this stuff's happening" he begins cautiously, with a wary glance at Kate. "It's like, I mean, we could be all day talking about it. 'Cos it's a very vast area of interest to me..."

Greater literary and journalistic minds than my own have already speculated links between this New Age spiritual awareness with the flashback potential of his earlier indulgence in 'perverse fun'. Indeed, his first intimations of 'otherness' come during a vividly described LSD trip. But it's during a later non-(directly)-narcotically induced sequence — what he calls his 'psychic death' — that he's contacted by 'alien intelligences'. His inner life is transfigured as a result, and his consciousness heightened. But after all, acid-guru Timothy Leary once claimed you could touch God through chemical drug-use, didn't he? "I think to a point he was probably right" he offers. "But it was kinda like, desperate times need desperate measures. Drugs are like using a sledgehammer to crack a walnut. But it has a relevance. Although I definitely don't advocate the use of hallucinogenics. But then again, I was talking to some kids about Ecstasy the other night. And these kids were actually functioning very well with each other. Talking about feeling the transmission of love between people. That's not crazy. Alright, so it's a chemical going off in the brain, making the nervous system or the brain do this. But is that so bad? Maybe — like, the whole universe is a fragment of my imagination? [he laughs] But if it doesn't cause harm. That's where we have to draw the line."

"To me, Buddhism is the most modern concept" he side-steps. "Because it relates to how you can function to improve your life, and the lives of other people around you. It's not necessarily God-related. It's an internal process. And aspects of it have been around for thousands and thousands of years. So that's why I tend to gravitate towards these Eastern things. But how come all these various wise guys had it, yet the world is in such a terrible state?"

I don't know. So he tells me.

"It's because they made it *convenient*! They made religion convenient and easy. And all it does is give people very little information, and makes them slaves of governments or religious organisations. I have some friends who are part of UFO groups. People say 'Oh yeah, but they sound like a cult to me'. But the Roman Catholic Church is a cult. Just because there's more of them than there are of me. I'm a universe of one. I'm a country of one. How many millions of Catholics are there around the world? Let's say

there's ten million — is that about right? I don't know, would *you* know?"

The *Observer* quotes 964.7 million worldwide baptised Catholics. "Okay, so there's a thousand million of them and only one of me, does that make me wrong? Y'know, might isn't always right. An individual's point of view is just as important. Particularly nowadays when there's so much misery, suffering, and shit happening. To me, the whole concept of spirituality is internal. It should be worked out internally. I... create... my own... spirituality... within me. The world will never change until we work on ourselves internally anyway. 'Cos that's where all the problems are. And all the problems *can* be solved."

Of course, it all ties in. It's not by accident that all this stuff's happening. Like, for example, Leonard 'Mr Spock' Nimoy introducing the Kinks on-stage at a Minneapolis concert. "That was *great*. He's a big Kinks fan. I had *no* idea. And that was a lovely moment. It was *really* exciting. You know? His voice, his projection! The only thing that was missing, he didn't have his pointed ears on. But you can't have everything."

He glances across to where Kate sits, colour co-ordinated with the orange upholstery. "Alright? So how're we doing?"

As the Leeds Town & Country gig finishes with an unexpected Twist And Shout, Dave holds his guitar out like a relic from Lourdes for fans to touch and to be healed by.

I swear I too was healed.
Thank you for the days,
I don't regret a single day,
believe me...

—The Kinks, Days

Kink: An Autobiography
by Dave Davies
ISBN 0-7522-1695-3 / Boxtree, 1996 / £16.99
ISBN 0-330-35377-2 / Pan, 1997 / £6.99

© Dogger

THE BYRDS
GENE CLARK
STRANGER THAN KNOWN

GENE CLARK, *founder member and main songwriter of the original* **BYRDS**, *toured Britain for the last time in 1985, during which this interview was taped. He died May 24, 1991, after his return to the States. This, then, is possibly the text of the last British interview he ever gave...*

 ashed in low vermilion light Gene Clark hefts his big acoustic guitar and goes into the opening lines of Mr Tambourine Man for what must be the 2010th time…

A fistful of years earlier, down around the turn of Punk, Gene and some other ragged ex-Byrds tour Europe to generally damning reviews. He appears 'listless' writes Steve Clarke (*New Musical Express*, May 14, 1977), "the epitome of the slightly stumbling overweight bearded Hippie who's drunk and smoked too much." Unless you happen to be Lou Reed, the late seventies isn't a good time for living legends and fully qualified survivors.

Here tonight, he grimaces at the memories, and at memories of the aftermath of that tour: "I couldn't get *anything* to do, it was *impossible*. People just weren't getting together and doing things. All my really good pals like Rick Danko and Michael [Clarke, ex-Byrds drummer] were kinda hiding out. Michael was on the road with Jerry Jeff [Walker] and Rick was somewhere up in Woodstock and didn't want to talk to anybody

— while I was in Hawaii for a year. Then, after some time had gone by, I'd done an album called *Firebyrd*. And Mike and I were sitting in a restaurant one morning and he says 'well man, what're we gonna do? Here we are, we've finished doing the album, so there's gotta be *something* to do!' So I said 'well Mike, what do you think we ought to do?' And he says 'let's get some guys together and just start going on the road playing music'. So we put together a group called Firebyrd, with some old guys from Spirit.

We went out on the road, just playing, and we really had a good time. Got quite a bit of press over there too, and suddenly it seemed as though everything kinda turned around. And you know the thing that surprises me now? It's the amount of young kids that have turned back to music with a little bit more roots to it — like the early Beatles, Byrds, and the early Rolling Stones. I swear we get kids — and I'm talking twelve, thirteen and fourteen! — and this is what's blowing my mind. I know young kids who love Willie Nelson, and he's an *old* man — c'mon, you know what I'm saying? *I'm* old compared to what they *think* of as old. I'm forty, while these kids are, what... fifteen? And they love it! I was doing a radio interview in Louisville Kentucky or someplace, and there were fifteen-year-old kids calling up who were just total *fans*. I mean they were *into* it. And I've seen them come to the concerts. They couldn't care less if those songs first came out twenty years ago. They're buying the records and they're loving them. So it seems we've ended up with some kind of a non-generation gap audience. Which is great."

The provocatively intolerant, but valuably iconoclastic revolution of 1976/77 ran its course ("You see, the Punk thing came and went pretty quickly, like a fad in the States," claims Gene a little prematurely). Icons got spat on. Guitar solos got mocked and reviled. Then new icons got themselves erected. Pretty much the same as the old ones. Yet on the more positive side, what follows is an opening out into a new, slightly more disciplined, less self-indulgent awareness of the virtues of certain elements of Rock traditionalism. Bands like REM, Lone Justice, Long Ryders, Rain Parade, and Green on Red — a whole phantasmagoric Paisley Underground — enthusiastically acknowledging the legacy of, and making it suddenly legit to confess an affection for the likes of Love, Buffalo Springfield,

and above all, the quintessential Byrds. Simultaneously, archivist label Edsel set about reissuing four Gene Clark solo albums in a shiny promotional package designed to meet the needs of this revamped interest. There's his *Roadmaster* set — originally released in December 1972, and then available only in Holland — featuring Byrds-friendly sidemen of the calibre of Sneaky Pete Kleinow, Clarence White and Byron Berline. There's the two Country-angled Dillard And Clark albums which Gene cut with Doug Dillard: *Through The Morning Through The Night* (Sept 1969), and *The Fantastic Expeditions Of...* (Oct 1968) which features contributions from future-

Eagles' guitarist Bernie Leadon — who, you might imagine, was furiously taking notes blueprinting his own soon-come high-profile chart career. Then there's *So Rebellious A Lover* (1985), a duo album Gene did with sometime Textones vocalist Carla Olsen, from 1984. All four were back on catalogue to coincide with this tour. Meanwhile Gene himself was guesting on the Long Ryders' excellent *Native Sons* album. While Hüsker Dü *and* Roxy Music were recording covers of Gene's Eight Miles High, and Flamin' Groovies were recording an electrifying take of his classic Feel A Whole Lot Better... as was Tom Petty for his *Full Moon Fever* album...

He does that one live tonight too.

SO YOU WANT TO BE A ROCK'N'ROLL STAR...?

And, as we speak backstage at the Wakefield Pussycat club in the lost wastes of West Yorkshire, it is *exactly* twenty years to the month (June 22, 1965) that the rarefied stratospheric harmonies and janglipop Rickenbacker guitars of Mr Tambourine Man peaked on the British chart at No 1, over the likes of the Yardbirds (Heart Full Of Soul), Elvis Presley (Crying In The Chapel) and Joan Baez (with Phil Ochs, There But For Fortune). It stays there two weeks, to be deposed only by the might of the Beatles' Help. In those far-off time-lost days a 45rpm single costs a precise 6s8d. And on a personal note — I get stranded in the Hull city centre with just enough carefully hoarded pocket-money either to go to Hammonds' record department with its luring listening booths to make the purchase I ache to make, or to pay for the long and winding bus-fare home. So, inevitably, I walk all the miles back clutching that orange-labelled CBS Byrds single tightly in my hand.

In what Roger — then 'Jim' McGuinn — calls a cross-Atlantic tennis match, America invents Rock music, the Beatles and the Stones throw it a few new curves and shapes, and lob it back, so that the Byrds — their harmonies carried on the futuristic mystique of Dylan's methadrine-fuelled poetry — can become the volley-back retaliation. Their horizons seem infinite. The epitome of Beat Hip with Mod(ernist) Cool. In their first promo shots they are five immaculately aloof fringes posed *With The Beatles*-style out of the black. Superior. Articulate. As cool as every promise of tomorrow. And this man — born Eugene

Harold Clark on November 17, 1941, in Tipton Missouri, an ex-Folkie one-time member of the Jet Set and the Beefeaters, was an essential ingredient of the band that opened the Day-Glo floodgates to all things West Coast esoteric and ultra-Hip. A band of awesome vision and wondrous innovation, the Byrds personified, and made flesh, a seismic shift in popular culture that still reverberates now, across decades, up to the Stone Roses, down to Travis and Teenage Fan Club. Pop seldom came better.

Perhaps that's part of it... part of its shimmering allure, but they're here tonight, teenage members of local bands cramming into the dressing room to pay homage. 'I've been waiting since before I was born for this' says one. "Do you still hang out with all those guys from the Byrds? You do — wow! How's Crosby doing?' gushes another. And he greets them all, as he greets me, with patience and indulgence.

There's also the obligatory first-generation Hippies who get him to autograph import copies of *Firebyrd* — his 'playin' favourites' album with the full four-verse version of Mr Tambourine Man which he performs tonight, plus Gordon Lightfoot's If You Could Read My Mind. The album is now into its second, or is it its third American printing? — according to Gene, but as the tour progresses it is still ludicrously without a regular European distribution deal!

And interview time? There's a studiously intense fanzine writer up from Cambridge who gets in first with a long itemised and typewritten scroll of questions going album-by-album from Gene's time with the New Christy Minstrels through the meeting with Roger McGuinn, then David Crosby in 1964, through the hits and the splits, and on up to, about... now. "The New Christy Minstrels? Oh yeah, I was on several of their albums. Well, see — oh God, I came in right after they'd finished Green Green. That was a *hit* single! It was starting to be a hit when I came into the group. Then there was an album called *Cowboys And Indians*. I think I did that one with them. Then I did a Christmas album, and another album with them — right? Then... we did several more, lots of TV and stuff, and toured all over. But the funny thing is it was *so* long ago, and we were travelling *really* fast for those days, I mean — man, one-nighters like you can't believe, y'know? And you have to remember that this was in the early stages of it all, jet flights had just come into existence in the few years before that. So the New Christy Minstrels, the Kingston Trio, Peter Paul & Mary, were the pioneers of today's jet-setting tours. Of course, today it's second nature, they all do it..."

THE FIREBYRD SUITE...

Gene Clark *looks* different. Baggy sweat-shirt top, sure. Denim pants, sure. And clean-shaven this time around...

On the early album sleeves, in promo stills and on ITV's cult *Ready Steady Go* show, he's there, basin-cut hair, sharp angular profile, gaunt, with almost haunted eyes. Tonight on stage, with the vermilion light cosmetically ironing out the ravages, he looks almost unrecognisably fresh, fleshed-out healthy. Backstage, with the unforgiving white light betraying the odd character-lines, you can see the odd visible reminders of a quarter-century on the road. But he still looks to be in good shape, better shape than the last tour, and the one before that. And he's *hungry*. Hungry for English Fish & Chips! The Pussycat club is a tarted-up variety venue more used to staging ribald Roy 'Chubby' Brown or Bernard Manning evenings than Folk-Rock Legends. And it sells every imaginable variety of American burger. But he wants *Fish & Chips*! So dutifully, I venture out to scour the late-night city precincts for a still-functioning chippie, it's the

least I can do by way of my own slight homage, getting back to find the fanzine interview already in session. "Say something so I can get a sound level," the scribe begins uncertainly, poring over his machine, with Gene grinning indulgently and now chomping huge greasy handfuls of *my* chips while answering someone else's questions! Life's unfair sometimes. But it gives me time and opportunity to study him at close-range and draw aforesaid conclusions.

At length he stands, washes his big workman's hands in the sink, carefully scrunches the chip-paper into a neat ball — "I'll just clear this crap away" — and shakes hands. "I didn't get your name? Andy? It's nice to meet you Andy." And so, with most of my archivist-type questions already spooled onto someone else's tape-machine we get into free-associating, he's well-loosened up now too, in a speed-jive motor-mouthing mood, derailing one topic into the other, anecdotes to drool over, name-dropping Bob, Rick, Roger, leaving me to pick up the connections like they're too obvious to explain...

Despite Roger McGuinn being the usually accredited group leader, it is this guy — Gene Clark — who actually wrote the majority of the original material on the first two official Byrds albums, classic material like Feel A Whole Lot Better, I Knew I'd Want You and Set You Free This Time. "Right," he agrees without rancour, like — *and where's the question?* "Actually — the thing is, there's always been streaks that I have in my life where I'll write a whole bunch of stuff within, like, two weeks. Then I might not write anything for ages. It just *comes*, like that, and I'll be waking up in the middle of the night for two weeks straight just scribbling stuff down, grabbing my guitar, putting it on tape. Usually it turns out that those songs are the best, because when you get a streak like that you're not trying to force anything, and you're not *trying* to come up with a song. And if something just comes to you, like that, it's real clear. Now those periods usually happen in two different ways — either on the road when you're with guys like Roger and David. People are trading ideas, y'know, and you're on the bus singing, playing or doing something like that. Or else they happen when I'm at home and I have some time to really relax, be quiet, and just kinda settle back down into my surroundings. Then things start coming in. But when it's a drag period I don't try. I don't even deal with trying to force it because it won't work. I've tried it a few times, and I've *never* liked any of the songs, so… y'know."

But the Rock'n'Roll history books state that with those albums — *Mr Tambourine Man* and *Turn! Turn! Turn!* — Pop began to intellectualise itself into Rock. "Right". And that the Byrds were one of the first bands to give Rock some kind of intellectual content. "A lot of that had to do with Dylan too, y'know. And John Lennon — bless his soul, man. I think he and Dylan are still probably the two most influential figures…"

"And I just found out" he drawls conversationally in a gravely David Janssen voice, "two more young groups have now cut Eight Miles High

over in the States — and one of them's doing a full-budget video on it." Featured on the Byrds third (*Fifth Dimension*) album, Eight Miles High was the last song Clark contributed to the group "before the thing started to fall apart." And it was released as Gene was in the process of becoming the first Byrd to quit, heading out, blazing Blue-Grass trails for his 'Fantastic Expeditions'. And although the remaining McGuinn-led Byrds had yet to deliver the incandescent *Younger Than Yesterday* — including some of their most beautiful moments — Clark's Country-Rock was by then already pioneering sounds that they too would follow in a couple of albums' time. So, besides being *my* all-time favourite vinyl of the decade, Eight Miles High is something of a watershed in Clark's career.

"You know how that song *really* started?" he asks casually. "It was me and Brian Jones sitting in a hotel room on the road when we — the Byrds, that is — were touring with the Rolling Stones. And we all got to be — me, Mick [Jagger], and Brian — real good friends. Brian was always a little more sociable than Mick and Keith [Richards], even though I really love Mick, I think he's great — he's definitely a tough guy, he stays out there and he does it real good. I respect him totally. But Brian was *always* real friendly. So he and I and Michael started hanging out together. I remember we were up in the hotel room. We ordered dinner one night and we were all sitting there eating a coupla steaks, talking and having a couple of scotches, and we started talking about William Burroughs. And somehow I just got this idea — it came into my mind — I don't know how the conversation led up to it or anything like that, but all I know is that I started scribbling down the poetry, y'know. And Brian said 'what're you doing?' And I said 'this' [he mimes showing him], and he looks at it, and he reads a little bit of it, and he says 'that's pretty good, you ought to work on that!' So that's how the song started. And then, I think… I worked on it kind of in private for — gosh, maybe about two weeks or something — almost every night in the hotel room or something like that. And then we were on the bus — there was all of us travelling across country on a Motor Home, and we were listening to a lot of John Coltrane, and a lot of Ravi Shankar, because we were 'programming' ourselves. And Bach — we were listening to a lot of Bach too. And I played the song on acoustic guitar for McGuinn. I remember our Road Manager turned around — God rest his soul, he's dead now — but he turned around and said 'that's good poetry!' And McGuinn goes 'yeah, I like that'. And then Crosby comes down out of his bunk — all the way down he goes, 'yeah, I like that too', and he says 'I got a line for that one place where the words are kinda shaky', so he threw a line in. And then McGuinn started working on it, he began getting into arranging it. So it ended up, the three of us ended up writing the finished thing. But the original idea came,

of course, out of Brian Jones, but he didn't know it. He never even got to know it. At the time he probably didn't halfway remember having the conversation, you know what I'm saying…?"

The stuff of legend. And that's just the beginning. I come out punch-drunk on the stuff.

TURN! TURN! TURN!

By the time he arrives in Wakefield this night on a tour supporting Lindisfarne, Gene Clark had been through hard times. He'd cut a series of cult solo albums — *Echoes* (February 1967) with the Gosdin Brothers, *White Light* (1971), *No Other* (1974) and *Two Sides To Every Story* (March 1977) — which took him through the seventies. Until, in a brief McGuinn, Clark And Hillman reunion, he found himself back in the US Top Forty with Don't Write Her Off Like That. Then, with the *Firebyrd* (1984) album, plus the groundswell of Byrd-maniax revivalism manifest in the Edsel reissue programme, he finds himself briefly back where the action is. Neatly coinciding with the amplifying echo of the Twentieth Anniversary whizz-bang of Mr Tambourine Man.

"It's funny how things come around" he muses in a moment of introspection as we wind down. "And the thing that still blows my mind is how you can go along and *nothing* is happening — and then, all at once, one thing breaks loose, and then everything snowballs. Maybe it's the time for it. I'm a little bit in shock that we still have — or have again — as big a following as we do. Whatever it is, it's definitely developing. But of course" he guffaws again in obvious pleasure, "it's not like I just started doing it yesterday either, you know!"

Gene Clark, Younger than Yesterday.

© Dogger

FLEETWOOD MAC
PETER GREEN
SPLINTERED

Joy it is to be here in the apple-blossom 'burbs, quietly seething with mysterious intrigue. And knowing it's all just a meandering bus ride from Croydon along the 'London Loop' of bridle-paths and picturesque country-style pubs with names like The Good Companions. But today, normality need not necessarily apply. For beneath all this apple blossom suburban respectability lurks one of Rock'n'Roll's most time-warped tales of teenage delinquency. Peter Green's story is a doosey among doosies. According to one of his biggest hits, he's a Man Of The World — it's just that for two decades the world in question happened to be Saturn. **PETER GREEN** *is the man who created* **FLEETWOOD MAC**, *wrote Albatross, then took twenty years out of his life to write the longest suicide note in Rock'n'Roll history. But now he's back, reclaimed from the Dead Zone and recording his first new Blues sides since his long, long absence from the music world... it's just that today he has hiccups. And a giant Klingon in his front room.*

nd of course, I've come to the wrong house. "The gentleman from Fleetwood Mac?" says the little old lady in a voice full of conspiratorial intimacy. "I've never actually *met* him. But I've seen him. And I saw the programme they did about him on television!" She means the BBC TV *The Works* documentary from October 1996, which did much to alert the nation to Peter Green's troubled history. And his return from the Dead Zone to active recording and performing.

The right house now. A gravel drive leads up to a porch. And after a long silence... Peter Green, in pale blue striped pyjamas and a hastily pulled-on dressing gown. Clumps of hair hang around his temples like wisps of lint. "Interview... what? I'm rehearsing today, I think. She's not here. I don't know whether I'm supposed to let you in. I'll have to find out." He's obviously agitated. I offer to return. Half an hour? He withdraws gratefully. I walk a little further down the avenue in no particular direction, past the tennis courts to the bridle path. Sit down, back hard up against a tree, listen to the cassette the record company gave me, and consider the strange

case of Peter G. The one-time 'Mr Wonderful' of Fleetwood Mac. A man who'd crossed the line. A line of fire. A man who poured gasoline on his career, and ignited it. I construct strategy. I always have strategy. But this one's important. Start with now. Then build a bridge of words back to the beginning, safe areas he's familiar with. Circle the black hole into which all his life was thrown, until he's at ease, then stalk that dangerous terrain carefully...

He lets me in warily. He's dressed now. Jeans.

Baggy sweat-shirt. He shows me into the front room... and leaves me there! Some long moments later he reappears. "What's the time?" he demands. "3:45." "And what time's the interview supposed to start?" "Four o' clock." "Right." And he disappears again, leaving me in the mid-afternoon gloom of his lounge. There's just me and him in the whole house. We're alone. But because the interview is scheduled to start at four, he scrupulously observes that punctuality, carefully making himself scarce until that time. And, although I'd prepared myself for all manner of odd scenarios, I'd not anticipated what comes next! I'm checking out his books and CDs (BB King *The Autobiography*, *Bumble Bee* by Memphis Minnie, and a *Mississippi Delta Blues* album collection, Muddy Waters' *20 Blues Greats*, Lonnie Johnson's *Blues In My Fingers*, Elvis' *Always On My Mind*, and Jimmy Witherspoon) when suddenly, over my shoulder, I catch sight of Worf — the giant *Star Trek* Klingon! Dark and brooding with menace, phaser on stun — and totally stunning. The kind of life-size movie promotional stand-up you get in the cinema multiplex foyer.

So has Peter Green, Fleetwood Mac's first and greatest guitarist, the man who boldly went deeper and further into unknown worlds than just about anyone else, the man who navigated Rock'n'Roll's darkest inner spaces, become a Trekkie? "What's wrong (hic)?" he demands later, obviously confused by my question. "What, me *Star Trek*? No. I think it's stupid. I watched it when it first came out, to see what it was like. When it was the original cast, Spock, Scotty and... the Captain... Captain Kirk. I watched it then. But when it changed... I didn't watch it anymore. *She* watches it most nights and... erm (hic), some of her friends bought that cut-out for her. I think it's stupid."

The 'She' he refers to is Michelle Reynolds,

former wife of Fleetwood Mac's manager Clifford Davis. And sister of Splinter Group guitarist Nigel Watson. She is now Peter's live-in 'companion'. She's wearing the kind of white top that would pass the Daz doorstep challenge, and joins us for the interview which — she suggests — would be best done sitting by the rustic table on the patio. She brings us coffee and doughnuts. "I'm just having my lunch. A late lunch". She's attentive. Discrete. Helps out when Peter stumbles details. Prompts as required. "We'll have to do something about your hiccups" she tells him.

"It's my sea lion" answers Peter, a little bafflingly. "My pet sea lion coming through." Then, to me, "have you ever interviewed someone with hiccups before?" And I have to admit that, no, I haven't. So we talk guitars instead. He has a growing collection of them. I glimpsed some very interesting ones hung on the wall of his room as I came in. He's enthusiastic about "a black one. A Berlioz flying-V. That's a special one of mine. You can have a good look at them if you like, before you go?"

"You'll have to make your bed first!" snipes Michelle piercingly.

Rock'n'Roll! Phew...!

I could tell you about my life
and keep you amused I'm sure...
　　　　　　—Fleetwood Mac, Man Of The World

Peter Green knuckles his eyes at the sun. In the garden, there's the rich scent of twice-blooming apple-blossom, and lilac overhanging the outer wall. A black cat prowls with affectionate intent. And Peter sits across from me at the rustic table. He's wearing a grey V-neck sweatshirt stretched over his portly gut, the short button-hole side folded annoyingly inwards at the neck, so that you have a persistent compulsion to reach forward and turn it right-side-out. His grey-white wisps and tufts of hair float around his temples, fanning in the breeze. He teases out the strands as he talks, then smoothes it all back close to his head. Sometimes he loses himself in his own trains of thought. But the emerging theme is obvious. He wants to be respected, if at all, for what he's doing now. Not for the tangled skeins of myth and half-truths that have accumulated around his life. The years of madness. The shotgun incident. The uncut finger-nails grown so unfeasible long they made playing guitar impossible. The religious torments that had him appearing on stage in a long white robe and crucifix.

So I deliberately start our conversation with what he's doing *now*. The Splinter Group. Then vault back over the madness to where he began. He's happy to talk. The current band is called The Splinter Group (which originally featured the late Cozy Powell on drums, and Neil Murray — formerly of Gary Moore and Whitesnake — on bass). There are new albums, blazing with some of his most confidently Blues wailingest material since... well, since his legendary last stint with Fleetwood Mac, the group he founded and which he originally powered to global stardom. And then there's a well-received

on-going tour. On the *Splintered* album, in the spaces between the live tracks, you can hear the audience warmth. Such levels of response must be gratifying. "The response is not what I worry about" he says dismissively. "I don't worry about audience response at all. I wouldn't mind if they didn't clap. In fact, it would make a change or something. I prefer it when we're just playing without an audience. But sometimes, when we play particularly nicely, then the response is more sensible, you see? More like something at Ronnie Scott's. At a Jazz club it would be more just, you know..." he claps his hands politely to demonstrate his idea of what would constitute suitable audience appreciation. Then he trails off into vacuum, "in-between numbers we... we, well, mmmm... I had a great word there... but it's gone, ah — yeah..."

Peter Green was born in October 1946, and spent a Cockney-Jewish childhood in Bethnal Green. "I was always a big fan of Little Richard, and Bill Haley & the Comets. Yeah, I liked them very much," he recalls. "But Bill Haley faded from sight when Elvis took over, didn't he? He suddenly appeared kind-of old-fashioned in some ways. Not much hair." By the time he was fourteen — going on fifteen — Peter was already bass-player with a group called The Tridents, the Shadows providing an early guitar model. One he's recently rediscovered. The Shadows early hits now provide ideal material for guitar rehearsal. "Hank Marvin was my first guitar hero. But I have to go back in time to admire him. I study melody by playing tunes like Wonderful Land. I don't know it off pat. I couldn't play it to you now without making a mistake — but I could probably get through Apache, and FBI. Peace Pipe is beautiful too. That's one of the all-time greats to me. But I could never play Man Of Mystery, in fact I eventually gave up on the Shadows because I simply *couldn't* play it." Elmore James. Willie Dixon. Robert Johnson. I'd expected names like that to occur. But *Hank B Marvin...?* Yet the debt has not gone unnoticed in the Shadows camp. "Hank was very pleased with Peter's version of Midnight on the *Twang* album," adds Michelle, referring to Peter's contribution to a Rock guitar tribute album, recorded in Francis Rossi's home studio.

But meanwhile, there are new idols. We've now reached around the mid-1961 mark, soon after Yuri Gagarin became the world's first spaceman, but before Christine Keeler had met John Profumo. The Beatles are still in Hamburg and Bob Dylan has yet to play his first New York concert. And the Tridents' lead singer gives 'Greeny' three Blues albums. And Blues — he soon discovers — by-passes the levels of verbal and logical understanding. It strikes directly at the intuitive. "You think, *c'mon,* you hear that great voice of inspiration saying 'play what *you* feel is music'. It talks, y'know. It's saying something." Even now, when he's on stage playing, it's a totally non-cerebral, completely 'natural' thing, a sensation that flows without thought processes for its expression. Only now it's a two-way thing, with no less a Blues giant than BB King saying "Peter

Green is the only living guitarist to make me sweat. He's got the sweetest tone I've ever heard." And when Buddy Guy plays The Shepherd's Bush Empire, he makes a special point of asking to meet Peter after the show.

But Peter is emphatic that the artists his style is modelled on are not 'heroes'. He distrusts heroes. Heroes are fantasy figures with supernatural attributes. Blues musicians are ordinary people who happen to have developed peculiarly expressive techniques for communicating experience. "I'm not one for heroes. Buddy Guy. Howlin' Wolf. Sonny Boy Williamson. They're not heroes to me. The whole thing is that they're ordinary people. I like to hear the records. Hear the music. But I never worry about meeting them. I don't have to go and seek them out. I don't have to forsake my privacy, or chance intruding upon theirs. I don't know what to say to these people. I really don't. But I've got no problem with that. I'd rather go and just be one of the audience."

The sixties cult of guitar heroes — a pantheon into which he was rapidly, if unwillingly included, made him feel equally uneasy. "People keep complimenting me" he complains. "They shouldn't really do that. Sometimes you wonder if they're jokers or not. When people come up to me and say 'you're my hero', I don't want to hear that. They shouldn't say that to me. 'Cos I haven't got any heroes, so I can't accept that anyone else has heroes either. That's the whole point. I'm a Working Class person. I hated school passionately. Going to school, getting up in the morning and rushing, doing everything. I just hated all those things that I had to do. Then when I got to work it was really strange too, it was like going back in time. It was a very, very strange experience. But I'll always have love for people who have that sense of their own mortality, people that see that they're going to die, who know that fear of death that comes at some point in their lives. That kind of *realistic* thing, you know? People who have spent time alone. People who have lived alone. And yet they're still just ordinary people. I can't have anybody as a hero. I could probably come up with some name for you, eventually. But it might be a jockey. Or it might be a cartoon character, I don't know."

For the moment let's restrict it to current guitar heroes. Who does he listen to? "Loads of them. I like Francis Rossi. He plays quite interesting notes." Or Lenny Kravitz perhaps? "I fancy 'is drummer, actually. That girl he has on drums. But I guess he's the nearest player around to Jimi Hendrix."

And coming closer to home, it must have been good having Cozy Powell playing on that first Splinter Group CD. "Why is that?" Why? Because he was a powerful drummer. "Naw. It's good to have *any* drummer. It's good to have *someone* on drums. But Cozy was a really great geezer. A good bloke. And *very* good looking. But eventually I'd like to play with mixed races. I guess Cozy was a bit like a mixed race himself in a way, wasn't he..." Mitch — that is, Michelle — adds "Cozy was part Red Indian, wasn't he?"

"Was he? I thought he was. Yeah. Not a bad drummer. I suppose." There's a brief silence. I look around. Beyond the garden fence there's the apple-blossom 'burbs seething with mysterious intrigue.

Can't help it 'bout the shape I'm in
I can't sing, I ain't pretty, and my legs are thin...
—Fleetwood Mac, Oh Well

When the Bonzo Dog Doo Dah Band posed the question 'Can de Blue Men sing de Whites?', it — the ability of the paler more northerly races to play music more normally associated with the Mississippi Delta or the Kansas City ghetto juke-joints — was a question of crucial subcultural importance. And the fanatically purist sixties Blues boom it describes, ignited by the evangelical highly-amped boogie of Cyril Davies, Alexis Korner and John Mayall, was to become a forcing house for much of the mega-buck Rock'n'Roll mayhem that was to follow — from the Rolling Stones, Led Zeppelin, Van Morrison and Eric Clapton... to the hyper-platinum MOR dross of prime-time Stevie Nicks-period Fleetwood Mac. And kingpin to it all were the lean, raw and hungry guitar heroes, Jeff Beck, Keith Richards, 'Slowhand' Clapton... and this guy, the outrageously precociously talented Peter Green who arguably took it all farthest. And then paid the most terrible price of all.

Robert Johnson was the doomed early Blues pioneer who legendarily traded his soul to Satan in exchange for his eerily awesome guitar genius. Peter Green must have hung around those same diabolical Crossroads. He's done a Robert Johnson tribute album with the Splinter Group. And even before that he'd already done Steady Rolling Man, with Peter singing and playing mouth-harp at its most authentic. And then there are two tracks done stark and stripped-back in the Fleetwood Mac Mobile studio. "'Stark' what? What did you say about them?" he queries vaguely. "'Stark' and 'Stripped Back'? What's that then? S–T–A–R–K and *stripped back*?" He samples the incomprehensible words like some baffling foreign language. "'Stark'…?"

"He means 'Back to Basics'," offers Mitch helpfully, her deep bronze hair fringing down to her knitted white sweater. "… and *stripped* back" he meanders on, each word pronounced carefully and very clearly. "I don't know what 'Stripped Back' is."

This is the man who spent twenty years re-arranging his sock drawer. So I guess it's unreasonable to expect snappy soundbites now. "I lost a lot of valuable years, maybe. But you can't say how it all works. I'm practising now, so I've got to be thankful for that. I'm learning. It's not work for me nowadays. It's pleasure. I can copy BB King solos with love. That's what people want. I ain't doing it for falsification. I'm doing it because I love copying BB King. I love his notations, his whatever-it-is you call it. There's no word for it. I copy them [the Blues masters] as best as I can. I'm Jewish. So I've got a little trapdoor there. The old Hebrew Testament thing, right back to

Moses. It could be worse, couldn't it?"

So he's fourteen-years-old — remember? — and already bass-player with a group called The Tridents, when he first hears Blues. "I was given three albums, a John Lee Hooker one. And one called *Rhythm And Blues*. It was a cheap Woolworth's album, and I didn't like anything cheap. I was very aware of all that kind of thing. I didn't like things from Woolworth's at all. But I love that album nowadays. It's one of my favourites. And the third album was *Folk Festival Of The Blues* with a dark cover, and Buddy Guy, Howlin' Wolf,

Sonny Boy Williamson and Willie Dixon on it. I didn't know what to make of them at first. I *really* didn't. I don't think I even wanted to play them. But the drums on one track with Buddy Guy slowed down, got slower and slower, and every time it got round to the start of another verse he kinda held it, and slowed it down a bit more. I don't know who was on drums, but he's a marvellous drummer. And that's what I first took to. The drummer. I took to the style of the thing. I *felt* what it was all about. I thought, I could *feel* this, feel what it was all about."

Then, "when I first heard Eric Clapton [with the Yardbirds] everything he played was pure enjoyment. Magic. Magicer than magic. And Paul Samwell-Smith, the group's bass player, what he played I enjoyed too. He played chords on his bass. He had a beautiful bass guitar and a lovely amplifier. And the whole group were rocking along to Chuck Berry and Bo Diddley things. And it was 'Wow, look at that!' And, you alter course, like a fish. I was onto Bill Wyman too. When you're young you kinda go on people who impress you. They're up there, strong and hairy, and futuristic I guess. So, I was a bass player for a while, and Eric Clapton was the person who led me here. He was the person who led me to this path. He put me on this path. Before that my guitar was a pastime. Then, when I got a job as a bass-guitarist I found I could make a little bit of money. Not very much at all. Enough to pay for a guitar, a uniform and an amplifier. Nothing else really. But I didn't make much money — as a *bass-player*. And... oh, I've forgotten what I was about to say. Oh yes — fingerboard study development, it's a direction, it shows you where to go from here."

After a brief spell in a group called Shotgun Express with aspiring Mod Rocker — and Joe Meek reject — Rod Stewart, switching from bass to lead, Green "followed Eric Clapton into John Mayall's Bluesbreakers. And John gave me lots of music to listen to. He was always very enthusiastic. That's the only discipline he ever imposed — we had to be enthusiastic. We had to have that emotion and that ability to portray and form a tune." Peter stays with the Bluesbreakers for a year, before the first Fleetwood Mac line-up emerges from out of its disintegration.

Peter Green doesn't believe in heroes. With a typically 'umble modesty he names his new band after its rhythm section, tall lanky drummer Mick Fleetwood and bassist John McVie, and he is violently opposed to the label titling their first album *Peter Green's Fleetwood Mac*. But it's his virtuoso guitar and driven creativity that powers that oddly unwieldy outfit of deadbeat scruffs from the twelve-bar ghetto of kludged-together Elmore James and recycled Freddie King riffs, and up into chart celebrity. Their three-year evolution is startling: Peter writes the delicately soaring instrumental Albatross — Fleetwood Mac's third single, their third hit, and their first No 1 — following it with the sparse economical guitars

PETER GREEN: THE HIGHEST HIGHS... AND THE LOWEST LOWS

29 Oct 1946 Born Peter Greenbaum in Bethnal Green, East London.

1966 After playing with The Tridents, joins Rod Stewart, Mick Fleetwood, Peter Bardens, and Beryl Marsden in Blues/Soul group, Steampacket.

17 Jul 1966 Replaces Eric Clapton in cult band John Mayall's Bluesbreakers.

4 Mar 1967 John Mayall LP A HARD ROAD (Decca SKL 4853), featuring Green, hits No 10. It includes Freddie King's The Stumble and Elmore James' classic Dust My Broom, plus Someday After A While.

Jun 1967 Mayall fires drummer Mick Fleetwood. Green quits, too.

12 Aug 1967 Peter Green's Fleetwood Mac debut at Windsor National Jazz & Blues Festival (Peter Green, Jeremy Spencer, John McVie, Mick Fleetwood and later Danny Kirwan). They sign with

of Man Of The World and the torrid Oh Well (another No 1), and then their final album together, *Then Play On*, which mutates into a supernaturally flaming morass of molten licks subsiding into brooding folderols of melting ambivalence. But despite their massive success, all is not well within the group. The mounting pressures, commercial as well as artistic, test the band's internal contradictions to destruction. "You can't do much without pressure. Because it's a physical thing, pressure, isn't it? Unless it is a pressure put upon you to come up with something that you can't do, and you have to admit 'I can't come up with it, I'm sorry'. John Mayall always insisted you love what you do. The same way that I do. I have that rule as well. Love what you do. But it's best playing for free. It's best playing for no money. I don't make no mistakes when I'm playing for no money."

With commercial success, Fleetwood Mac became increasingly strange. Peter now claims that, standing stage-front and concentrating on his playing, he wasn't always aware of the antics going on behind him, or that slide guitarist Jeremy Spencer's behaviour was becoming particularly erratic. But at one point Fleetwood Mac even got banned from The Marquee Club following Spencer's appearance there with a sixteen-inch pink Dildo protruding from his flies! "I don't know how much trouble we all got into, we lost our hair through Jeremy Spencer. The whole lot of us ended up bald doing all that rubbish. I think he saw a joke in it. He had some things that were blatantly obvious. Mick Fleetwood used to see the joke. But I didn't understand his sense of humour at all."

Those with long-term memories may recall Peter's Messianic appearance on *Top Of The Pops* dressed in long white monk's robes and a huge wooden cross around his neck. It was 1969, and sartorial weirdness was hardly exceptional at the time, but to Peter Green it was the outward expression of a mounting mental and spiritual crisis. Peter's natural aversion to 'stardom' was by now causing him the stress apparent in the lyrics of Man Of The World ('I guess I've got everything I need / I wouldn't ask for more / and there's no-one I'd rather be / I just wish that I'd

---

Mike Vernon's new Blue Horizon label and release their first single I Believe My Time Ain't Long.

2 Mar 1968 LP PETER GREEN'S FLEETWOOD MAC (Blue Horizon BPG 7-63200) hits No 4. It features Elmore James' Blues standard Shake Your Moneymaker.

24 Apr 1968 Single Black Magic Woman (Blue Horizon 57-3138), written by Green, hits No 37.

21 Aug 1968 Single Need Your Love So Bad (Blue Horizon 57-3139) hits No 32. It's a cover of a song by Little Willie John, and, controversially innovative for a Blues record at the time, it features lush strings.

7 Sept 1968 LP MR WONDERFUL (Blue Horizon CD 4746122) hits No 10.

29 Jan 1969 Single Albatross (Blue Horizon 57-3145) hits No 1.

28 May 1969 Single Man Of The World (Immediate IM 080) hits No 2.

30 Aug 1969 Compilation LP PIOUS BIRD OF GOOD OMEN (Blue Horizon 7-63215) hits No 18. BLUES JAM AT CHESS (Blue Horizon CD 480527-2), recorded during 1968, finally released in Dec. This period is

never been born'). He is a man of sincere self-doubt and personal fragility, brought to a breaking point of strangeness magnified by the group's seismic introduction to LSD by New York acid-guru Stanley Owsley. Peter's drink gets 'spiked' with LSD in New York — and it catalyses a revelation, compelling him to re-evaluate his entire moral and spiritual value-system, leading to what sleeve-notes call his 'years in a personal wilderness', and what *Mojo* magazine terms his drug-damaged 'two-decade Dark Ages'.

Later, *Rumours* will become Fleetwood Mac's biggest selling album, and *the* biggest selling album of all time until Michael Jackson's *Thriller* comes along. Its songs form a complicated soap opera of veiled and not-so veiled references to the groups marital breakdowns, various deceptions and multiple affairs. It came some time after Peter had left, but confusions of intrigue and rumour seems to persistently dog the Mac throughout its lengthy career and frequent personnel changes.

His memories of his time as leader of Fleetwood Mac are still tinged with confusion and suspicions which seem to nag and worry him to this day. Do you look back with pleasure on the records you made with Fleetwood Mac? "No. I don't actually. I like Danny Kirwan's thing — Dragonfly — which was done when I first left. I think that's the best thing they did But I was just glad to get out of that group. They all seemed to be older than me, or taller or more fashionable than me, or friends with someone or something. That group was a load of clowns of some kind. But Green Manalishi of ours was *quite* good, it was on the way to brilliant, but it should have been a little bit quieter… "

I tried so hard not to remember
and I've tried so hard to forget,
but I can't stop my mind wandering…
—Fleetwood Mac, Trying So Hard

Let's take a reality check here. A deep ultrasound scan: Peter Green doesn't believe in heroes. And necking down fistfuls of E's or microdots of acid is not, in itself, heroic. Any fool can do that. It's the nightmare of creative tension that he wrings

also retrospected in a double-CD of studio out-takes issued in 1998, THE VAUDEVILLE YEARS OF FLEETWOOD MAC 1968–1970 (Receiver Digipack RDPCD 14).

4 Oct 1969 THEN PLAY ON (Reprise RSLP 9000) hits No 6.

15 Nov 1969 Oh Well (Reprise RS 27000), spread across both sides of the single, hits No 2.

11 Apr 1970 After a period of increasingly erratic behaviour, and a series of fall-outs with the group over his wish to transfer all 'excess' profits to charity, Peter Green announces he's quitting Fleetwood Mac during a tour-date in Munich. However, he agrees to complete the tour, leaving the group in May following a final concert at the London Lyceum — at which, tripping on LSD before the show — he tries to set fire to the amps! He rejoins Fleetwood Mac briefly during Feb 1971, to help them out when Jeremy Spencer also leaves (to join the Children of God religious cult).

20 Jun 1970 Final Peter Green Fleetwood Mac single Green Manalishi (With The Two-Pronged Crown) (Reprise RS 27007) hits No 10.

21 Nov 1970 Green's composition Black Magic Woman is a US Top Ten hit for Santana, as

EXCLUSIVE By GORDON BLAIR

THE ROCK STAR WHO TURNED HIS BACK ON A MILLION

As they were—Fleetwood Mac in 1969 with Peter Green on the right

THE man local schoolchildren call The Werewolf shuffled through the morning traffic—head and face a mass of matted hair and fingernails a menacing two inches long.

People who stepped aside as he ambled towards them don't realise he was once regarded as the world's greatest rock guitarist—Peter Green of Fleetwood Mac.

The scruffy, unwashed figure has lost or given away more than a million pounds earned when he reigned as a pop king.

Shoulders rounded and coughing violently from a chest complaint, 40-year-old Peter was heading for his favourite cafe in Richmond, Surrey.

say mental hospital."

Mick Fleetwood and Christine McVie flew from Los Angeles to talk about getting back together with Lindsay Buckingham and Stevie Nicks. Their first album for five years will be released tomorrow.

Mick said of Peter Green last week: "It's a great waste that he left. I rung him a few months ago but he didn't seem to want to talk. It is so sad."

Christine McVie said of Peter's spurned cash: "He began to believe it was evil to be rich, and started giving his money away."

Peter's solicitor Margaret Bennett

mous litigation about money.

"Following a recent judgment, Peter can hope to regain £40,000 eventually."

Meantime Peter seems happy with his life, living in a modest little cottage.

Will he ever pick up the guitar again? "I had one a while ago," he said. "But it broke."

As he started to walk home after his breakfast of bacon, eggs, sausage and cups of tea perhaps remembering the words of one of his song, Man Of The World.

"I can tell you about my life and,

Peter's solo LP **END OF THE GAME** fails to chart.

1972 Maggie Bell attempts to lure the increasingly reclusive Green back to live work as a replacement for Leslie Harvey, killed on stage with Stone The Crows. She fails. Instead, he spends time on an Israeli Kibbutz, then returns to England sleeping on various friends' floors, including that of Thin Lizzy guitarist Snowy White.

23 Jun 1973 Re-issued single Albatross (CBS 8306) reaches No 2, as Green guests on new Fleetwood Mac LP **PENGUIN**.

26 Jan 1977 Green, now working as graveyard gardener, lab assistant, and hospital porter, allegedly attacks an accountant with an air rifle. The accountant is attempting to give him a £30,000 royalty cheque! He's sent to Brixton, then to St Thomas' Mental Hospital

where he's diagnosed schizophrenic, and undergoes the controversial ECT (Electro-Convulsive) treatment. He later spends time at The Priory, the £500-a-week private clinic.

9 Jun 1979 Peter Green solo LP **IN THE SKIES** (Creole PVLS 101) hits No 32, despite his blowing out scheduled TV promotion dates, and playing only a one-off concert, at London's Dominion Theatre.

from the process that makes Peter Green's hideous mental collapse exceptional. Green Manalishi, Fleetwood Mac's final chart single to feature Peter Green, is a spookily Satanic documentary that captures the crawling terror of a mind splintering, coming apart, fragmenting into insanity. Its unsettling emotional intensity is spiked with white-hot jets of pure feral violence, riffs unfolding like bloody flowers in a speeded-up educational film. It's like being flung bodily through a wall of laser knives. It catches Peter Green passing through an LSD-fuelled Quantum Singularity to emerge… altered. As though he's changed places with the Peter Green from some alternate universe. Seemingly identical in every external respect. But different.

He woke up one morning. He ate some bad karma.

And beyond the lost years, it's his return from that Dead Zone that gives it all meaning "You lose your mind with LSD" he tells me now. "It puts you somewhere you don't know where you are. And you're very meek. You become very meek, very exceptionally truthful. Very, very… you have

a necessity to tell the truth. Like you *need* something, you *need* to go somewhere. A need as strong as the need to go to the toilet or something. You *can't* fuck this up. You *can't* really miss one. It's like at school when you say 'can I be excused' when you want to go to the toilet. Can you be excused. Well, it's like that, it's like pissing and shitting yourself. I did that when I was at school. I didn't know what was happening actually. I was four-years-old. I was walking home like this…" he apes walking around, ludicrously splay-legged. "And my Mum said 'I saw 'im walking up the road like this, and I thought what's happening now?'" He guffaws deep and throatily at the memory. I've lost track of it all. I just tape what comes. "But — 'Can I be excused' they say. CAN I BE EXCUSED. I mean — what a funny concoction to say! 'Can I be excused'. But anyway — so, it's like that when you're on LSD. It's like everything you say is said as a *necessity*. As necessary at *that*, you know? Or 'would you like something?' You're replying, but you are asking, too. You're offering something. There's something funny about LSD. I'm still trying to work out what it was. It's marvellous. I don't know if you've ever taken it? It makes you very meek. Very docile."

I'm not sure, I could be wrong, but I'm sure I see a yearning terror behind his eyes as he pauses. "I was taking tablets. I was really bored. I was falling asleep. I was sleeping all of the day, all day long. I had very bad trouble in the night. I had a hiatus hernia. I was being sick sometimes. Even now I do, occasionally. But I'm moving slowly. Sometimes it's a little too slow to tell you the truth. But there you go. I can play chords quite nicely. I can play Beatles tunes that sound roughly like them, to me. But listening to them today there's a lot of subtle chords which I'm not familiar with, so I don't play those tunes. I only play basic chords, but I can't be a single-note person…"

Peter Green might not believe in heroes, but others regard him in that light. Judas Priest do a ham-fisted Heavy Metal cover of Green Manalishi, Santana go US Top Ten with his Black Magic Woman, Gordon Giltrap does a more creditable version of Oh Well, and… "the only good versions of my own songs that I've heard, the *best* one I've heard of mine, the *only* one of one of mine that I've *really* liked is Rory Gallagher's Leaving Town Blues," he offers. "He does a version of that, and it's a different arrangement, but it's a really, really good one." He produces a thick wedge of lyrics that Rory Gallagher once faxed to him, intended for future song-writing collaboration.

Peter Green has spent the years since Fleetwood Mac deliberately deconstructing his own myth. With Michelle becoming an important part of his recovery from what he terms 'my illness'. "I'm really very thankful to Mitch for losing her husband and coming to get me from where I was…" He's now killed off 'Peter Green: Rock Star'. And he's returned to the Blues. Di-

rectly, in the case of The Stumble, an instrumental he did originally with the Bluesbreakers. He performs it again on *The Peter Green Splinter Group Album*. "Mmmm. Yeah. We put the thing together at short notice, so we were scrambling material together" he explains dismissively. "We were practising and rehearsing with it, then we ended up doing it on stage. The other members of the group wanted me to do it, they were saying 'let's do…' and I was saying 'no naaaargh… oh alright, I suppose I could…'. We *were* very short of material." After that came *The Robert Johnson Songbook*. 'Nice idea' comments *Observer* journalist Neil Spencer, 'get the revived Brit Blues legend back in harness with a tribute to the Faustian, legendary figure of Johnson.' Like Robert Johnson, Peter Green has faced his own personal demons. Unlike Johnson, he's survived. Both albums are enthusiastically received.

But "I worry about whether the music will come through properly on record" Peter confides quietly. "Whether it will ever be polished. I want that glossy look on it. I wonder how they get that glossy production look? — where it's all, like, toffee-apple glossy and sweet. Even with this group now I want to polish it a little bit more than we are doing. But I'm trying." A pause. Then "do you know any good producers?" he asks suddenly. "We're looking for a good independent producer, do you know one?" I mention names. Stephen Street. John Leckie. "What colour are they?" White. Does it matter? "Yeah. We want a dark one. A more mixed-race African orientation."

I'm thinking Jazzy B perhaps, or the Massive Attack collective, when Mitch comes up with "what about Quincy Jones, Michael Jackson's finest producer?" "He'll do then" says Peter Green decisively. "See if you can get 'im!" There's a hesitation as I try to decide whether that's a deliberate joke or not. But he's already moving out beyond it. "I never used to work at home for some reason, but I do nowadays. I can practise here. I play at home a fair amount of the time. I sit in my room and play. It's very convenient. It's wonderful. And it's no longer work to me. It shouldn't be 'work'. It should be a pleasure. There was a long, long, long, long time when it wasn't. When it was just very, very slow development. But it's worked out nicely, I'm doing my stuff, and I can play it all with a nice feeling."

What do the neighbours think of Peter Green's amped-up home rehearsing? Does that conspiratorial little old lady down the road complain about the noise? "*Mitch* always comes and tells me if I've got my new hi-fi on a bit too loud!" he agrees amiably. "It's not *that* loud" protests Michelle. "Peter usually practices on an acoustic guitar." "And they throw me a fish now and again" he adds "a red herring. What *is* a red herring anyway...? A *dead* herring...?"

Rock'n'Roll! Phew...!

His hiccups have now subsided. The only demons left in his life are a 'stupid' cut-out Klingon in his front room. And finally, he gets to show me his guitars, proudly unhooking them from the wall one by one. "I'm collecting guitars now. I'm copying Francis Rossi. You know Francis Rossi from the... erm... [Status Quo] he's got about 122 guitars. He buys Telecasters, all different shapes, all different colours, different designs and so

forth. That's left it open for me to do something similar because I do love collecting things. Look at this one. A black Gibson. And I've another one... somewhere, let's have a look. Ah yes, a dark blue Fender Stratocaster. But for the next few live dates I'm thinking of using a guitar that people haven't seen before. Shapes they haven't seen before. I might use this big Baldwin, if I get round to it. But I'm taking a chance, 'cos I'm only as good as... only as *reliably* good as the instrument I use."

There's one with a silver glitter-logo stuck on it. The lettering says 'MILLER LITE: MUSIC'. 'Is that a case of commercial sponsorship?' I suggest jokily. "Miller Lite. That's golden beer, isn't it?" he asks. "That'll do for me. But no, no. Do you think people will think a thing like that? Do you think so? Will they think I'm advertising Miller Lite?"

Actually no. It was my attempt at humour. But "I bought it for the shape of the body. And that sticker just happened to be stuck on it" he explains earnestly. "Perhaps I should have it painted over? Apparently you *can* remove the lettering. And if they can, perhaps I should get it done." Then he grins decisively. "I know — I'll get them to remove the 'MILLER LITE', but they could leave the 'MUSIC' there, couldn't I? Don't you think?" And with this crisis avoided, and with a triumphant "Yes, I'll do that!" he begins strumming the guitar contentedly.

© Dogger

COUNTRY JOE & THE FISH
RETURN OF THE SUPERBIRD FROM HAIGHT ASHBURY TO WOODSTOCK... AND LEEDS

Country Joe McDonald, the one-time front-man of **COUNTRY JOE & THE FISH**, *hero of Woodstock and radical star of sixties counter culture, remains a confrontational and challenging artist with a continuing agitational-propoganda agenda of issues and concerns. His return to England as part of a tour of European dates is a great opportunity to check out Country Joe's present, by way of his past. And it's an intriguing trip...*

Put down your books and pick up a gun,
we're gonna have a whole lotta fun...

—Feel Like I'm Fixin To Die

ever got to Woodstock. Too young. And Temple Newsam Park is some way from 'the three-day nation' — temporally, geographically, and sub-culturally. Drizzle ghosts relentlessly through the trees, shading the billowing Andyspan Marquee, real-ale tents, vegan food and CND merchandising stalls. No-one rain-chants, but drifts of figures in blue and green cagoules trudge on melancholy highs through mud-slick grass. Beards and beer guts predominate, children from the brave circle of trailer-tents and campervans adding implications of weekend outings from safe nuclear family units.

"You must get pissed off with people asking you about Woodstock and the sixties" I nudge tentatively. "N-o-o-o-o-o," comes Joe, chomping mouthfuls of organic white pulp forked from a polystyrene tray. "At least they've got something to ask me about. I can't remember much of it, but I don't mind being asked." This night there are three of us bathed in leprous white calor-gas light in the caravan that doubles as a dressing room: me, Joe, and Geoff Francis, some-time Supremo of the Animus/Rag Baby

record labels. The lights flick and pop, irradiate noxious fumes and fluctuate a lurching unsteady dance of shadows. Rain whispers subversively on the roof, while Robin & Barry Dransfield harmonies seep in muted from the nearest soundstage. "There are two realities" Joe asserts, by way of further explanation. "One reality is the media — all forms. The other reality is, er, reality, you know? The media chooses to focus on certain things at different times. But as far as the Woodstock Nation or the counter culture or whatever you want to call it, that was going on before the sixties, it went on straight through the seventies and eighties, and it's still going on now. Nothing ever stopped. The media stopped covering it. That's what happened. There was a certain backlash within the industry regarding sixties musicians. That was a little disappointing. They weren't really treated with the respect that they should have had, perhaps. But all that's water under the bridge now, y'know."

Joe McDonald delivers a most entertaining interview spiel. He's a poor example of the acid-casualty theory of Rock History. He's too sharp to fit it. His bristling hair brushed back, his large loose lower jaw articulating personal histories in a uniquely lazy drawl, his lucidity spiked with laconic humour and seeded with tabs of information casually dropped in passing, illuminated by strange lights from the past. Listen…

GIMME AN F, GIMME A U, GIMME A C, GIMME A K… AND WHAT'S THAT SPELL? WHAT'S THAT SPELL…?

Maybe you ought to try a little bit of LSD
(only if you want to),
shake your head and rattle your brain
makes you act just a bit insane
give you all the psychic energy you need
L-S-D, for you and me…

—The Acid Commercial

"Daddy, Daddy, who were the Vietcong? And why does the man in the funny T-shirt wanna drop bombs on them?" Well, lemme tell you son, a long, long time ago in a galaxy far, far away there was Country Joe & The Fish. They start out as the Instant Action Jug Band, where Fixin To Die begins as early as 1965 on a privately-pressed EP. By then Joe is already a fully-quali-

fied survivor, discharged from the US Navy that same year following his own harrowing Vietnam tour-of-duty. But soon CJ&F (Joe, Barry 'The Fish' Melton, 'Chicken' Hirsh, and Bruce Barthol) are playing Bay area Happenings, gatherings, stu-

dent anti-Nam protests and Be-Ins, with a sound somewhere between early Airplane Folk-Blues, fractured Magic Band solos, strange tunings and tales from peacenik Beat bohemia. Their first album, *Electric Music For The Mind And Body* (1967) splices absurd acid-fuelled psychedelia to erratic political assault and flavours it all with some ephemeral weirdness. Superbird poses Joe as the comicbook crusader with the kryptonite necessary to send LBJ (President Johnson) home to Texas with the refrain 'pull him off the stand, / clean up the land'. Then there's the shimmering instrumental Section 43… And drugs! — a stoned hitch-hiking road-movie called Flying High ("it was the first song linking drugs and hitch-hiking, and it was a true story. I was hitching with my guitar in the rain, and two guys in a Cadillac picked me up, exactly as the song says…"), and Bass Strings which opens 'hey partner, won't you pass that reefer round', before closing with a whispered 'LSD'. While elsewhere, skewed romances use strange time signatures: there's Porpoise Mouth, and then there's a paean to Not So Sweet Martha Lorraine who 'all she's learned she's had to memorise', a story complete with phoney I-Ching mysticism. "I was walking on the Berkeley campus tripping on acid, and my eye was caught by a ball-point pen lying on the ground… so I picked it up, and it had a name printed on it — 'Martha Lorraine'… so I figured that if I was tripping and found a pen saying 'Martha Lorraine', it was there only for me to see. It made perfect sense to my brain at the time… why else would I see a pen like that? Naturally, I changed the title of the song to 'Not So Sweet Martha Lorraine'". That's the way he explains the song's genesis to journalist Pete Frame. A song John Peel is destined to play on his first ever BBC Radio One *Top Gear* broadcast.

"Our first album was cut on a sixteen-track tape recorder" Joe recalls now. "We were in the studio for four days, and that was it." And if current technology had existed at the time of psychedelia, then Country Joe & The Fish would have used it. "We *did* use what was State Of The Art at the time" he nods sagely. "Which was an echo machine, and reverb. So we had echo, and we had reverb! And we could splice tape together. We did a little sound effects on that album, a little influence from John Cage, and some David Tudor concepts. At the time that was very radical stuff…" Those who read Brian Eno, Chemical Brothers or Prodigy interviews will know that Cage/Stockhausen/Tudor are still considered pretty relevant names to drop.

But back in '67 there was a second album from 'The Fish's Multiple World' (as described in the sleeve notes) in less than twelve months, reviving *Feel Like I'm Fixin To Die* as its title track. Less consistent than its predecessor there's nevertheless the pointed Mingus-related wackiness of The Bomb Song ('please don't drop that H-Bomb on me, you can drop it on yourself') and The Acid Commercial, plus Magoo with its reverb and echo overdub effects, and Eastern Jam which makes the perfect instrumental soundtrack for the Hippie Crash-Pad sequence from an imaginary psychedelic-exploitation movie. A contemporary review describes the track Colors For Susan as 'prettily frightening' and the Fish as 'one of the most bizarre, and most talented of the West Coast psychedelic groups' (*Record Mirror*, March 23, 1968). And of course, they reprise the singalong 'way down yonder in Vietnam' war-a-go-go title track in the *Woodstock* movie (alongside Rock'n'Soul which ends with Joe yelling '*marijuana*'). And it gets them freeze-framed into posterity for their pains, becoming part of a generation's collective memorabilia.

I never got to Woodstock. Too young. But now Country Joe McDonald is back playing European dates. And although he's written into mythology as the guy in the Beach Boys' California Saga who 'sang about liberty', and the politico-Folkie draft-dodger spokesperson of Tom Wolfe's *The Electric Kool-Aid Acid Test* (chapter sixteen — check it out!), 'Country' Joe McDonald has moved on. "In fact, I really had no business to be in a Rock band at all. I just wanted to play my guitar and do my own songs" he confesses. While there are some people who've refused to grow out of those years. People who deny the decades since ever happened. Most of them seem to be here at the Leeds Folk Festival. But what of the Fish? The last album with the original line-up — *Together*, came in 1968. *Here We Go Again* was marketed as CJ&F, but was created by Joe with input from the likes of 'Peregrine Pickle' (Airplane's Jack Casady), Peter Albin, and Dave Getz from Big Brother & The Holding Company. Finally there's *CJ Fish* from 1969, with Greg Dewey of Mad River. Of course, there have been other collaborations since, including the *Superstitious Blues*

ELECTRIC MUSIC FOR THE MIND AND BODY
Country Joe & The Fish
STFL6081(S) TFL6081(M)

album recorded with Jerry Garcia (Ryko, 1991). And there's been a continuous working relationship with ex-Fish in various guises over the three decades since way back (including a disappointing 'partial' *Reunion* in 1976/77), with regular

rumours of reunion tours and albums too. "We've always broken up and come back together, so sure, it's nothing new. But I'm not into doing a nostalgia trip. It's just a matter of the right time, y'know? We thought 1984 was a good year for Country Joe and The Fish to re-emerge, to show Orwell he was wrong...." But of course, things don't work out *quite* that way.

Meanwhile, long-time partner and alter-ego Barry Melton does some recording with San Francisco supergroup The Dinosaurs, then "yes, he's an Attorney now! He passed for the Bar, and he never went to school for it. He did it all by correspondence course. Took him ten years." Pause. "So there you are," drawled with perfectly-paced timing, "it just goes to show you what perseverance can do!" So let's speculate. If there *was* to be a major Country Joe & The Fish re-union tour *now*, what'd it be like? "Ah... well, it'd be a big co-ordinated show, a two-hour concert, high-lighted with a light-show visually showing you something about the sixties, seventies, and then into the eighties. I guess there'd be about twenty-five songs, a few new ones, but mostly the hits from all the different areas. Hopefully the sound would be... not quite as shocking as *Electric Music For The Mind And Body* was in the sixties, but it certainly *wouldn't* be what you expect. It'd be a *new* Country Joe and The Fish. It'd have synthesisers in it too, I've been talking with Jack Lancaster from Blodwyn Pig (and ex-Jethro Tull). He's now into synthesisers, and there's a reed-instrument synth, y'know? Definitely we would use that sound..."

Such fantasies temporarily shelved, for his Festival set in Leeds, book-ended by the Battle-field Band and Moving Hearts, Joe changes into Jesus sandals and grey socks, frayed denim pants torn a precise one-and-a-half inches up the seams, and a white 'Vietnam Veterans Against The War' T-shirt. What war? Vietnam?

Afghanistan? The wars in former Yugoslavia? Or war in general? Backstage in a copious tide of beards, beer-guts, and Moving Hearts roadies, Georgie Fame slouches in a long off-white trenchcoat, bumming cigarettes off strangers and sneering derisively about 'Vietnam Veterans Reunion Night'. While over the public address system Joe's doing an acoustic Tricky Dicky, guitar

COUNTRY JOE AND THE FISH
I feel like I'm fixin' to die
STFL6087(S) TFL6087(M)

phasing from a foot pedal, and I'm forced to concede some sympathy with Fame's stylish put-downs. We've had Gerald Ford, Jimmy Carter, George Bush, Reagan, Clinton *and* Bush again, since 'Tricky Dicky' Nixon got his. In 1969 this song might have been cutting edge satire, but time has moved on, and it means less than zero today.

But already Joe's shifted, he's doing Eric Bogle's searing And The Band Played Waltzing Matilda, one of the starkest and most moving versions of this pacifist killer I've ever heard. Then, just as fast, he switches acoustic for a cherry-red Gibson and runs a perfect Here I Go Again, a song he wrote that went Top Twenty for

Twiggy(!). Tonight it comes enlivened by some melting slide guitar and a hook so insistently contagious it dissolves all trend-dialectics to nonsense. In *this* reality Joe has no problems. It's the journalist in me — the representative of the 'media-reality' — that watches during Feel Like I'm Fixin To Die Rag ('Just follow the bouncing ball, kiddies!'), and divides the audience up into those old enough to sing along, and those who aren't, then interprets this as some kind of credibility watershed. Behind him, no matter what he does, there's always going to be the ghost from the *Woodstock* movie, where he's haranguing the audience with "Listen people, I don't know how you expect to ever stop the war if you can't sing any better than *that*. There's about 30,000 of you fuckers out there. I want you to start *singing*... C'MON!" Now Joe sings his 'hits from all the different areas', it would be ludicrous for him to do otherwise. He's no fashion-slut chasing the charts, but he's no washed-up Hippie either. He was doing this politico Folk-Populist Rock before the temporary psychedelic circus hit town, he enjoys his coupla years of Counter culture media celebrity with some cynical amusement ("... if the revolution ever comes for real, they'll probably use Andy Warhol munitions. You throw it and this big sign comes out — POW!!!," he tells *Village Voice* in 1968), but he never loses his footing. He isn't suckered by Hippie politics, he *precedes* it, to a degree even shapes it. His political concerns and strategies now are just as personal as they've always been. Joe McDonald is a poor example of the 'Boring-Old-Fart' theory of Rock History.

So now, in the next century, what does he think of Hip Hop, digital-electro Dance, and the sample-delic House music that's currently all over the clubs and the underground radio stations? "Syntho-Rock? Techno-Rock?" He forks food contemplatively, tasting the words, as I notice a blue plastic security band on his right wrist, and a tattoo on his fore-arm. "Well, I like it. I really love it. I mean, 'cos in spite of our attachment to traditional music, or traditional *anything*, as a general rule the past is wrong and the future is correct. You can really count on that. The facts are coming in all the time. Today there's more facts than yesterday, and tomorrow there'll be more facts than today. In the sixties I really knew that electronic music was the music of the future, and synthesisers are the future of electronic music, and computers and synthesisers are the future musics of the planet. That's for sure."

THE COLLECTED CJ & FISH
A SAGA OF LOOSE STRINGS
AND FAST MUSIC
AN UNTITLED PROTEST...

I dance to the wonders of your feet
and sing to the joy of your knees,
I whistle symphonies of your face
I hunger for your porpoise mouth
and stand erect for love...

—Happiness Is A Porpoise Mouth

The 1998 compilation *Something Borrowed* (on Ace Records) draws material from seven solo Country Joe McDonald albums recorded throughout the 1980s. *Peace On Earth* emerges in February 1985, with fine songs of the calibre of Garden Of Eden, Pledging My Love and War Hero. And despite the inevitable self-indulgent stoned humour on the *Child's Play* album (1983), there's also evidence in his 'sound environment' technique suggesting his audial radicalism is still intact. Side one, track one, creates a kind of mock-up virtual reality holophonic Chinese restaurant setting with Joe as resident stage vocalist; it's an almost Rock *vérité* effect as incidents complexify and the fabricated scenario extends

into your head. Close your eyes, you're there.

But increasingly Joe's social awareness now takes the form of benefits and agit-prop work on behalf of Animal Liberation and various environmental issues. Of all the West Coast bands with subversive revolutionary aspirations, Jefferson Airplane contributed a late 'up-against-the-wall-motherfucker' *Volunteers*, the Doors' 'erotic politician' gave it a mystic visionary dimension, but only Joe McDonald succeeded in fusing the Old Left street-fighting Woodie Guthrie tradition with New Left satiric irreverence. He even rebuked Dylan for his political abdication (on the *CJ Fish* album track, Hey Bobby: 'where you been?/ we missed you out on the streets'). Now, a song like Coyote ('I don't much like the Federal Government / but I like coyotes some') has Blues chords shining through its skeletal frame, while the anthemic Save The Whale subsumes English Folk to the same effect that Fixin

To Die once colonised vaudevillian satire. And there's Blood On The Ice with vocal back-up from Airplane's Marty Balin. Joe uses such songs to carry the issues that most directly concern him.

In much the same way, the seventies brought his radical proto-feminist All-Star Band, with anti-sexist songs like Sexist Pig and Coulene Anne challenging gender stereotyping (on the 1973 *Paris Sessions* album). "It was kinda in at the roots of feminism in a way, y'know, from a male point of view. It was the only thing of its kind around at that time. We had three women musicians in the group (Dorothy Moscowitz, ex-vocalist with United States Of America, Tucki Bailey, Anna Rizzo, plus vocalists Sally Henderson and Susan Lydon too)." In retrospect it seems to have been a brave project? "It wasn't so brave

```
S.B.A. by arrangement with HAROLD DAVISON
                   present
       AN  EVENING  WITH
COUNTRY JOE
            AND THE FISH
   LONDON    ROYAL ALBERT HALL
   MONDAY, 22 SEPT., at 7.30 p.m.
 TICKETS: 4/- (standing), 8/-, 10/-, 14/-, 17/-, 21/-
   Available from Royal Albert Hall Box Office
     (KEN 8212) and all usual ticket agents
```

actually because no-one understood it. And by the time they *did* understand it — say, about ten years after the event — I was gone by then, I was into something else. It only survived a year-and-a-half, but I have a *million* stories from that band. People could *not* understand that there was a woman playing the piano, a woman playing the

drums, and a woman playing saxophone. The promoters didn't understand that, the press didn't understand that, and the audiences didn't understand that. They all saw and heard something else. We toured Europe, and they wouldn't let Dorothy come up and play the piano at the soundcheck. They'd say 'this is Country Joe's piano-player's piano, get away'. And she'd say 'but I *am* Country Joe's piano player'. And they'd say '*don't touch it, I'm telling you,* this is serious business. There's going to be a soundcheck here in a few minutes, and the piano player's coming up here'. And she'd say 'well, I am the piano player'. And they'd say *get away!!!* It'd just go on and on."

It's as if, then, the industry was only prepared to accept women in the role of groupies or fans. Now it's a far healthier situation where female musicians co-exist on their own merits. Suddenly it's Joe's turn to crack up laughing. "They're all over the industry! It's really getting hard for a *man* in this business nowadays! But then it was like Alice in Wonderland. That was a common occurrence with that band. It's a case of, sometimes you're doing something which is, like, advanced. And it's incomprehensible. It does not compute. In fact, it's exactly like that with Animal Liberation at the moment..."

Blood on the ice pack in Labrador,
in Paris New York and Madrid
High Fashion moguls all agree
white coat seal pup trim is so chic...

—Blood On The Ice

© Dogger

JEFFERSON AIRPLANE
GRACE SLICK
BETTER LIVING
THROUGH CHEMISTRY

Van Morrison called **GRACE SLICK** *'Daphne Dildo'. Others call her the Chrome Nun or the original Acid Queen. She lost her virginity to a watering can. Became the most visible face of* **JEFFERSON AIRPLANE** *and* **JEFFERSON STARSHIP** *(later just* **STARSHIP**). *She had hits in the 1960s, and wrote White Rabbit, the definitive sixties drug song. She had bigger hits in the 1970s. Then she had even bigger hits than that in the 1980s, went mega-platinum and Built This City On Rock'n'Roll with Starship. Now she makes her final entries in the flight log in book form. So perhaps now is the time to get all the psychedelic sleaze, LSD flashbacks, group sex and cannibalism(!) from Jefferson Airplane's self-proclaimed Rock'n'Roll Slut...*

nd this night Grace is on Tom 'Big Daddy' Donahue's show — "300 Pounds of Solid Sounds" — on KSAN-FM Frisco's Rock'n'Roll radio. But she's taking sulfa due to a kidney complaint, so when she necks down a couple of beers, she gets totally wiped out, blanks and does ten varieties of weird shit. She and Paul Kantner are doing an interview for Starship's *Dragonfly* album with Donahue, after which Paul leaves the studio. But Grace doesn't. In fact, Grace *refuses* to leave. Tom's reading commercials and traffic updates while she's wrapping her legs around his neck. Now Van Morrison comes in, and Grace starts on *him*, yelling stuff like, "You can't sing your fucking way out of a fucking paper bag." So he goes, "'Grace Slick'? I don't give a shit if your name is 'Daphne Dildo' — get the fuck out of here!" Tom and Van escape into the studio to do an interview. They lock the studio door, but of course Grace wants in, too. Meanwhile, one of the station's other jocks is picking up on the thing in his car, and all he can hear is these crashing sounds and someone mumbling obscenities in the background. It's all *Kerrrrash! Kablangggg!!!*

"Open this fucking door you ass-holes" *Ker-Smash!!!* He thinks construction work must be going on in the studio! Finally, a couple of gay guys come into the station to listen in person to what's happening. 'Cos they just can't *believe* what they're hearing on their radio. And Grace grabs one of them and hauls him off into the station restroom with her. Some considerable time later he comes out sobbing "I've never had a woman before. I only came in here to listen!"

This is Bill Thompson, some-time Starship

manager getting nostalgic in *Oui* magazine. But Grace Slick stories all tend to be like this one. So I ask her now, as carefully as I can, so as not to fall from grace with Grace. "What!? I can't remember ever *meeting* Van Morrison!" she retaliates genially. "I can't remember doing Tom Donahue's show either. But I *could* have done that. I mean — it sounds like something I *might* have done. It sounds reasonable to me, I just don't remember. Maybe I was drunk as a fart — who knows?"

Imagine. She's in her front room now, looking out over the Malibu beach-front, a mist is coming in over the Pacific softly blurring definitions, while her fax-machine subversively whispers messages from her publisher. This same Grace Slick was singer and writer with Jefferson Airplane, then Jefferson Starship, then finally just Starship. She was the most visible face of a band which took in the Monterey, Woodstock, and Altamont festivals. She was the original Acid Queen. A self-celebrated Rock'n'Roll Slut'. In the late 1960s they sang "Fly Jefferson Airplane, get you there on time..." and Grace Slick's flight-plan takes in the high — and low points of Hippie-dom. She had hits in the 1960s. She had bigger hits in the 1970s. And then she had even bigger hits than *that* in the 1980s when the Starship enterprise boldly took her to new highs — three American No 1 hit singles with slightly less adventurous, but monstrously mega-platinum MOR Rock. And it's all here in her book. Three decades of the most outrageous Rock Life-style excesses. David Crosby writes Triad — a song about three-way sex which so shocks Roger McGuinn that he refuses to allow the Byrds to record it. Grace is delighted. She's not only eager for Jefferson Airplane to do their own version (on their *Crown Of Creation* album), but adds an extra gender twist of her own — taking it from a two-girls-one-guy scenario to a two-guys-one-girl triad. And it's electric, sensual, seductive, and irresistible. But then Grace has already worked her way sexually through each male member of the Airplane. Except Marty Balin. But, by way of compensation, she has a one-nighter with Jim Morrison instead...

Now she makes what she claims are her final entries in the flight log in the form of this book, *Somebody To Love?...* and it's *all* in here! For Grace, it is a product of 'my old fart' years. The book-jacket is a luminous confection of reflective silver foil. And from it she looks out at you as mesmerisingly beautiful as ever. Long black hair. Eyes laser-bright. Insolently intelligent. Subversively mischievous. "I don't like old people doing Rock'n'Roll" she asserts dismissively. "It's kind of pathetic. I'm sure if the person *doing* it likes to do it, then that's fine. It's just that I'd feel *sappy* at the age I am now, singing '*UP AGAINST THE WALL MOTHERFUCKERS!*' It's stoooo-pid. Or — as a non-practising alcoholic, singing 'feed your head' — it's not *pertinent*."

As you'd expect, her book tells it all in intimate, often startling detail. A psychedelic swirl of perception and sex. Mind-crunching drugs and humour. She is born Grace Wing on October 30, 1939, to a former Hollywood Movie understudy and sometime nightclub singer and her investment-banker husband Ivan Wing. Both are graduates of the University of Washington, Seattle. And young Grace's childhood is a self-confessed 'WASP caricature of family life'. Look in vain for early symptoms of radicalism. On her first day at pre-school in LA she pisses herself, leaving a trail of yellow liquid

> My entire life has been an exercise in counter-programming. You say 'white'. I say 'black.'
>
> 'Amazing Grace' Slick *the wit & (stoned) wisdom*

across the classroom floor. But beyond such mishaps, blonde and plump until puberty, she lives largely in her imagination. She does — with some strange 'feed your head' prescience — wear an Alice in Wonderland costume to a school Halloween parade. And her first exploration of pre-pubescent sexuality comes as a tryst with a watering-can, inserting the spout carefully up her vagina. Then she gets hit by the big "blasts of hormone-driven shrapnel", and there are Kleenex-in-bras dramas and heavy petting in the backseat of a 1955 Oldsmobile — until she 'got poked for the first time' for real while double-dating with David 'who wasn't [even] really my type'. Meanwhile Grace goes to private school, and Finch College in New York, "a finishing school for girls from wealthy or prominent families," later also attended by President Richard Nixon's daughter Tricia.

But Rock'n'Roll? She goes to the record shop to buy La Bamba by Ritchie Valens — and winds up listening to a Lenny Bruce album instead. So for Grace, "I didn't grow up with an intense dream of being a singer. I didn't have this *big* moment where I went *Oh my God, I have to do that!*" Instead, the major influence is not so much a musician, as a foul-mouthed iconoclastic Jewish stand-up comedian… and now she devotes more text-space to describing the effect that Bruce had on her than she does to *any* musician. "Sure, Lenny Bruce, Miles Davis, and Edvard Grieg [Norwegian composer of the *Peer Gynt Suite*], *did* have an impact on me, and *did*

> Are nude young girls shit-dancing a good example of freedom of expression? Sure, let 'em dance.
>
> 'Amazing Grace' Slick *the wit & (stoned) wisdom*

influence the music. Lenny Bruce influenced the way I speak, and how what I'm saying comes out. He had a very powerful influence on me, and so he *did* influence the music. He could have influenced the way an artist *draws*, the way an actor *acts*, or the way somebody views *politics*. But he was important to me in how I thought about politics; which end I wanted to be on; who I was fighting for, or not. He brought to light some extreme problems in the so-called marvellous democratic society that we think we have in this country. And instead of just going along thinking you're fabulous, he brought to light that *no*, we aren't quite as marvellous as we think we are — and *here's* where the problems are. And he did it with a sense of humour. So that was just irresistible to me. Lenny Bruce lived in this country. And he loved this country. But just because you love something doesn't mean you don't notice when something inappropriate is going on. So you do two things at once, and it's kind of a paradox — that is, you love the country, but you also try to improve it, or try to stop something that you can see is going wrong, if you can. And you use whatever your voice is — ballet or movies or whatever — to do that. You state what you think, and you let it go out onto the airwaves or into print or on record, or in movies or whatever. And that's all you can really do. It all comes from you. You try to be as honest as you can. And if you get nailed for it — that's *TOUGH SHIT!* So, that's where Lenny Bruce comes in… and he would have had a *ball* with that Clinton/Lewinsky thing. [she cracks up laugh-

> We [Jefferson Airplane] would dose the young reporters with acid until they thought a whole new world was emerging on the West Coast. And maybe it was…
>
> 'Amazing Grace' Slick *the wit & (stoned) wisdom*

ing huskily] There were people in this country got all pushed out of shape 'cos he got some head from some young girl. Who cares? It's not important, it's just so innocuous. Yet people get all goddam worked up about something that has no importance at all on things like poverty or the nuclear thing… and it's so DUMB! I just wish Lenny Bruce was alive to make comment. The Clinton/Lewinsky thing is a joke. Nobody, none of the people I know could care less."

But this is 1957. Things are different. And she never does quite adjust to the suburban mould and lifestyle mapped out for her. She meets Jerry Slick in Sixth Grade, aged ten, and marries him eleven years later, a big formal white affair after which they honeymoon in Hawaii. But "was there passion? Nope. Just cultural imposition… it was probably inevitable that my first marriage would be temporary." But let's be positive… already there are station-wagon trips 'south of the border' to Mexico's Baja Beach to score dope. And from that first marriage she gets a song (Jerry's brother Darby wrote Airplane's first US Top Ten hit Somebody To Love). And she gets a name. 'Slick' is a good Rock'n'Roll name. But then again, so is 'Wing'. Just that Wing — although her given name — would've sounded made-up as part of Airplane. Geddit? Grace fails an audition for a black record label, singing Summertime. But instead winds up writing her own first song for a forty-five-minute 16mm student movie called Everybody Hits Their Brother Once, filmed with Jerry…

Meanwhile, in another part of town, Paul Kantner and Marty Balin (Martyn Jerel Buchwald), a couple of ex-Folknix, are hooking up to Blues guitarist Jorma Kaukonen, with the result that the first Jefferson Airplane takes off in July 1965. And soon after, Grace and Jerry and Darby are forming the nucleus of *their* own band while simultaneously experimenting with peyote — and then

LSD. And suddenly, it's like "hey, this is *not* Kansas, Dorothy". But, in the light of such chemical interactions, should they call their new band Acid Faction? No — it becomes Great Society. BBC TV once ran a docu-series called *The Cold War* retrospecting the fifties and sixties years, which showed President Lyndon Johnson giving his 'Great Society' speech, from which they presumably take the name. "Yeah, well, we were just doing that tongue-in-cheek. Because we had at that point listened to Mort Sahl and Lenny Bruce, we'd read about the turn-of-the-century Parisians

and Gertrude Stein and what-have-you, and we viewed the Government with some degree of amusement. In other words — I viewed it then the same way I do now. So, you just do the best you can." And soon Great Society is a communal thing inhabiting a shared Mill Valley house. Was it the Hippie extended-family idyll? No — it was more "you don't have to watch five rats in a small cage to understand claustrophobia". But Great Society *did* leave vinyl evidence of their existence. There's a live at the Matrix Club tape featuring Father Bruce, Grace's tribute to Lenny Bruce (a tape which later surfaces as an album called *Conspicuous Only In Its Absence*). And there are studio sessions with San Francisco's indie label Autumn, including a cover of the Mamas & Papas Free Advice, and a fine version of Somebody To Love (which Grace would soon re-record for the Airplane), both of which eventually appear on *The Autumn Records Story*.

Gene Sculatti, writing the history of Autumn Records, recalls Great Society as "the epitome of the city's emerging anti-Pop underground. When an Autumn staffer asked Grace to provide info on herself for a teen mag questionnaire, Grace told her to fuck off. And when the Society put Sly [Stone, producer] through some fifty takes to get a satisfying version of Somebody To Love, he threw up his hands and stomped out of the studio. Worlds were colliding."

Great Society play at Tom Donahue's Mothers — "the world's first psychedelic night-club, a pulsating ultra-violent cavern doing weird business along the topless Broadway sin-strip in North Beach". But the big turning point for Grace comes later that same year, when she sees the Airplane play at the Matrix, a small San Francisco club co-owned by Marty Balin. And, when Airplane's first vocalist, Signe Toly Anderson, quits with immaculate timing, Grace joins Airplane. Although, to hear her describe it, the equation seems to be more financial and lifestyle than it is artistic. "I was working as a model at a department store when I saw Jefferson Airplane play. But it wasn't so much — ah — a *big deal* as it was just, Hey! What they're doing looks like a lot more fun than what *I'm* doing. And if you're gonna work, that looks like a better *job* to have. It looks like a good way to make a living and goof off at the same time."

> Drugs, groupies, limos, five-star hotels... we lived the all-expenses-paid life that everyone dreams about while they're wiping off the countertops at Burger King.
>
> **'Amazing Grace' Slick** *the wit & (stoned) wisdom*

Like the *Star Wars: Phantom Menace* trailer puts it: 'every generation has a legend, every journey has a first step, every saga has a beginning'. And by joining Airplane she not only first-steps into a hedonistic anti-materialist lifestyle uniquely attuned to her talents, but ignites the Hippie Dream too. "The sixties idea of sexual freedom was something I actually related to quite easily, despite my earlier programming". In the fifties the girl never got to ask the boy out. "Ask them *OUT*?" protests Grace. "How about asking them if they want to *FUCK*?!" Still technically married to Jerry Slick she has sex with Airplane's 'extremely well-hung' bassist Jack Casady, and then drummer Spencer Dryden (she later writes the tragi-comic idiot-wise Lather about him — 'children call him famous / what the old men call insane / and sometimes he's so nameless / that he hardly knows what games to play' — for the *Crown Of Creation* album). Nevertheless, Spencer gets eventually 'fired' from Airplane for his 'incessant complaining'. So she has a one-off night with guitarist Jorma Kaukonen. And finally, as "the acid was clarifying some aspects of our friendship that I'd been previously unaware of" she gets around to group leader Paul Kantner. That's pretty much *all* of the original Airplane — except for Marty Balin. He once told an interviewer: "Grace? Did I sleep with her? I wouldn't even let her give me head!" But, no regrets. "Loving the people you work with is wonderful," she insists now. "Fun. Interesting. A way of connecting, y'know. It's hard *not* to love people. It's a very *good* thing to love people. But possessiveness gets in the way. People are very possessive. It's too bad that we have the possessiveness that we do. *That's* what gets us into trouble. But loving people is a whole hell of a lot better than *hating* them!"

Outside of sexually working her way through Airplane members, there's also a 'strawberry fuck' with a stoned immaculate Jim Morrison in which "I was, again, the perpetrator". It occurs during a joint Doors/Airplane European tour, but turns out to be so memorable an event that when writing it up for the book she has to 'phone Doors biographer Danny Sugarman to work out, by a process of tour-date elimination, where exactly it happened.

And yeah, the 'Summer of Love' is now stock

newsreel cliché. Dumb flowers-in-the-hair idiot dancing, Haight Ashbury Beat bohemia, recreational chemistry-a-go-go, blowing bubbles (and each other) in the Park, naked breasts spiral-painted with CND symbols in Day-Glo colours and blahdy-blah. And of course — it's all down to the sudden eruption of the as-yet legal LSD, not technically outlawed in California until October 6, 1966 (666!). And of course, it is this newly synthesised cult wonder-drug distributed by Grateful Dead electronics wizard Augustus Owsley, that puts the 'acid' into Acid Rock and

gets itself eulogised by Timothy Leary in his *Politics Of Ecstasy*. And more by some kind of beautiful cosmic accident than by fuzzy logic design, Grace finds herself a central part of this emerging 'Frisco counter culture, going to the Marin County Merry Prankster's Trips Festival, the Kool-Aid parties you read about in Tom Wolfe's *The Electric Kool-Aid Acid Test*. It's here she first meets the Grateful Dead's Jerry Garcia ("even in his twenties he projected the wise old rascal image of an Eastern guru") and Neal Cassady — 'Dean Moriarty' of Jack Kerouac's *On The Road* ("stand here long enough, and you'll catch up with all seven of the conversations he's having with himself"). Soon after these events, in what's probably her first ever interview with the British press, Grace describes the evolution of that scene:

"Because it's a small cosmopolitan sort of community, San Francisco has always been a breeding ground for individualists. And they've always been accepted there. The 'Flower People' aren't really new — it's just the old Beatnik scene revitalised. The only difference between the Beatniks and the Flower Children is that the kids now are more positive in their beliefs and actions. A lot of people regard us [Jefferson Airplane] as a spokesman-group for this new scene, but we didn't start off as that — it just happened really, because of our music." (Record Mirror, October 21, 1967)

And of course, there have been other psychedelic ripples since then, more knowing, less eyes-wide naïve, more deliberately contrived. But Airplane and their Bay Area cohorts are inventing it all for the first time. At one point in the book Grace writes: "psychedelics can offer a spiritual gift or issue a death sentence. Aren't you glad there are extremist guinea pigs like me who've already performed the nuts-and-bolts experiments?" "That was a snide sarcastic remark" she laughs now. "That's just 'aren't you glad there's screwballs like me that you can *watch* and you don't have to do it…?' That's also kinda saying 'why don't you get up off your *ass* and go experiment with something your own self? Actually *do* something rather than just being a voyeur.' Voyeurism is interesting for a while, but if you can never do it yourself…? Life is kinda short, why spend eighty years doing *nothing*? Ignore the fear…!"

When history arrives it often looks like the latest fad, and it often comes disguised as journalism. Airplane were there. Not only there, but pivotal to it all. It was Acid Rock. It was Hippie mystique and the Head community. A huge amorphous mass of drug-crazed dropped-out Uncle Freak-Out weirdness. Concerts and musicians interacting on and with each other. Country Joe

& The Fish, Grateful Dead, Quicksilver Messenger Service, Big Brother & The Holding Company (with Janis Joplin). But "I didn't call myself or anybody else a 'Hippie'" she stresses now. "Herb Cohen, a San Francisco columnist, made that term up. These are *people*. They're not *Hippies*, they're people."

But even within that definition of individualism, Jefferson Airplane was always a collective organism made up of separate personalities performing *for each other* as much as for their audience, in the manner of Crosby Stills & Nash. Kantner's polemical trips often seem at odds with Balin's love songs, or with Slick's ironic humour and dark angel of glacial poise, her vengeful beauty and diction like daggers. But together Balin and Slick's keening laser-guided harmonies spin a diet of the strangest food for the spirit and mind, played out over Jorma Kaukonen's disturbingly unpredictable guitar lines. And Marty Balin, who comes across in Grace's book as the band's most enigmatic figure, has a voice that can go from the seductive to the supersonic in seconds flat. "He *is* enigmatic" she agrees. "I think he'll even cop to it. Some days he'll be delighted with the world, y'know — 'I felt wonderful and I walked on the beach blah blah blah' — and then the next day he'll be gone. And we'd say 'well, what happened?' He wouldn't show up. 'Well, I had to walk on the beach' or 'I had to go…' You just never knew what was happening there. But he's fascinating. Children can move very quickly from one emotion to another. And he's very much like a child in that he can move quickly from one frame of mind into another. But the thing I liked about Airplane was that Jorma [pronounced 'Yorma'] and Jack did Blues. Paul did his anthemic political stuff. Marty did love songs. And I did this kind of weird sarcastic stuff. So you had at least four different styles, which kept it from being boring. I *liked* the fact that

at
The GREAT South Coast
Bankholiday
POP FESTIVITY
to be held at
Ford Farm, Nr. Godshill

Isle of Wight Tickets 25s
with
The Crazy World of Arthur Brown
Jefferson Airplane

The Move Tyrannosaurus Rex Fairport Convention
Plastic Penny Pretty Things Aynsley Dunbar Retaliation
Orange Bicycle Blonde on Blonde The Mirage

Festival compered by JOHN PEEL

August 31st from 6 p.m. to September 1st 10 a.m.

Tickets available from
London Chapman Agency Ltd Tel 01242553L 7 8 Aldgate High St EC3 184 Bishopsgate EC2
(opposite Liverpool St Station)   65 Fenchurch St E C 3 (opp Fenchurch St Station)
Davis s Records 8 Allscar High Street EC3   Apple Ltd 94 Baker Street W1

there were different types of things. But also there is — if not stated overtly — there's an underlying thing of 'well, I think *my* stuff is really far out, and there should be more on the album'. So yeah, I'm sure that went on too."

The *Surrealistic Pillow* album, which costs just $8000 to make, sells eight million copies, goes Top Ten and spawns two gold singles: Somebody To Love and Grace's twisted White Rabbit. The latter is reviewed rather cautiously by *NME* who stipulate that 'the lyric is very off-beat and, all things considered, it's a strange disc' (October 7, 1967). 'Tonight,' writes Richard (Oz) Neville, 'I rest my head on *Surrealistic Pillow*, praying it weaves its magic warmth.' And she's there, looking directly and pro-vocatively out at you from the sleeve, long black hair, supernaturally piercing eyes, the perfect Hippie-chick dream incarnate, mocking all of 'straight' America's phoney aspirations with her beauty, her intelligence and her acerbic subversive wit. And despite Airplane's "lazy and somewhat sloppy attention to cranking out the hits" their splintered muddle-headed flight-log keeps them there as underground America's top band through to the end of the decade. An Airplane on glide path, Eight Miles Higher than high. They even get to hook up with Jean-Luc Godard to shoot a short underground film (*One American Movie*) live on the Manhattan rooftops, a stunt that results in arrests for 'disturbing the peace'. "U2 did the same thing in LA in the process of shooting a video. There were no arrests" she adds tartly. Then comes *After Bathing At Baxters* and *Crown Of Creation* featuring Triad as well as Grace's very strange Lather.

Live, "our music… because of the technology that became available, was the first music that was so *fucking LOUD* that you could not stand up in the middle of a Jefferson Airplane concert and say…" she drops expertly into a perfectly mimicked loud stupid heckler-voice *"Hey, I don't like what you're playing, why don't you fuck off…?!* 'Cos we'd never *hear* you."* She says it clearly, carefully and very deliberately, recalling a time when their gigs are already upgearing to concerts and benefits organised by Bill Graham, for whom Airplane become regulars of the Fillmore (where the live *Bless Its Pointed Little Head* album was recorded in 1969) and the Carousel. Then, inevitably, they'd gone from doing the Monterey Festival (1967), to opening the final day of Woodstock — where Grace announces from the stage, "Alright friends, you have seen the *heavy* groups. Now you will see morning maniac music, believe me — yeah, it's a new dawn!" opening with the title track from their *Volunteers* album. "At such events, there's no way the audience could reach us. Our music covered *everything* else that was going on. You'd have trouble hearing an *atom bomb* exploding while we were playing. So technology changed things in that sense. But apart from that, the things we were saying and doing are the same things people have always done and talked about. We want peace. We don't want to kill each other. We like to fuck a lot. We like to have a good time… so, hey! What else is new?"

But wasn't the responsibility of such sudden success a little, um, frightening? "No. Because there were about twenty bands at that time — some from Europe, a couple from New York, a couple from LA — who were out on the road doing that, and I felt that *we* were doing it to-

> 'Rock'n'Roll tradition' could be an oxymoron, but God knows, there are plenty of traditional morons in Rock'n'Roll.
>
> **'Amazing Grace' Slick** *the wit & (stoned) wisdom*

gether. It wasn't a matter of narrowing it down to Airplane. I thought it was a *generation* of people making various remarks through music. It wasn't like I'm here doing this all alone. It was a whole bunch of us. So, it wasn't frightening, it was kinda fun as far as I can determine."

But Airplane go on to do the Altamont concert later that same year (1969), sharing the bill with the Rolling Stones. And watching the *Gimme Shelter* video, there's some *scary* footage of the Hell's Angel violence taking place there, where Angels called in to do 'community policing' murder a black youth. That's when the Hippie 'dark side' really comes through. A long loose spacey Airplane jam dissolves into a frightening mêlée of movement and figures. "Easy" says Grace over the mounting confusion, "it's getting kinda weird up here." Marty Balin jumps offstage to intervene in a fight that's suddenly taking place in the audience directly beneath them. "Hey man" announces Kantner from the stage, "I'd like to mention that the Hell's Angels just smashed Marty Balin in the face and knocked him out for a bit. I'd like to thank you for that". A huge Hell's Angel is on stage now, grabbing the mic: "Let *me* tell *you* what's happening!" "I'm not talking to you man" counters Kantner, "I'm talking to the people who hit my lead singer in the head…" while in the audience the Angels are fighting each other and the assembled Hippies with sharpened broken-off pool cues. "That's really *stupid, stop it!*" yells Grace over the mounting anarchy, "you've got to keep your bodies off each other, unless you intend love." Then she tries a slightly more conciliatory "people get weird, and you need people like the Angels to keep people in line. But, the Angels also, y'know — you don't *bust* people in the head for nothing. So both sides are fucking up temporarily. *Let's not keep fucking up…!*" It's a scary, *scary* film with the fear burning off the video-tape, as Angels bludgeon the Hippie dream to death with pool cues and chains.

"There you go," says Grace brightly. "The Monterey Pop Festival was the bright beautiful event. And the dark side of that is Altamont. With Jagger fully dressed as the devil [an explosion of hacking laughter], he had a devil outfit on that day. [Not on my video he doesn't.] That was perfect, perfectly apt." But it remains chilling to watch Grace trying to deal with the violence at that concert. "Yeah. But the truth is, I couldn't see. I didn't have my contacts on. So, it wasn't a matter of *dealing* with it. I had to go over and ask the drummer what the Hell was going on! So I didn't really know what was happening. Who knows why I didn't wear my contact lenses that day? I think we were in Miami the night before, and we'd been on a plane all night. So maybe I'd lost them. But I didn't actually *see* a lot of that day up close — fortunately. It doesn't sound like it would have been very interesting to watch anyway."

Volunteers sees the Airplane fully charged up for perhaps the last time. In the book — and now — she talks about recording Jefferson Airplane albums, and the constant consumption of chemicals taking place while they do it. Perhaps, just perhaps if they'd been under greater control — at least in the studio — the albums might have been in some ways better? Grace responds "yes" immediately, without hesitation. "I always wanted to do more practising. I always wanted it to be so that we knew a song so well that when you go on stage or into a recording studio, *then* you can elaborate on it, or improvise on it or something. I was always jealous of the tightness of Crosby Stills & Nash harmonies. Their harmonies were so beautiful and so pristine. But, on the other hand, that not knowing led to a lot of improvising that would not otherwise have happened. So, either way, it's okay. If you practice a lot, then you get a really pristine clean sound. And if you *don't* practice then you get some, er, interesting improvising. So, either way is okay. It's just, at the time, I would have liked to have practised a bit more than we did." But, acting as Devil's Advocate, it's that unpredictability and the occasional unevenness of the Airplane albums that makes them artistically fascinating. "Oh good. Thank you, I like to hear that. [laugh] That makes up for a lot of wanting more practice."

But in fact, when Airplane — or Starship as they were now becoming — do get more controlled and more digitally perfect, particularly approaching the time of their 1980s successes, they get more commercially accomplished, but less artistically interesting.

EVERY JOURNEY HAS A FIRST STEP...

We record buyers have been inculcated with the belief that the holy grail of now-ness, of hip-defining leading-edge socio-musical quintessence is a vinyl commodity purchasable across the counter. Sometimes, just sometimes, that vision comes true. Jefferson Airplane was a psychedelic confection, a game of musical beds, a trip down the rabbit-hole, a barbaric divinity, and a band always way ahead of the curve. Everything you read about them was already out of date. Looking like "a pimp and a go-go-girl" in a miniskirt that "went all the way up to the beaver", Grace and Yippie Activist Abbie Hoffmann go to a Whitehouse reception organised — bizarrely — by Grace's former Finch College, with an invitation addressed to 'Miss Grace Wing'. "When I went to the White House it was with my tongue planted firmly in my cheek" and with the intention of dosing 'Tricky Dicky' Milhous Nixon with LSD, she recalls now. In the event the hip coun-

ter culture intruders get muscled away by alert security gorillas, but "we didn't *have* to dose Nixon. He overdosed himself on love of power, driving himself out of office without any outside help."

With acid, the perceptual centres of the brain go into hyper-stimulation. Yet it is the pivotal ingredient of the scene, and sometimes works out in the final edit. Sort of. "Yeah. It's a *real* powerful drug," Grace agrees . "It's not like just getting kinda loaded on alcohol and putting a lampshade on your head. It's not an *easy* drug to take. If you're not psychologically in balance *it–is–a–rough–drug!* But if you're in a good frame of mind — which fortunately I was when I took it, then it's very exciting and very eye-opening and mind-altering, and all those other sort of clichés. But what if you're *not* in psychologically good condition…? It's best to have somebody with you. People assume they can fly. I mean — and you know, you *can't!* So you've got to have somebody there saying 'Ah, not now, maybe later' [laughter]. So it's a good idea to be 'in nature'. It's a good idea to have somebody be a guide with you, and it's also a good idea to take it with somebody else. So that you have a frame of reference."

Are there similarities between that sixties psychedelic scene and today's Ecstasy and Acid House cultures, which take E's like Hippies took acid? Are there similarities or only differences in attitude to, say, the spirituality, or the hedonism of it? "I haven't taken any of those drugs, so can't make a comment on something I haven't experienced… I've never *had* Ecstasy, and unless I've taken a drug, I don't make comment on it because I *can't* do it coming from an experiential place. I can only make broad comments the way everybody else does: *'Oh, you're gonna kill yourself'* [in hectoring mum voice], and y'know, some people *will*. But we just figured LSD is a new chemical. Young people generally figure *'Uh? Hey! Let's go dere and do dat'* [in moronic brain-dead voice]. It's not *that* unusual. Nothing we did is *that* unusual."

But the Airplane were not just for the Summer of Love — they were for life. They don't crash. They don't even nose-dive. More a process of sequential 'baling out'. Marty Balin "went off to be an 'honest artist', creating art that suited his muse". While elsewhere, the Paul and Grace union was proving to be an 'interesting combination' ("both of us are fairly strong and obnoxious, and it was fairly inevitable that the daughter they had together would inherit "both of those characteristics"). It was Grace's original intention to call their child 'god' "with a small 'g' because we wanted her to be humble", but she later became China, and featured on the cover of her parents' joint album *Sunfighter*. A symptom of maternal sentimentality? Maybe — but it's still an album full of cannibalism and lycanthropy (werewolf tendencies). "We were living in Bolinas at the time which has a lot of Hippies around there and the kinda deal was you gotta make your own bread, you gotta be a vegetarian, you shouldn't shave your armpits, don't wear any make-up, you gotta be *real*. And I thought fuck all that shit.

> Jim Morrison was a well-built boy, larger than average, and young enough to maintain the engorged silent connection right through the residue of chemicals that can threaten erection.
>
> **'Amazing Grace' Slick** *the wit & (stoned) wisdom*

GRACE SLICK: THE ALBUMS

1980 CONSPICUOUS ONLY IN ITS ABSENCE (CBS) Recorded live at the Matrix in 1966 by The Great Society (Grace Slick, vocals; Darby Slick, lead guitar; David Minor, rhythm; Peter Vandergelder, bass; Jerry Slick, drums) and includes Somebody To Love, White Rabbit, Outlaw Blues, Father Bruce, Sally Go 'Round The Roses. '[Grace's] voice is a little more raw and inexperi-enced, occasionally even going out of tune but is inexplicably innocent and direct… Grace attempts innovations on this record which are not detectable in… later albums' (*IT*, May 1968) 'Psychedelia's first flowering…' (*Melody Maker*, Mar 29, 1980)

1986 THE AUTUMN RECORDS STORY (Edsel) Various artists' album featuring previously unissued studio versions of Great Society's Somebody To Love and The Mamas & Papas' Free Advice.

Aug 1966 JEFFERSON AIRPLANE TAKES OFF (RCA) First Airplane album featuring vocalist Signe Anderson (*not* Grace Slick) with regional hit Chet Powers' Let's Get Together. 'Its lovely original

You're going around thinking you're pure? You've got your head up your ass. At the same time there was a news story about some people coming across from the East Coast to the West Coast who got stuck for months in a blizzard in a Pass in Colorado. They were there some months 'cos there was no way to get in, no way to get out, too much snow. People were dying. Pretty soon they ran out of food. So they had to eat the people who'd died. So I was sorta making a song ('... what if you were starving to death / and all you had to eat...') that asked what *would* you do? In certain circumstances you do things you ordinarily would not. And is that wrong? The guy's dead! Who cares? It's just food. Everything on this planet *kills* to eat. You may be killing a broccoli. But you're killing. So I was just objecting to their flat-out statement that 'this is wrong'. Who knows? You may have to eat your *sister* at some point. WAKE UP!"

After *Volunteers*, the personnel changes, spinoffs and side projects get increasingly complex. Balin, Kantner and Slick quit — then rejoin, then quit again. Others pass through, including Liverpool-born ex-John Mayall drummer Aynsley

"WHEN SHE SAYS, 'FEED YOUR HEAD!' IS SHE REALLY ENCOURAGING THE YOUTH OF AMERICA TO TURN ON? YES, IN EVERY SENSE."

GRACE SLICK
OF THE
JEFFERSON AIRPLANE

sleeve featuring pictures of them with short hair and drainpipes, is still highly enjoyable, from Signe Toly Anderson's harsh, driving vocal on Chauffeur to the best-ever version of Let's Get Together, the anthem of the Haight Street Culture.' (*Melody Maker*, Sept 1971)

Feb 1967 SURREALISTIC PILLOW Classic line-up of Grace Slick (vocals), Marty Balin (Martyn Jerel Buchwald; guitar/vocals), Paul Kantner (guitar/vocals), Jorma Kaukonen (guitar), Jack Casady (bass), Spencer Dryden (drums, ex-Peanut Butter Conspiracy, and later of New Riders Of The Purple Sage). Album features White Rabbit and Somebody To Love. 'This top American vocal-instrumental beat group weave rich sounds...' (*NME*)

Jan 1968 AFTER BATHING AT BAXTERS Features The Ballad Of You, Me, And Pooniel. 'One of those gimmicky sound LPs, yet not without some good instrumental work.' (*NME*) 'Unfortunately the music doesn't match the title — thus the whole LP comes across as pretentious.' (*Record Mirror*, Apr 6, 1968)

1990 LIVE AT THE MONTEREY FESTIVAL (Thunderbolt) and

Dunbar, ex-Turtles John Barbata, ex-Quicksilver David Freiburg, Papa John Creach — a sixty-three-year-old violinist — and Mickey Thomas who once sang lead on Elvin Bishop's chart hit Fooled Around And Fell In Love. Then, with the arrival of the seventies, commercially, the regrouped Jefferson *Starship* go stellar, becoming "a veritable gold-record machine", while Grace hooks up with their lighting manager — Skip Johnson, a "good-looking dark Irish Catholic boy... a cute goofball with a foul mouth". By September 1975 Jefferson Starship's *Red Octopus* album sells 2.5 million copies as Balin's Miracles tops the US chart. Commercially they're bigger than Airplane had *ever* been, but they've ceased to be essential and become merely 'pleasant'. Their 1978 European tour gets complicated by Grace's growing booze problems, with her acting — according to journalist Andy McConnell — as "a pathetic adult version of Shirley Temple" (*NME*, June 29, 1978). There are riots at the Hamburg Lorelei Festival, and she effectively quits, reputedly saying, by the time the tour reaches Knebworth, "I don't give a fuck about any of you guys." While Kantner retali-

ates that Airplane/Starship without Grace — despite their having two other lead vocalists — would be 'The Stones without Jagger'.

In the meantime, she does solo albums: *Manhole*, *Dreams*, *Welcome To The Wreckers Ball*, and *Software*. Until the disintegrating band reforms yet again. This time Kantner refuses to get involved and takes the rights to the 'Jefferson' prefix with him, so the Starship enterprise continues without it. By the mid eighties, in those lush days

MONTEREY INTERNATIONAL POP FESTIVAL Vol3 (1992 Rhino) Live material.

Sept 1968 CROWN OF CREATION Cover photo of 'Hiroshima courtesy USAF'. Features Triad and Grace's Lather ('putting drumstick on either side of his nose / snorting the best licks in time').

Mar 1969 BLESS ITS POINTED LITTLE HEAD 'Alive' at the Fillmore East/West. Features Donovan's Fat Angel, which *he* later re-worked live as 'Fly Jefferson Airplane / get you there on time'). 'Grace Slick's trilling and thrilling vocals soaring over a backing that dives and roars.' (*NME*, Aug 1969)

1969 VOLUNTEERS Features Kantner/Crosby/Stephen Stills' Wooden Ships as done by CS&N at Woodstock where Stills announces it as 'a kind of science fiction story... it's about these people who are escaping the holocaust, or whatever it may be, leaving it behind and escaping in the wooden ships'. Lines include 'can you tell me please, who won the war?' Guests on album include David Crosby, Nicky Hopkins, Jerry Garcia and Stills. 'Marks the group's entrance into what the

of digital seduction and market-driven manipulation, she's back in the chipped-up Starship fold, but as the only surviving link to the original *Surrealistic Pillow* line-up. The first single under the new designation is the multi-platinum We Built This City (US No 1 in October 1985). "Everybody assumes we're talking about San Francisco," she says dismissively. "But it was *not* written by us. It was *not* written about San Francisco. It was written by a British guy — Bernie Taupin — about a grey time in the early seventies when cops were closing clubs or something in LA — and I couldn't give a shit whether they close the clubs in LA. They're gonna re-open them all in a month anyway. So okay, it's a good song. But it doesn't have anything to do with me."

Next there's Sara (US No 1 Jan 1986), and then Nothing's Gonna Stop Us Now, used in the mindless trash-movie *Mannequin*. Written by Diane Warren and Albert Hammond, produced by Narada Michael Walden — of Whitney Houston notoriety — it tops both US and UK charts (in February and April 1987), and becomes the year's biggest-selling single in, ironically, the same year the Grateful Dead finally crack the US Top Ten. But Diane Warren is a name associated with a whole roster of MOR hit songs. "Yes. It was written for us by Diane Warren. And I like her — as a person. She's amazing. And she's very bright. Loves writing. She stays in her little studio and writes *all day long* — sixteen hours a day. I was amazed, 'cos I just saw her on TV the other night, and she can write for *anybody*. She has written for Rock bands like Aerosmith. But, Nothing's Gonna Stop Us Now? I don't *believe* that. I *don't believe* that nothing's

> Alice (in Wonderland) uses chemicals that literally get her high, tall, and short -- DRINK ME, EAT ME. She takes a bite out of the Caterpillar's magic mushroom (psilocybin) and pulls a toke from his hookah (hashish). The girl is thoroughly ripped all the way through the book. And our parents wondered why we were 'curiouser and curiouser' about drugs!
>
> 'Amazing Grace' Slick *the wit & (stoned) wisdom*

Americans might call politico-rock...' (*NME*, Mar 21, 1970)

WORST OF JEFFERSON AIRPLANE (1970) Greatest hits.

FLIGHT LOG (1966–76) (1976) Compilation.

200 FULTON STREET (1987) Compilation with previously unissued material, including Levi Commercials. Title refers to Airplane's then-communal home in San Francisco.

EARLY FLIGHTS (1974 Grunt) Out-takes and rarities.

WOODSTOCK / WOODSTOCK 2 (1970/71 Atlantic) Various artists recorded live, including Airplane (playing Volunteers). See also **WOODSTOCK — 25th ANNIVERSARY COLLECTION (1994 Atlantic).**

BLOWS AGAINST THE EMPIRE (1971) Credited to Paul Kantner & Jefferson Starship. Features guests Jerry Garcia, Graham Nash, Mickey Hart, David Freiberg, Joey Covington and David Crosby, and gives thanks to Kurt Vonnegut, AA Milne, Robert Heinlein and Jean Genet. Lyric booklet proclaims 'Search out Atlantis. It lives and breathes inside of you. Join us — a plunge into Reality'.

gonna stop you! That comes from Diane. I'm cynical. A truck will stop you in five seconds flat. I think it's probable that this romance is not gonna last more'n six months. I've got a little darker eye. I'm a little bit more sceptical, and cynical. It's not *necessarily* more healthy that way. I'm not saying that I'm right either, I'm just saying that I happen to view things that way. I'm not going to *assume* that that flower's gonna bloom. I wait till it *blooms* before I get *real* excited. You know what I'm saying? Romance doesn't last that long. Wait until he sees the younger girl at the supermarket, and you're out *on your ass*. I would not have written a love song in that way. So I'm basically singing something I don't believe. And I don't like that. It's a good song. But not for me. Somebody who *believes* that song ought to sing it. *That's* what's important."

So Starship has become — by Grace's own admission — an MOR sell-out, a congenial "mu-sical Shopping Mall". "The people in Starship had families," she explains carefully, "and there was a lot of fear around money. They didn't want to experiment with weirdo songs, because they were afraid they wouldn't sell. It was a *commercial* band, and Starship actually sold more, had more No 1 singles and all that kind of stuff, than Airplane ever did. We'd all played our instruments and sung long enough to know what we were doing. So it was relatively *easy* to go into a recording studio and make a hit song. But they weren't as interesting. I'm singing songs that I really don't care about, and lyrics I don't believe in. And that's a mistake. You shouldn't do that. I had fun during the eighties. It was okay. I can *do* it. It's not like I *can't* do it. I'm a professional in the sense that I've been doing it over a long time, but I would prefer to sing songs where I *know* the lyric, I *know* what I'm talking about because I *WROTE* it."

> The truth is that I'm just not into vaginas. Because they're pretty much a mucous membrane, gushy and hot, and they can develop an awful lot of strange bacteria. My idea of Hell is putting my face in somebody's pussy.
>
> 'Amazing Grace' Slick *the wit & (stoned) wisdom*

1971 SUNFIGHTER Credited to Paul Kantner & Grace Slick. Cover photo shows baby China Slick. Inner artwork includes Frank Frazetta — courtesy of SF Book Club — plus childhood snaps of Kantner and piano-playing Slick.

1973 BARON VON TOLL-BOOTH AND THE CHROME NUN (Grunt) By Paul Kantner, Grace Slick & David Freiberg.

1973 MANHOLE (Grunt) Solo album. 'Gaudy, garish and indulgent... if a Novocained nun shrieking Spanish civil war songs in a Chinese brothel is your idea of tomorrow's music, you can enjoy it today: Grace Slick's there first.' (*Rolling Stone***, Mar 1974)**

1971 BARK Features Slick's Never Argue With A German sung in spoof-German, Joey Covington's fifties a cappella-style Thunk, and final Airplane single Pretty As You Feel. Their first album for their own Grunt label, and first without Marty Balin. 'The controlled quality of a ***Rubber Soul* with none of the (albeit worthy) inhibition of a ***Workingman's Dead***, and it's highly recommended.' (***Melody Maker***, Sept 1971)**

1972 LONG JOHN SILVER

The final get-out comes around 1987 when Starship's co-vocalist Mickey Thomas begins cold-shouldering her out of sessions, "singing with the old broad clearly wasn't his idea of the ultimate Rock band line-up". For Starship, it was a lucrative slide into the artistic oblivion of albums like *Nuclear Furniture*, selling to an audience located "sadly adjacent to the people she'd once warned Woodstock against" according to Bill Graham (in *Hot Press*, July 1987). So inevitably, she felt it was a good moment to quit. Finally dis-Graced, Starship fly gracelessly apart and vanish from commercial visibility. Simultaneously her relationship with Skip effectively ends. He goes on to work on projects with Prince.

A brief re-union of the *original* Jefferson Airplane line-up comes minus Spencer Dryden, who is replaced by Kenny Aronoff. They tour and produce a single album called *Jefferson Airplane*. "No-one bought Lear jets on the pro-

ceeds" she jokes. After which you only hear about Grace Slick through her involvement with the twelve-step Alcoholics Anonymous Rehab programme. Or the 1994 shotgun incident (hunt down the book for the full amusing story)... "I haven't been in a Rock'n'Roll band for ten years. And I don't even think about it," she says now. Doing promotion for the book is "a little like going around representing an airline company when you don't fly anymore. It's like 'huh, what am *I* doing here?' But if I were to write an album of songs talking about the way I feel and am right now, it would be rude to an audience, because they'd go, understandably, 'Why don't you play White Rabbit, why don't you play dada-dada-dada.' But I don't want to do that. And you can't go out and say to an audience 'I'm not gonna *sing* that' [in bratty little girl voice]. Well then — don't sing. So I don't."

As a strong woman she's always taken her

> I was comfortable having sex during my pregnancy. I viewed it like feeding the baby. You know, sperm must be healthy. It's protein. So I just went ahead and did it, because what are you going to do, poke its eyes out...?
>
> 'Amazing Grace' Slick *the wit & (stoned) wisdom*

1973 30 SECONDS OVER WINTERLAND Live.

1974 DRAGONFLY First as Jefferson Starship, with Ride The Tiger and Be Young You.

1975 RED OCTOPUS With Miracles and Play On Love. 'A bevy of beautifully vacuous melodies and lyrics but no inkling of how good the Starship could be. At least it has the saving grace of Marty Balin's delicious voice.' (*Melody Maker*, Feb 28, 1981)

1976 SPITFIRE Includes Your Love.

1978 EARTH With Runaway, Take Your Time and the single Count On Me. 'Dreck of the most monumental redundancy.' (*NME*, Mar 18, 1978)

1980 DREAMS (RCA) Grace Slick solo album, with Do It The Hard Way, Full Moon Man and Garden Of Man. 'Alternates between banks of swamping synthesisers and the use of gentle acoustic guitar and piano. But the main instrument is that powerful voice.' (*Melody Maker*, Apr 26, 1980)

1981 WELCOME TO THE WRECKING BALL (RCA) Grace Slick solo album with Mistreater, Shooting Star and

own strengths for granted without ever seeing the personal need for a 'Woman's *Movement*'. Indeed, Feminism itself gets swiftly dismissed as being just "a new slant on an old Tupperware party". Instead her book starts off by defining what she terms her 'Betty Grable' philosophy which accepts "no whining or lobbying against sexist attitudes" but advocates instead a credo of "say what you mean, mean what you say, and throw a joke and a song in the mix now and then". "I didn't really have that big of an interest in women" she admits now. "I didn't think they were *that* interesting. At that time it was kind of all stuff about — 'which diapers are better than another' or 'what kind of bread to buy', or 'what to wear to the Social' — and none of that stuff *interested* me. I didn't hang out with women that much, though I had some friends. I didn't *dislike* women. But it was never a matter of "Oh, I'm gonna go out and do this for *US* women". It was just... I didn't *care*! It's like, I don't *care* about — for example — Algebra, so I don't do anything about it. It's not that algebra is right or wrong, it's not *interesting* to me. That's something like what it was like. It's different now. It has changed.

GRACE SLICK
Somebody to Love?

A
Rock-and-Roll
Memoir
with Andrea Cagan

Shot In The Dark. 'Has the ingredients of a fine album, but not quite the finesse she's capable of.' (*Record Mirror*, Mar 7, 1981) The press-ads say: 'A powerful & exciting Rock album as far removed from *Dreams* as Rainbow is from Mantovani.'

1981 KENT STATE Grace contributes Dance Around The Sun and They All Look The Same to soundtrack album of TV-movie about Kent State Student shootings of 1970. Back-up musicians include Richard Manuel, Garth Hudson and James Burton.

1980 FREEDOM AT POINT ZERO Jefferson Starship, with Jane and The Girl With Hungry Eyes. 'Grace Slick and Marty Balin are gone, and with them her confused and meandering lyrics.' (*Melody Maker*, Dec 8, 1979)

1981 MODERN TIMES With Find Your Way Back, Stranger and Stairway To Cleveland. 'Mickey Thomas will never believe in miracles the way Marty Balin could.' (*Washington Tribune*, Jun 4, 1981)

1983 WINDS OF CHANGE With I Came Back From The Jaws Of The Dragon, Keep On Dreamin' and I Will Stay. 'After her return to the fringes of the ranks providing

I enjoy being around women now because they *are* interested and they *are* educated. They might be still supporting families but they *do* go out in the world."

So how does this self-proclaimed some-time 'Rock'n'Roll Slut' view acts like the Spice Girls? They were celebrated for personifying a 'girl power' that Grace was not only practising but already taking for granted thirty years ago! Is that a continuity of feminine individualism, or are such current pretenders just industry puppets? "Ah, it seems like there's room for all of us" she comments — for once, tactfully. "In other words, if you want to dress up, sing four-part harmonies, have big production numbers, and do all that stuff — fabulous. If you want to pick up a guitar and have hairy armpits and sing about politics — wonderful. It doesn't really *matter*. It's all just entertainment. So, there's room for everybody."

EVERY SAGA HAS A BEGINNING...

Today Grace lives in Malibu overlooking the

Pacific. She paints. And she writes. She's not only veggie, but vegan too. She feeds the racoons that infiltrate her garden. And she conducts what she terms 'Bio-Medical Research' ("the business of a war on drugs is just comical" she pronounces it 'Karm-ical'! "Man has *always* taken drugs and always will. Even animals do it"). The Doors and Velvet Underground are universal Rock Esperanto. Joplin's dead. So is Nico. We've still got Courtney Love — but she has yet to write anything as powerful as White Rabbit. And that Grace is still around should be a cause for celebration.

At first, I was iridescent

then I became transparent

finally, I was absent

—Starship on the *Blows Against The Empire* album

Somebody To Love?
by Grace Slick with Andrea Cagan
ISBN 1-85227-738-6 / Virgin / £16.99

background vocals and one shared lead on *Modern Times* the dark angel of Rock, Grace Slick, makes the opening statement on the new Starship album and firmly re-establishes herself as synonymous with the band's best recordings.' (*Soundmaker*, Dec 18, 1982)

1984 NUCLEAR FURNITURE With Layin' It On The Line, No Way Out (written by ex-J

Geils Peter Wolf), Showdown and Rose Goes To Vale.

1984 SOFTWARE (RCA) Solo album, with All The Machines and Fox Face. 'A rather desperate attempt to sound modern... uncomfortably out of her depth in such blatantly forced modern surroundings.' (*Melody Maker*, Mar 31, 1984)

1985 KNEE-DEEP IN HOOPLA First LP as simply Starship,

with We Built This City.

1987 NO PROTECTION With Nothing's Gonna Stop Us Now and It's Not Over ('Til It's Over).

1989 LOVE AMONG THE CANNIBALS

1989 JEFFERSON AIRPLANE (Epic) Re-union of original line-up, featuring Summer Of Love, Planes and The Wheel.

© Dogger

LED ZEPPELIN
ROBERT PLANT
HEAVY PLANT
CROSSING

In through the out door. It has to be...

London splurged with the blizzard-white light of early Spring greenhoused into heatwave. And from its slow dazzle I go into the huge silent gloom of a hotel silted with dignified ritual and polite establishment observances, as calm and grandiloquent as psalms. But I go in through the out door, in ritual observance of some other cultural tradition.

Then a sound, distant at first, but growing startlingly fast — like the planet Saturn coughing out moons of phlegm — until it roars and resonates and shakes the foundations atremble like an amplified Krakatoa at maximum throttle. And K-E-R-R-A-N-G! Splattering ferns and exploding potted plants into shrapnel, the jet black'n'chrome-gleaming machine comes hurtling, jouncing and growling through the plush-piled corridors, down the richly carpeted stairs, and banshee-screeching into the foyer. Juddering and throbbing to a halt that rips Axminster fibre, revving down, comes the huge 10,000cc Harley Davidson with quad exhausts. A Romano-Celtic warlord sits astride its power-glide' metallic sheen. He wears a python around his throat and a naked woman draped across the pillion. Her long dark hair is threaded with chrysanthemums, and there's a daisy woven into her pubic bush. Strutted up against the shocked Reception Desk, unleaded gas-fumes dancing in contrails of dry ice, he dismounts shaking sweat-matted ringlets of golden hair from his piercing blue eyes, brocade jacket open over glistening bare chest.

He grins, bounds up to me and pumps my hand. "Hi Andy, I'm **ROBERT PLANT***..."*

Except it doesn't happen quite like that.

"Hi, Robert Plant here" says the voice flooding through the 'phone. "I'm speaking from a little office by the side of the rehearsal place that we're working in right now. Yeah, Devon, that's correct." Interviews courtesy of British Telecom are not ideal. "No, they're not. Where are you? Where are ya. You're in Wakefield...!"

LED ZEPPELIN *— still over the hills and far away.*

Hey there Mama, said the way you move
gonna make you sweat, gonna make you
groove…
—from Black Dog (*Led Zeppelin 4*) and
Your Ma Said You Cried In Your Sleep
Last Night (*Manic Nirvana*)

B
ut this is March 1990. And Robert Plant has no time for 1970s Heavy Metal dinosaurs any more, he has no musical corpses or Rock behemoths to drag around either. Heavy Plant is crossing over into the new decade, and that's his main preoccupation now. The current band. The current album *Manic Nirvana* ("fast bliss"). *"We've got a Band. A big positive workforce.* And people have got the ticket now. The reviews have been very positive, very up. They've really kinda given great credence to the job we're trying to do. They understand what's going on. *Finally, now, I'm allowed to get on with my own career. And this music is that strong.* It's undeniably another phase of my life. Which means I don't have to keep on dipping back into the past all the time. And *references to the past are becoming less and less necessary…"* Despite the quote from Black Dog on side two track two? "Yes, this band is a very positive work environment. We'd just come back from an American tour after playing to slightly under a million people, and we came back wanting to make our next statement *together*. It was a case of 'let's make this record', and my young

chums were pushing and encouraging me and saying 'Yeah, let's go, let's go, c'mon'. I would have it no other way than that."

Fact is, *Manic Nirvana* is an album worth gloating about. It's ten years since Plant sloughed off the stale Zep skin. And it's been a decade of false starts and half-realised projects. His retro revivalist Honeydrippers group, a belated Top Twenty single with Big Log (Plant's first ever UK chart hit; No 11 in July 1983), and a series of flawed and only occasionally impressive LPs: *Pictures At Eleven* (July 1982), *The Principle Of Moments* (July 1983) which features Big Log and Messin' With The Mekon, *Shaken'n'Stirred* (May 1985) featuring guest harmonies from Kirsty MacColl, and *Now And Zen* (February 1988). *Manic Nirvana* easily bests them all, fusing the finest aspects of his heritage with what the *NME* calls 'an eagle eye fixed on the nineties'. "Yes" he concedes, "and it's a lot of fun as well!"

Here and now, in this rehearsal suite, he introduces me to the band. Doug Boyle is his best, flashiest and most incendiary guitarist since — it has to be said — Jimmy Page. Chris Blackwell his best, solidest, and most inventive drummer since, yeah, John Bonham. "Chris also plays guitar on the Tie-Dye On The Highway track. He plays drums, and he plays keyboards, he *thinks* he writes songs, he smiles, he plays straight. He's a musician. An all-round musician. He's not *just* a drummer, and yet he's a *great* drummer. But that's only one string to his bow." He neglects to add that this is a band that also works together as smoothly as a finely-tuned 10,000cc Harley at maximum throttle: Plant, Boyle, Blackwell, Phil Johnstone (keyboards) and Charlie Jones (bass). A solid unit formed for *Now And Zen*, honed in by touring, and now kicked well into its stride, making their *Manic Nirvana* an oddly disconcerting mix of the expected and the destabilising. Like rambling through a strange, unfamiliar and fantastically haunted forest, but glancing up through the tree-tops to glimpse the same reassuringly familiar old constellations in the same starry firmament.

"Doug Boyle? How did I meet Doug Boyle? Through Chris Blackwell. Track record? He hasn't got one really, yet. He's played in pubs, playing jazz basically. In fact that's what he's doing over there now — the bastard — while I'm over here doing this. You can hear him warbling on like…

I dunno, like Steve Reich's dad. And yes — if I sound a bit dopey at this time it's because somebody else over there is trying to recreate the sixties about ten feet away from me… look at 'im!" He delivers this line to general laughter.

But the album doesn't *try* to recreate the sixties — it samples it *direct* from the *Woodstock* soundtrack (on Tie-Dye On The Highway, a track "that's just saluting the glorious days of my adolescence"). Because continuity and innovation don't necessarily conflict. Here they co-exist. The song might remain the same, but at least this is very much today's remix. He quotes Black Dog, samples from *Woodstock*, and goes even further back — on the set's only non-band composition. 'The surface noise is unavoidable' say the sleeve-notes. "Oh yeah, you mean the drum-track on Your Ma Said You Cried? The rhythm track is a bass-drum sampled from the original record. It was a great song done first by Kenny Dino. Doug Sheldon had the English version, on Decca [F11416, fact fans]. But the one we sampled was the American version. I read in one review that it got to No34. I thought it did a little better than that." (He's right, of course. Kenny Dino charted April 12, 1961, and reached No24 on US *Billboard*. Doug Sheldon entered January 4, 1961, and hit No29 in the UK *Record Retailer* chart.)

Are there other antique Rock'n'Roll/R&B tracks you intend covering in the future? "No. Not really. I tend to write 'em. I mean, that's what I was saying about *Manic Nirvana* — it's 'panoramic Rockabilly'. That's what *it* is. It's just contemporised a little bit. It doesn't pretend to be anything other than that. It's basically extended Rockabilly." There's an obvious continuity with the Honeydrippers project. "Well, I think that with things like the tracks Nirvana and Hurting Kind you've got a continuation of the Honeydrippers there. I see Nirvana having little smacks of things I was trying to do on the

G ENT with the beard, the solemn expression and the beads is Robert Plant, recently out with a CBS release "Long Time Coming". So happens I specially liked this record and checked into his background. He's 18, Birmingham-born, grammar-school educated, with 'A' levels in English, history, civics and maths. Started singing two years ago with a group called Listen. First disc solo was "Our Song", recognised by Robert as a gigantic flop. He plays violin, piano, organ and guitar. Now he works, all over the country, with his backing group "The Band of Joy". Already his disc has hit the Birmingham Top Twenty which is at least Plant-ing the seeds of his talent.

Shaken'n'Stirred album, where you try to make a piece of music into almost a detective theme from the sixties. You know? A kind of 'The Unwritten Detective Movie'. And you start getting that wacky sinister edge to things. So yeah, I think Nirvana and Hurting Kind are really where the Honeydrippers should have gone…"

Conversation rambles on in this disjointed manner, until "Okay, Andy, I'm getting the nod. I've got about another two minutes, 'cos the whole rehearsal has ground to a halt." So, let's dip back into the past just a little. How about some quick *Hammer Of The Gods* salacious tour stories before I have to go, Robert? "I've got no *Hammer Of The Gods* salacious tour stories." Curt, sharp, and with obvious irritation. "And I can't *believe* that anybody wants that shit. *Tell them to fuck off!* "

Carry me back, carry me back, carry me back
Baby, to where I came from…
—Rock And Roll, *Led Zeppelin 4*

Even in an industry based on hyperbole the Led Zeppelin statistics are stunning. Between 1969 and 1982 they shifted enough vinyl product to plug the hole in the ozone layer. Made enough money to bail out the Russian economy. Travelled more tour-miles than the Voyager 2 space probe. And played to more people in a month than the Pope (even with U2 as support) could manage in a year. They played at punishing volume, and with as much adrenaline as a riot.

In one of his final interviews John Lennon said "I am still a Beatles fan". So is Robert Plant still a Led Zeppelin fan? Is he happy with his legacy? "Yes. I am. I'm very much a Led Zeppelin fan. I wouldn't be a fan of Led Zeppelin *now*. But I'm a fan of what they did — what *they* did?" He corrects himself. "What *we* did then. It was reasonably honest. And it was certainly very inspired at times."

Robert Anthony Plant was born August 20, 1948, in West Bromwich, Staffordshire. Is Kenny Dino the kind of music the pubescent 'Percy' used to listen to? "When I was a kid? Yes, in a sense. But my taste was a bit, I don't know… left of centre I guess. I used to listen to anything that was enticing, alluring. I liked material that made me shudder, and that kind of wild American Pop used to really seduce me. I've always tried to put some of that sound into what I do. To make my music seductive, without being stupid, you know? I really used to enjoy Gene Vincent — his early stuff. In fact I've always enjoyed his voice. Even up until his death he was singing beautifully, even if the material was sometimes a bit questionable. And at the moment I'm trying to collect Joe Meek stuff if I can. And er… yes, there's other stuff, like rare Ral Donner's material…"

Perhaps Donner's Presley-sound-alike, You Don't Know What You've Got (Until You Lose It), I suggest? "Well, that was his big hit. But I had to wait three years to get an even *rarer* Ral Donner track on the Red Bird label!"

The early 1960s saw Plant sucked into the burgeoning Birmingham Blues Scene. "It was the Black Country, actually. Not just Birmingham." As later, Zeppelin would draw exhaustively on roots music too, most obviously the Blues. It is the Blues that validates and gives organic inputs to what they create together. The Blues roots that made Zep more *real*. They double-head a bill with John Lee Hooker at the Roundhouse in 1969. But perhaps sometimes they even get *too* Blues rooted! After all, Willie Dixon has valid grounds for serving writs over his You Need Love (written for Muddy Waters), which forms the basis for

Whole Lotta Love. A situation rectified by the CD reissue of *Led Zeppelin 2* which belatedly adds Dixon's name to the composer-credits. Nevertheless, Blues gives Zep music some kind of solid foundation, whereas subsequent bands — like Guns N' Roses, Bush or Therapy — draw only on secondary sources. On sources like Led Zeppelin themselves. "Exactly. It's lost its plot, really. It's a little neutered. It's just a bit of a drag."

Yet Robert Plant's own first 45rpm single is recorded with a band called Listen. "Oh yeah… You Better Run." His vinyl debut coming in the form of a 1966 cover of an American Young Rascals hit. "That's right. I put it out the same week as a version by a band called the Inbetweens. And of course, later those same Inbetweens turned into Slade. We were all from the same part of the Black Country, so it was quite funny really. We probably only sold about 800 copies each." Two Plant solo singles followed: Our Song c/w Laughing, Crying, Laughing, and Long Time Coming c/w I've Got A Secret, both for CBS. Both now extremely rare and collectible;

people are prepared to pay incredible amounts for such obscure early sides. Are you aware of the collector's value of your first single? "About £80 innit? Yeah, well, I pay money for records if I *really* want to get something, y'know? So I can understand that."

Plant left the Midlands with just his rail fare in his jeans, following up an invitation to join The New Yardbirds for a Scandinavian tour — the band's contractual final tour before its name-switch to Led Zeppelin. Then Zeppelin vamp the media on a learning curve. It's already a band made up of entire fanzines full of muso trivia, even before they play their first gig at Surrey University, October 15, 1968. Jimmy Page's session pedigree is breathtaking. It's his note-bending guitar you hear on Dave Berry's The Crying Game. He plays on the Rolling Stones' *Their Satanic Majesties Request*. He plays on the Jet Harris & Tony Meehan No1 Diamonds, The Who's *My Generation* album, as well as Kinks,

★★★ LED ZEPPELIN (Atlantic 588171).

Way-out blues sounds that go mad at times, that's the forte of this new group formed by guitarist **Jimmy Page**, who produces the disc. **Robert Plant** is an inconsistent lead vocalist, who sometimes sounds good and sometimes bad to me. He also plays harmonica. **John Paul Jones**, well-known helper out on various records hitherto, is on bass and organ, and **John Bonham** on drums. All three back Plant vocally. They perform their over-dramatic songs well and thump up a storm on their instruments, but I felt they overdid it a bit at times. Seven tracks written within the group and the other two are by **Willie Dixon** — You Shook Me and I Can't Quit You Baby.

Other titles: **Good Times Bad Times, Babe I'm Gonna Leave You, Dazed And Confused, You Time is Gonna Come, Black Mountain Side, Communication Breakdown, How Many More Times.**

Pretty Things, Them, Paul Anka, and Cliff Richard records. He first evolves his notorious violin-bowing guitar technique (used to such devastating effect in the Madison Square Gardens film during Zep's Dazed And Confused sequence in *The Song Remains The Same*), while helping out on the *Painter Man* LP recorded by flamboyant Pop Art band Creation. Then, as a Yardbird, he appears alongside Jeff Beck's petulant amp-trashing sequence in Antonioni's movie, *Blowup*. And on and on.

As more-or-less simultaneously the young John Paul Jones is acting as a Mickie Most staff producer, and sessioneer for the likes of Herman's Hermits, Lulu, Cat Stevens, Donovan's *Sunshine Superman* album, the controversial Downliner Sect, and on and on...

And, coming full circle, *Manic Nirvana* is recorded at Olympia studios, where *Led Zeppelin 1* was cut, in thirty-six hours. "Yes, that's true. Was the ghost still there? Yeah, the ghost was still there. The ghost was there alive and well — and laughing at me. I managed to get my best vocal performance for such a long time. I think that was partly to do with the ghost of all that wildness."

From the start Led Zeppelin cultivate class via mystique. A ruthlessly protected exclusivity. Peter Grant, their carnivorous manager, determines their policy of no British singles and no TV shots, ensuring their status as cult gods. There are no sugar-coated bullets of radio-friendly noise from the Zeps, only rhythms broad-brushed with an awesome power, guitar-breaks machined to within one-thousandth of an inch, and there — beneath the sonic machinery — the wet velvet rub of soft human sex. But image is more than just logo, and Zeppelin has the power to flesh out the myth. Album by album their music edges forward along the rim of a precipice. Their sound developing like a shiny spring uncoiling in gut-tightening curves, flashing shoot-to-kill riffs at audio health-hazard volume.

On a day-trip to Calais I once smuggled home a secret stash of a French single coupling Communication Breakdown with Good Times, Bad Times, for massively marked-up resale to other fourth-formers, and to add to my impeccably cool personal credibility (in fact I wound up keeping it, and still have it). More recently I lurch in (through the out door) of a local HMV shop where they're playing Good Times, Bad Times cranked up really loud. For a millisecond it doesn't really connect who it is, the synapses don't close, registering only the hard sharp fast guitar grenade-fragmentation. It sounds remarkably contemporary. Until it clicks that I'm listening to a record made over twenty years earlier! Plant laughs as I retell the anecdote, "I know. Makes you think, dunnit? What next?"

LED ZEPPELIN:
AN UNNATURAL HISTORY
THE SEVENTIES

The Beatles in pieces. The Rolling Stones' quality-control plummeting. Led Zeppelin the world's uncontested No 1 band. Metal at its densest, its heaviest, its most speed-crazed and inventive. But never *just* metal. The electronic techno is always there too — from the swirling theramin vortex running (vinyl) rings around the chaos in the mid-section of Whole Lotta Love, to In The Light, which fades in with an insect's hollow drone, shifts into a vivid crimson *whooosh*, leads into an arc of purple curves through red surrounds going scarlet with animation. Slash its veins and it bleeds ice and lava. Just as their range is wide enough to encompass traditional songs, from as early as Babe I'm Gonna Leave You on *Led Zeppelin 1*, through Gallows Pole and on to the 11:08 minute In My Time Of Dy-

ing on *Physical Graffiti*, as well as absorbing Folk elements from the likes of Sandy Denny and Roy Harper.

Is it fair to assume that the electronic side of Zeppelin is down to Jimmy Page, while the acoustic whimsy was due to Plant's influence? "No. The electronic side would come from whatever was going on at the time. And whoever you could see at the time who would encourage you into doing things in certain directions. But the acoustic side, no, I think that was everybody too. Y'know? I mean, the more extreme of the extremes came from Pagey — sonically. Then John Paul was also there with his early use of synthesisers on things like Celebration. He was always one step ahead of everyone else. He had the first Yamaha G1 — even before Stevie Wonder got his! Which Bonzo just lifted off the ground once when he was a bit drunk. It was so heavy he dropped it about three inches — and totally wrecked the thing." Plant dissolves into tides of laughter, before resuming, "of course, he was only doing it for a bit of a joke..."

Ten albums, plus batches of after-the-event digitally remastered compilations. *Led Zeppelin* and *Led Zeppelin 2* (both in 1969, March and

October), *Led Zeppelin 3* (in October 1970), *Four Symbols* (November 1971) featuring Stairway To Heaven and guest Folkie Sandy Denny, *Houses Of The Holy* (April 1973), the *Physical Graffiti* double-set (March 1975) featuring Kashmir, *Presence* (April 1976), *The Song Remains The Same* soundtrack double-set (October 1976), *In Through The Out Door* (August 1979), and the posthumous *Coda* (November 1982). Plus six American Top Forty singles, from Whole Lotta Love (No 4 in 1969) to Fool In The Rain (No 8 in 1980). Yet unlike the evolution of comparable-status bands like the Rolling Stones or Queen, which are almost excessively documented by film-clips and promo video compilations, pretty much the only visual legacy left by Led Zeppelin is their 127-minute self-indulgent performance-and-fantasy sequence movie *The Song Remains The Same* (Warner Video).

Does Robert regret the decision not to do TV or to make singles for the British market? "Naw. Not at all. I think, in a way, it's better that the records speak for themselves. You haven't got to see the sort of aping and glamour too much. It's just fine the way it is. Any more of it and it would have become an industry." In the movie Peter Grant does his gangster bit, John Bonham goes drag-racing, Jimmy Page sets off on a mystic quest to self-realisation — and Robert Plant enjoys the otherworldly rural Hippie idyll, riding horseback, children frisking in the stream, the full Pre-Raphaelite deal. Is that *really* the way the members of the band saw themselves at that point in their lives? "Well, I don't think I saw myself as a Romano-Celtic warlord. Not really! But I do still see that the countryside was beautiful. And I did like the evocative imagery of the place in which I was living. I was there on the Welsh border surrounded by all that incredible past, all the history of conflict between the Saxons and Celts. That sort of thing. And sure, it was wishy-

ELODY MAKER, September 19, 1970

And Soon

washy. A bit sloppy. Romantic. A pre-Mary Whitehouse ramble. But yeah, I'd do it again."

Filmed live from a camera positioned in the second row of Madison Square Gardens the movie captures Black Dog, Stairway To Heaven, and a manic Dazed And Confused — with Plant roaring in his full sex-god persona, projecting the erotic stage and lyrical satyr doppelgänger that's continually attracted attacks for sexist offensiveness and shallow phallocentric posturing. Yet Feminist par excellence Germaine Greer provides as escape clause by describing him as 'the sexiest man in the world' (in her notorious *Playboy* interview). "Good Lord…" He's momentarily thrown off balance. "Yes, but if I'm being levelled as sexist because of the lyrics on these records then, the thing is, *none* of it is developed around male dominance, or around the use of the female as being some kind of subservient being. Occasionally it can actually be *fun* to have people who are attractive to one's desires. Rock'n'Roll and Rockabilly was built on that. I'm no 'Brain of Britain' but I like to think that I'm aware of different aspects of what I like. And these things are particularly funny."

Do you get pissed off with people making these accusations? "No. I don't care. It doesn't matter. It is what it is. Ultimately all the waffling in the world doesn't make it any different. I like it. And it sounds good. It makes sense. It's non-offensive. It's only offensive to people who are looking for things to be offended by."

The Led Zeppelin entry in the Phil Hardy/Dave Laing *Encyclopaedia of Rock* (Panther) identifies the humour and spoof elements of Plant's performance. They find him 'a golden ringleted Adonis marvellously parodying the sexual superstar while singing in a voice of limitless power'. "Exactly" he concurs. "How serious can you be? The songs are okay. The records are made of steel, you know? And they're made by men who

are, if you like, craftsmen. And anything else that goes off is just downright repetition. To play a role every night is a bit of a joke — however, it's much better that watching television. And I really like to do it. I like to sing. So yes, parody does come into it. And when it comes down to basics, ask anyone about anything — it's all repetition. There's not many times in your life when you can go, 'God, this is absolutely NEW, this new gesture of mine.'"

Yet Led Zeppelin make perhaps more original gestures than most. While their tour performances repeat those moments more often, and to more people than most. Their tours remain legendary in their scale, their cash-generating potential, their excess… but first, I've got to ask this…

"Why have you got to ask?"

Because I'm interested. He laughs indulgently. "So ask." Plant's long-time infatuation with Elvis Presley is evidenced by Zeppelin soundchecks and encores of A Mess Of Blues or Don't Be Cruel. The Honeydrippers continue the obsession by revamping Presley's retread of Ray Charles' I Gotta Woman. While even now he's contributing to the various-artist charity compilation *The Last Temptation Of Elvis*.

So is it true you got to meet and play for Elvis at the Los Angeles Forum? "We didn't exactly *play* for him. But we met him, yes" he concedes. "The circumstances were that we were both represented by the same agent. He wanted to meet us, and we met him. We were all in a circle in the middle of the room, which was full of people who'd come to fawn over him. And yes, it was a very nice experience. We talked for about an hour-and-a-half, about… *every single thing* you could imagine. It was remarkable. He was definitely loose, and he was very lucid as well. It was great fun. We were inseparable, the five of us. He wasn't particularly aware of whatever was *that* contemporary at the time, unless he was exposed to it by accident. He didn't even know who Elton John was, which was quite funny — 'cos neither did we! Jimmy told Elvis that all I ever do is sing Elvis songs at soundchecks. Which is true. So later, on the way out of the room Elvis asks me which is my favourite song, and I said Anyway You Want Me — oh no, it was Love Me, which is a big ballad that goes 'te-reat me like a fool / treat me mean and cruel / but lu-u-rve me…' And as I leave and we're walking down the corridor going '*What a nice guy*', he sticks his head round the door and says 'Robert', and he starts going 'te-reat me like a fo-o-o-ol' — and so I sing back to him 'treat me mean and cr-o-o-ol'. And at that moment we became the buddies that we always remained. Two rampant sexists!"

Yet when Presley met the Beatles a few years previous it seems to have been a tensely formal and awkward situation. "Yeah," dismissively. "I guess you've just gotta catch people right, y'know."

So what about some more *salacious* tour stories now Robert? The sex'n'sleaze stuff served up by Stephen Davis in his fuck'n'tell book *Hammer Of The Gods*? "I've got no salacious tour stories. The salacious stories of the past are not what I deal in right now. Tell them to read the book if they *really* want to!"

Then just tell me about one incident. Tell me about the 1973 John Bonham Birthday Party where you drive motorcycles down the corridors of the Sunset Strip Hotel, and throw George Harrison into the Swimming Pool. "Well… yeah… but that wasn't Bonzo's birthday party. That was another *outrageous* time! But yes, we used to rent small motorbikes, but they were only circus bikes. And I couldn't ride mine very well anyway because I had a python round my neck, and a naked woman on my face, and so on… and so on…"

In a decade when the critical rottweilers snarled but seldom savaged, when most bands could be bought (and judging by their subsequent product can't have come too expensive), Led Zeppelin stand aside in their own immaculate game. No full metal jack-offs they… but we are not here to praise the myth. We are here to build new ones…

Despite all this alleged excess and posturing, Robert Plant's demeanour in this rehearsal studio webbed with cables and instrument leads, is remarkably unaffected. He comes across re-

Robert Plant embarking on the Non Stop Go Tour 1988

tinental Drift (on their *Steel Wheels* album) incorporates the Moroccan Master Musicians of Jajouka. "I suppose the whole writing of that track took about eight minutes. Until recently I was living near Monmouth, and I had a house with a room where we had a little mixing desk, and we could set everything up and play around the desk. And it happened like that. It was Chris [Blackwell] and Phil [Johnstone] together. It was just a case of guitar, keyboards, and a drum-loop that Chris had already developed. So, I just wanted to get some kind of vocalising that swirled right across the top of everything, rather than keeping with the strict metre of the track. And, um, it's a bit pompous you know. It's a bit overly grand. But I was listening to The Mission for about half-an-hour that morning. Giggling at Tower Of Strength (their attempt at replicating Led Zep's Kashmir) and hearing that sort of mock-grandeur. So the melodic input began from that angle. And then became more focused later on. Watching you — yeah, it's great, because it's like there's a lot of torment in the song. And I'm not a stranger to that."

laxed, totally without pretensions, no artistic affectations, or hang-ups. He's matey. He's 'I'd love to spend more time with you because I can tell that you're quite a historian.' He's 'Oh, well, have a good life'. Perhaps part of that is due to the uninhibiting effects of the 'somebody trying to recreate the sixties about ten feet away' from us. I can smell the sweet heady aroma from here, where I'm sat. But no, it's there in the grooves too. His music says 'stop patronising the public'. It says 'no wonder Rock is sinking into apathy'. It says 'let the heads, the good times and the cameras roll'. Apathy is still a crime. Can anyone seriously justify anything other than full-on attack in 1990?

Listen to Watching You. Classic spiky Rock spraying World Music across the mix. It samples the Arabic chant of Siddi Makain Mushkin in much the same way that the Rolling Stones' Con-

Torment. Yes. It's not always been so *up*. It must have been difficult following the demise of Led Zeppelin. The sudden crash from whizz-kids to was-kids. The going back to square one and reconstructing a career from the ground up. "Yeah, well. Basically I hate careers. I hate the idea of it being a career. I just wanna *sing*. It's what goes with it to be able to do that reasonably successfully that makes it problematical. But it's been an 'interesting' struggle. I've learned how short-tempered I am. And how impatient."

Following the final implosion made irrevocable by John Bonham's death (on September 25, 1980), Zeppelin fragments spun off into sometimes improbable orbits. Perhaps most bizarre of all being John Paul Jones' exploits in production knob-twiddling for metal upstarts The

Mission. And in particular their aforementioned Tower Of Strength — which, as already observed, blatantly reconstructs and rewrites Kashmir (long before Puff Daddy would sample Zep's sublime epic original for his inclusion on the *Godzilla* movie soundtrack). "Yes. I know. Crazy innit? I've said a coupla daft things when people have asked me about it. Somebody in an interview said 'what about John Paul Jones?'. And I said 'I think he's a double-glazing salesman now'. Because basically *you can see right the way through that piece of music*. You have to be really a fool to buy it. Or at least a fool to buy it *emotionally*. It surprised me. But for what it was — it wasn't

bad. It's just that it's a bit negative to have to take that into account. When I see it I *want* to like it. I really *want* to embrace it. And I want it to be more than just a hollow gesture. Mission played with us for quite a while in America. They supported us on the Non Stop Go tour in 1988. And they were good. But I was waiting for the skies to open... and they didn't..."

Following the final Zeppelin product, *Coda* — a compilation of previously unissued studio out-takes from earlier albums — Jimmy Page hooks up with Bad Company's Paul Rodgers for

dodgy supergroup The Firm. And finds time to score the soundtrack album for Michael Winner's ever dodgier *Death Wish 2* movie. But connections remain. Page, Plant and Jones reform (with Phil Collins on drums) for their forgettable Philadelphia Live Aid slot. They re-reform (with Jason Bonham drumming) for a one-off bash celebrating Atlantic Records fortieth anniversary. Then Plant guested on Jimmy Page's surprisingly lacklustre *Outrider* solo LP, while Page contributed to Plant's *Now And Zen*.

So there's a continuing Plant/Page association? "Well, it isn't continuing *now*! I don't know about later. Then it was just the right time to develop and keep the friendship going, y'know? But this time, for this album, I was concentrating so much on the music I was doing that it just seemed inappropriate to ring him up and say 'hey, come on, come on over and have a play'. Jimmy's presence on this album would have created a talking point. But it probably wouldn't have been the best way of cementing the future of the band in people's imagination..." Whereas the remaining Led Zeppelin connection — the drum chair vacated by John Bonham, whose relationship with Plant extends clear back to their pre-Zep Birmingham group Band of Joy — seems to have been more difficult to fill. Plant's first solo venture, *Pictures At Eleven*, runs through a battery of drummers: Phil Collins, Cozy Powell, and ex-Jethro Tull Barriemore Barlow. "Yeah, drummers are usually a cranky breed. Cozy didn't really want to get involved too much with the technology of drumming, or the technology of creating rhythm tracks. It was more like 'I'm the drummer, and I play drums.' When really, when you're going out to try to create moods and textures, there's a lot more to it than just that. Particularly now, when there's so much technology there to expand on ideas. Tracks like Watching You could never have even come to life at all if that was the attitude of the crew on board! Phil Collins was as busy as ever. He's great fun and a hellishly eager guy. Very, very positive, a great encourager. But obviously he has his own career, so there could be nothing full-time about that. Barriemore Barlow — his contribution was Reckless Love and Stranger Here And Over There, which are tremendous. I think they're two of the best solo tracks I've ever done. Especially Reckless Love. Then I also worked with Ritchie Hayward of Little Feat, he was technically excellent, but at that time everything seemed to happen at once. So when Chris Blackwell came along..."

Led Zeppelin was a democracy. Now it's Plant's band. He's the leader. "Yes. That's true. But democracy is gaining. We now have free elections here. I'm not so much the leader, as just the petulant lunatic vocalist. And from time to time — like now — I have to sit over here in the corner while somebody else takes over. But that's good. I would have it no other way."

And the future? "There's a track coming out on some CD thing, called Oompah-brackets-Watery Bint, which is about a relationship with a woman. [Did this track ever emerge? I've no idea.] A relationship which is always very questionable because her hands are so cold, and her skin's always wet. And basically — what it is, the guy is trying to figure out what it's all about. And why he's so quizzical about it. Until he realises that she, in fact, lives underwater. That she might even be descended from 'The Lady Of The Lake'. This *ridiculous* song burbles along, and then suddenly — at the end, it goes into something that sounds like a cross between Cozy Cole's Big Noise From Winnetkah meets... goodness knows what! And it's that sort of wacky

unwritten theme music again. It's funny. It's a funny track — 'oh porous love, what can I do / but drift forever in a sea of you'. That's how it goes..."

Then: "Okay, I'm getting the nod. I gotta go." An audible hesitation hangs in the air between us, until he adds, "Tell them to forget about *Hammer Of The Gods*. The, erm, salacious stories of the past are *not* what I deal in right now. Or make it up. Just put anything you like. *Make it up*. That's what usually happens anyway!"

PRESENCE

So, okay Robert.

In through the out door. It has to be...

London splurged with the blizzard-white light of early spring greenhoused into heatwave. And from its slow dazzle I go into the huge silent gloom of a hotel silted with dignified ritual and polite establishment observances as calm and grandiloquent as psalms. But I go in through the out door, in ritual observance of some other cultural tradition.

Then a sound, distant at first...

© Dogger

KRAFTWERK
RALF HÜTTER COMES TO SAY HELLO TO THE MACHINE SPIRIT

KRAFTWERK *means 'Power Station' — regardless of what you read elsewhere. They are also the Teutonic four-piece responsible for such soundtracks for science as* TRANS-EUROPE EXPRESS *and* COMPUTER WORLD. *They are the musicians who first encrypted the transcript from the handbook of neuro-electronic tomorrows, the fountainhead of all things digital-sterile, and took it into the minimalist technological zeitgeist. Their sound — from its early 1970s beginnings — was already aerodynamically styled for the next millennium. The journey from Joe Meek's suicide, to the ignition of* AUTOBAHN *takes just seven-and-a-half years — but covers a million persecs of evolution. Now the legendary prophets of modernism and all things digital-sterile are here in London for a brief tour, and a limited number of meet-and-greet press interviews. So I get to corner* **RALF HÜTTER** *in a cluttered backwater of* EMI *House, for a conversational nexus in which we poke theories at each other through the language barrier... Frank Zappa said 'writing about music is like dancing about architecture'. This is the sound of dancing architecture...*

EINS. TECHNO-POP AT THE ELECTRIC CAFE

We play the machines, but the machines also play us. They should not do only slave work, we try to treat them as colleagues so they exchange energies with us...

—Ralf Hütter, *Mojo* (April 1997)

ed man. Stop. *Eins, Zwei, Drei, Vier.* Green man. Go. People respond, regulated by the mechanical switch of coloured lights.

Crossing the Pelican towards EMI House it's easy to submerge in a long droning procession of Kraftwerkian images, pavement thick with lumbering showroom dummies reacting to Pavlovian stimuli, parallel lines of thruways, multi-legged ferroconcrete skyways, glass-front office-blocks waterfalling from heaven, individuality drowned, starved to extinction, etc, etc. This could get boring. This could be cliché. Ideas prompt unbidden, strategies of sending my cassette recorder on alone to talk to the Kraftwerk answering machine. That's Kraftwerk, isn't it? *I got news for you. It ain't.*

Ralf Hütter (electronics and voice) is neat, polite, talks quietly with Teutonic inflection, and totally lacks visible cybernetic attachments. He's dressed in regulation black — as per stereotype — slightly shorter than me which makes him five-foot-eight-inches, or perhaps nine, hair razored sharp over temples not to allow traces of decadent side-burns. Shoes are black, but sufficiently scuffed to betray endearingly human imperfec-

tions. He walks up and down reading review stats thoughtfully provided by EMI's press division. Seems it's a good review in *The Times*? Strong on technical details... yes? "No. The writer says we play exactly as on the records, which is not so." He is evidently chagrined by this particular line of criticism, which is an interesting reaction. I file it for reference. But then again he's just got up and come direct from his hotel. He wants breakfast. Coffee and cakes. An hour or so to talk to me, then down to Oxford for the dauntingly exacting Kraftwerk sound check rituals. The other Kraftwerkers — Florian Schneider (voice and electronics), Karl Bartos and Wolfgang Flur (both electronic percussion) are otherwise occupied. So every vowel must count.

I extend a tentative theory. The image Kraftwerk project of modernity, it seems to me, is largely derived from twenties and thirties originals: the Futurist dedication to movement and kinetic energy; the Bauhaus emphasis on clean, strictly functional lines; the Fritz Lang humans-as-social-ciphers thing. Even an album 'inspired' by Soviet Constructivist El Lissitzky with all the machine-art connotations that implies. Doesn't Hütter find this contradictory? "No. In the twenties there was Futurism in Italy, Germany, France. Then in the thirties it stopped, retrograded into Fascism, bourgeois reactionary tendencies, in Germany especially…" And time froze for forty years. Until the Kraftwerk generation merely picked up the discarded threads, carried on where they'd left off. After the war "Germany went through a period with our parents who were so obsessed with getting a little house, a little car, the Volkswagen or Mercedes in front, or both. All these very materialistic orientations turning Germany into an American colony, no new ideas were really happening. We were like the first generation born *after* the war, so when we grew up we saw that all around us, and we turned to other things." Kissing to life a dormant culture asleep four decades?

But computers only print out data they're programmed with, so working on this already grossly over-extended mechanistic principle I aim to penetrate Kraftwerk motivations. The dominant influences on them then were — what? American Rock? "No." In that case, do Kraftwerk fit into the Rock spectrum? "No. Anti-Rock'n'Roll." So their music is a separate discipline? "Yes, in a way, even though we play in

places like Hammersmith. We are more into environmental music."

So if not Rock, then what? — Berio? Stockhausen? "Yes and no. We listened to that on the radio, it was all around. Especially the older generation of electronic people, the more academic composers — although we are not like

that. They seem to be in a category within themselves, and only circulating within their own musical family. They did institutional things — while we are out in the streets. But I think from the sound, yes. From the experimenting with electronics, definitely. The first thing for us was to find a sound of Germany that was of our generation, that was the first records we do. First going into sound, then voices. Then we went further into voices and words, being more and more precise. And for this we were heartily attacked." He mimics the outrage of his contemporaries — "You can't do that… *Electronics*? What are you doing? *Kraftwerk*? German group — German name? It's stupid. Music is Anglo-American — it *has* to be, even when it is in Germany." The incredulity remains: "Still today, you know. Can you imagine? — German books with English titles, German bands singing English songs. It's ridiculous!"

Of course it is. But didn't the Beatles do some German-language records at one time? "Sure" shrugs Hütter, friendly beyond all reasonable expectations. "They were even more open than most of the Germans…"

ZWEI. RADIO ACTIVITY THE VOICE OF ENERGY

I think our music has to do with emotions. Technology and emotion can join hands…
—Ralf Hütter, 1991

I'd anticipated some mutual incomprehensibility interface with his broken English and my David Hockney Yorkshire. You find the phrasing strange? I'll tell you… when the possibility of doing this interview first cropped up I ransacked my archives and dug out everything on Kraftwerk I could find. Now it occurs to me that each previous press chat-piece, from *Creem* to *Melody Maker*, have transposed Herr Hütter's every utterance into perfect English. Which is not the case. His eloquence is daunting, but it inevitably has very pronounced Germanic cadences. Sometimes he skates around searching for the correct word, other times he uses the right word in the wrong context. When he says "we worked on the next album and the next album, and just so on", it *really* emerges as "ve vork on ze next album und ze next, und just zo on". It might be interesting to write up the whole interview tape with that phonetic accuracy, but it would be difficult to compose and impossible to read. Nevertheless, I'm not going to bland out his individuality by disinfecting his speech peculiarities, or ethnically cleansing his phrases *entirely*…

But now he's in flight and I'm chasing, trying to nail down details. In my head it's now turn of the decade — sixties bleeding into the seventies, and this thing is called Krautrock. Oh, wow!

Hard metallic grating noises, harder, more metallic, more grating and noisier than Velvet Underground, nihilistic Germanic flirtations with the existential void. Amon Duul II laying down blueprints to be electro-galvanised into a second coming by PiL, Siouxsie & The Banshees and other noise terrorists. Cluster. Faust. Then there is the gratuitous language violence of Can, sound that spreads like virus infection from Floh de Cologne and Neu, and Ash Ra Temple who record an album with acid prophet and genetic outlaw Timothy Leary. Was there a feeling of movement among these bands? A kinship?

"No." One note on the threshold of audibility, shooting down fantasies. "In Germany we have no capital. After the war we don't have a centre or capital anymore. So instead we have a selection of different regional cultures. We — Kraftwerk — come from industrial Düsseldorf. But Amon Duul II came from Munich, which has a different feeling. Munich is quite relaxed. There's a lot of landscape around."

Now for me it's not just some off-the-top-of-the-head peripheral observation, but the cornerstone of my entire musical philosophy that this affable German is effortlessly swotting, and I'm not letting him off lightly. I restate histories carefully. American Rock'n'Roll happened in 1954 — Memphis, Sun Studios. From there it spread in a series of shock waves, reaching and taking on the regional characteristics of each location it hit. By the mid sixties a distinctive UK variant had come into being, identifiably evolving out of exposure to US vinyl artefacts, but incontrovertibly also home-grown. Surely Krautrock was evidence that Germany had also acquired its own highly individual Rock voice? It seems to me there *is* a common feeling, a shared voice among these diverse groups. But he's not buying.

You don't think so? "No. At least not as far as we were concerned. Maybe it seemed that it was that way to the Hippie generation. But I don't think we had anything to do with those other bands you mention." I'm unconvinced, but ask why, out of that plethora of sound, only Kraftwerk survive? "Maybe it's because we are more... tough. Where we live is the toughest of them all, I think. The hardest situation to live. So maybe we are most trained, from childhood on, to..."

Trained for survival? "In a way, yes. Because we got always knocked on the head. Put down. I think it has to do with that, basically. We had our Düsseldorf studio since 1970. And the city is so extreme in its steel and glass output that you either disappear in the street somewhere, you go down — or you stand up, and those people standing up just combine and maybe manage to stay together, work together, and be productive. So when you travel somewhere abroad, and you don't get the feedback you imagine, you don't get disillusioned. We call ourselves 'musical workers'. We are an industrial unit. I think that what happened to the other groups was that they went into it as *artists*. As guitar players or whatever. But they got carried away with the Pop scene." He gestures like the smoking of imaginary joints.

Perhaps this emphatic denial of Rock roots has something to do with his charges of American cultural imperialism? His search for a 'German voice' for Kraftwerk? Surely there was more Elvis Presley and Beatles on Düsseldorf radio than there was Stockhausen and Berio? Surely the Rock influence was unavoidable? Unless he is deliberately excluding it in retrospect for reasons of cultural purity, substituting only German reference points — like Franz Schubert? I don't know. Kraftwerk — to Ralf Hütter — is an industrial unit manufacturing environmental soundtracks for European cities. A separate development. Modern music. But could it have evolved in that form — issuing stylised riff-based Pop singles like Pocket Calculator, *without* exposure to US radio? Perhaps the assimilation was subliminal, and not a conscious thing? Perhaps he's too close to be objective?

I'm gonna work it round to my point of view eventually, but meantime I buy time and ask what story lurks behind the track Franz Schubert on their *Trans-Europe Express* album. "He played it himself. I was switching on the sequencing machines and then it was playing," he hums the spiral theme. "It was something else we'd been setting up before. Something much speedier. The machines just happened to be tuned to that thing the next day, and they played it. So I changed the octaves, and I thought it was Franz Schubert playing. As if he's saying 'hello', because he's the acknowledged master of German melodies. Now in England they say 'New Romantics', but what we said in 1975 when people ask 'what is "Autobahn"', we said 'it is Romantic Realism'. Because we are existing now in the gap between the *reality* of cars, and still the *romanticism* of cars. So it's like Franz Schubert just came in for a few minutes and said 'hello' to the machine spirit."

How much of Kraftwerk is tongue-in-cheek? Ralf Hütter delivers these lines deadpan, almost expressionless, identifiably the voice from the records. But also, it seems, he is a man with a sense of devious humour. "Yes. We have a special type of black humour. We always wear black. It has to do with truth and certain aspects of the truth. Funny and serious at the same time. Revolutionary, and funny." Creative absurdity? "Yes. Somebody says we are very absurd, in front of truth and things." But absurd in the Dada sense that it is a *serious* assertion of absurdity? He nods enthusiastically. "It makes you smile, not really laugh or break out. That's what we find when we play a good thing, or find something in the studio, then we start to laugh. It opens up. Breaks down barriers anew..."

DREI. MAN MACHINE
MENSCH MASCHINE

We feel that the synthesiser is an acoustic mirror, a
brain analyser that is super-sensitive to the human
element in ways previous instruments were not, so it is
really better suited to expose the human psychology
than the piano or guitar...
—Ralf Hütter, *Mojo* (April 1997)

Breakfast becomes manifest. Mushroom quiche — no meat — followed by a choice of apricot or apple flan, plus two coffees. I sit opposite him, tape machine on the floor between us picking up air, the windows of EMI House blanding out over the trees of Manchester Square. I'm marshalling scores. So far, not content with winning each verbal exchange hands down, Ralf Hütter has also squashed each of my most cherished illusions about Krautrock. But on the plus side, massive giga-jolts of respect are due here. Long before the world had heard of Bill Gates or William Gibson, when Silicon Valley was still just a valley and mail had yet to acquire its 'e' prefix, Kraftwerk were literally inventing and assembling their own instruments, expanding the technosphere by rewiring the sonic neural net, and defining the luminous futures of what we now know as global electronica. So perhaps it's time to probe more orthodox histories?

It seems to me there are two distinct phases to Kraftwerk's career. Or perhaps even three. The first five years devoted purely to experimental forays into synchromeshed avant-electronics, producing the batch of albums issued in Britain through Vertigo — *Kraftwerk* in 1972, *Ralf Und Florian* the following year, the seminal *Autobahn* in 1974, and the compilation *Exceller 8* in 1975. Then they switch to EMI, settle on a more durable line-up and the subsequent move into more image-conscious material, a zone between song and tactile atmospherics. The third, and current phase, involves a long and lengthening silence.

"No, it wasn't like that" says Hütter. "It was..." his hand indicates a level plane. "There was never a break. It was a continual evolution. We had our studios since 1970, so we always worked on the next album, and the next album, and so on. I think Düsseldorf therefore was very good because we brought in other people, painters, poets, so that we associated ourselves with..." his sometimes faulty English — interfacing with my even more faulty German — breaks down. The words don't come. So he switches direction. "Also we had some classical training before that [Ralf and Florian met at the Düsseldorf Conservatory], so we were very disciplined." Others in this original extended family of neo-Expressionist electro-subversives included Conny Plank (who was later to produce stuff for Annie Lennox' The Tourists, and Ultravox), Klaus Dinger and Thomas Homann (later of Neu), artist Karl Klefisch (responsible for the highly effective *Man Machine* sleeve), and Emil Schult (who co-composed *Trans-Europe Express*). In the subsequent personnel file, as well as Hütter, there is Florian Schneider who also operates electronics and sometimes robotic vocals. While across the years of their classic recordings they are set against Karl Bartos and Wolfgang Flur who both manipulate electronic percussion.

I ask if they always operate as equal partners. "Everybody has their special function within the group, one which he is good at and likes to do the most." It was never just Ralf und Florian plus a beatbox rhythm section? "No. It's just that we started historically all that time ago and worked for four years with about twenty percussionists, and they would never go into electronics, so we had to step over, banging away and things like that. And then Wolfgang came in."

What about the review stats which emphasise

the static elements of Kraftwerk on stage, their presence animated by vastly visual lighting and videos, slides and effects? Isn't that a deliberate playing down of the human element? "Yes. But it's not important. Because we find, especially in the music business, that individuals are over-blown until they explode. It's all bullshit. We don't need that. In Germany we can walk down the streets and work like everybody else. We are just another profession, nothing special. We do our work like everybody else does, like doctors or taxi drivers, dentists or bus drivers. The other ex-treme," he adds, "is the American star system. For the first five years we toured always in Ger-many on the autobahns, that's where that album came from. Since 1975 we do other countries as well."

They first tour the USA in March 1975, top-ping the bill over British Prog-Rockers Greenslade — leaving an American Top Thirty hit in place. How much of that early music was improvised? Was the earlier material 'freer'? Kraftwerk num-bered Karl Klaus Roeder on violin and guitar back then, so are the newer compositions more structured? "No. We are going more... now that we play longer, work longer than ten years, we know more, and every afternoon when we are in the Concert Hall or somewhere in the studio we just start the machines playing and listen to this and that. Just yesterday we composed new things. Once in Edinburgh we composed a new piece which we even included in that evening's show. New versions on old ideas. So we are al-ways working because otherwise we would get bored just repeating. And it's not correct what he [a hostile gig reviewer] was saying — that we play on stage exactly like we sound on the record. That's complete rubbish. It means people don't even notice and they don't listen. They go instead over to the bar for a drink! Our music is very basic, the compositions are never complex or never complicated. More *sounds* — KLINK! KLUNK! Metallic sound. We go for this sound composition more than music composition. Only now they are thematically more precise than they were before."

But when Autobahn broke Kraftwerk world-wide, it lead to a direct confrontation with the contradictions of American hype-biz. "Certain ideas of the robots came from there because we were doing sixty concerts in two months. And through doing that we discover new qualities in the way we play. In the robotic life of automa-tism. You think you're actually playing, but you're not playing — it's your *fingers* that are playing. Your nerves play automatically, and your system plays. We tried to bring that out because no-one was talking about it. Everyone was talking about California, sunshine, 'Hey, let's go on holiday'. So we said 'no, let's go to work'. People disas-sociate themselves from their work, and it's a very dangerous, very strange tendency of Western society. Mentally, people are *always* on holiday. And music plays a very big part of that. It is purely escapism. It is a leisure industry, projecting biki-nis and sunshine. It is a form of advertising which says 'smoke this cigarette brand' and you go on holiday — which is not true. Smoke and you ruin your lungs."

In their press files, journalists are constantly angling Kraftwerk on the 'machines take over' theme, which is basically phoney. Machines are neutral. They merely perform the functions that their operator feeds in. Right? "But that's an ob-session that comes from English writers. It's a fear. There's so much fear involved, so that in order to forgo that fear, they feel they have to control everything." So that impression is the product of writers putting their own paranoias on what you do? "I think so." What about the dehumanised aspects of the Showroom Dummies single, then? "They say it's dehumanising. You use the word 'dehumanising'. I would not say that. That's negative thinking. What we're trying to do is bring something about. Maybe speak for the dummies. And we get a very big understanding in Germany from young people that it is a robot society." He acts out clockwork movements, clone dancing, monotoning — "I'm a robot — I'm doing this — I'm doing that. I'm not a human. I'm a robot." Then he dismisses it all. "We speak for the underprivileged."

A legend on the *Computer World* sleeve lists 'Interpol & Deutsche Bank, FBI & Scotland Yard', implying that traditional political divisions have

now been superseded by transnational organisations co-ordinated through electronic links. So it's not the machines that have taken over, but those who *control* machine technology to manipulate the underdogs, the dummies. A political statement. Correct? "Social-political. The control functions of computers today are an English obsession, but this is also true in Germany. The 'Captain' must have everything under control — the sea, the wind, the crew. But computers have been called the 'universal machines', and we can do other things with them than just control. Lots of people, when they think of comput-

ers, get complications of Interpol and Deutsche Bank. But such control thinking is very limiting. 'Leave this out I can't control it.' They never go and say 'Okay, let's see what we can do' first."

Now things are starting to fall into place, and rather than the shallow motor-reflex clichés I'd been half-expecting, I'm reeling on Kraftwerk psyche-spiel. This is *anti*-Rock, in that it opposes phoney industry hype. This is also environmental soundtrack, music that flows ponderous and huge as the encroachment of glacial ice. My preconceived expectations groan, and some of them shatter. But hang on a minute, Ralf. Surely there's a difference between *your* work — which is creative — and some poor guy stuck on a factory assembly line? "We work in a music factory. We established a small factory, a studio with four people, one engineer, and a video guy. It's like a co-operative. We establish a working situation. I think that you must first change, you must establish a working-type situation to be able to love your work."

But you control what you do. You are the artists. "Sure, but nobody gave it to us. You could make music in an assembly-like situation. If you're a session musician you play whatever comes. Someone tells you this is the new work — you look at it, and then you play it. Then, ten minutes later, someone else comes in with a new film idea or record concept, some new dance music, and you play that too. What we want is to establish a productive situation for human beings, or several humans. But it only becomes a political situation because we *own* our machines." So the point is *positive choice*, you can submerge your individuality in the mass: conform, be a dummy, be a robot. Or you can control your own destiny: create yourself, and through freedom, become truly human. Kraftwerk at once parody the robotic, pointing it out, using it, but also, by example, indicating that there are alternatives. This I like. This is worth coming for.

I suggest an analogy with the proliferation of Indie record labels. "Yes. That's how we started. Our first recordings were done with a cassette recorder, a Revox. Then we had to go to certain studios to mix and finish. Then, over the years, we get more and more [equipment]. Concentrating on our studio. It can be done. Everyone can record. As people have found out. Why should we spend £10,000 in a big studio where we must finish in one day because it's so expensive? Why? You can record at home and the quality can be nearly the same. People don't *need* to go to London to record. They can do it in Sheffield or Manchester or Birmingham. Just as we didn't *need* to go to Hamburg and deal with a record company. We could record in Düsseldorf."

He smiles around a mouthful of mushroom quiche thoughtfully provided by EMI, sitting on an EMI studio couch in EMI House, London W1. A perfect situation in which to stomp all over the corporation ethic, volte-facing opinions and spreading enlightenment. The smile becomes a grin. "Everybody that Phil Spector recorded sounds the same, because he imposes his 'sound' upon them. Spector is creative, but he just uses people like puppets, marionettes. He used to change the personnel of those groups — one guy gets drunk, so right, send in the next one. Manipulation. It becomes so sterilised. Everything and everybody sounds the same. My voice sounds the same as your voice, and everybody can hear it. But *here* is where the difference lies. *We* are the actual persons who control what we do, we put *ourselves* in front of the microphones. That is what is so good about England now. And Germany also. The situation with the new music."

So to Ralf, the *real* music industry robots are not those who use the automata-image as a mar-

keting device, but the assembly line dance hits masterminded by anonymous production teams; where the name on the label (and the 'fronting' face on *Top Of The Pops*) are reduced to ciphers. This is a line of argument that shows up the Gary Numan-oids — who all leech off Kraftwerk's pioneering thrusts — for the one-dimensionally posturing clowns they are. Where Showroom Dummies is agent provocateur, Numan's We Are Glass is bland acceptance, a boring cliché of mindless defeat. In many ways Kraftwerk's outlook seems the *opposite* of the way the press has represented it. Individuals can *liberate* themselves through their work. This is a very *positive* approach. A full three-hundred-and-eighty-degree turn from technological dehumanisation.

"Oh, I see." But now things start getting weird again...

VIER. THE COMPUTER WORLD INTERFACE

Kraftwerk's music is promoting the virtues of cybernetic cleanliness and European culture against the more sensual, body-orientated nature of most Afro-American derived music.

—*Mojo*, August 1987

Hütter's opinions on machine technology have been known to inspire hacks of lesser literary integrity to sprees of wild Thesaurus-ransacking adjectival overkill, their vocabularies straining for greater bleakness, more clone-content, *Bladerunner* imagery grown bloated and boring through inept repetition. And sure, Kraftwerk is all geometrical composition, diagonal emphasis, precision honed etc, but their imagery is not entirely without precedent. Deliberately so. Their *Man Machine* album track Metropolis obviously references German Fritz Lang's 1926 proto-sci-fi Expressionist movie. The album sleeve also acknowledges the 'inspiration' of Bauhaus constructivist El Lissitzky. I went on to hazard the connections with German modern classical music bizarro Karlheinz Stockhausen — particularly on Kraftwerk's *Radio-Activity* album, where they use the 'musique concrete' technique of surgical-splicing different sounds together from random areas. Radioland uses drop-in short-wave blips, bursts and static twitterings, Transistor has sharp pre-sample edits, alongside the pure found-sound audio-collage The News. A technique that resurfaces as late as *Electric Cafe*, where The Telephone Song is made up of 'phone bleeps and telecommunication bloopery. He's familiar with the input. Immediately snaps back the exact location of the ideas — *Kurzwellen*, from Stockhausen's back-catalogue. And what about the aural applications of Brion Gysin/ William Burroughs' literary cut-up experiments? Is there any interaction there? "Maybe" he concedes. "'Soft Machine', contact with machines. But we are more Germanic." He pauses, then suggests "we take from everywhere. That's how we find most of our music. Out of what we find in the street. The Pocket Calculator in the Department Stores."

The music is the message — 'the perfect Pop song for the tribes of the global village' as Hütter once described it. The medium *and* the form? "If the music can't speak for itself then why make music? Then we can be writers directly. If I could speak really everything I want with words then I should be working in literature, in words. But I can't, I never can say anything really, I can't even hardly talk to the audience. I don't know what to say. But when we make music, everything keeps going, it's just the field we are working in, or if we make videos we are more productive there."

I quote back from an interview he did with Q magazine in July 1991 where he suggests that traditional musical skills are becoming increasingly redundant. "With our computers, this is already taken care of," he explains. "So we can now spend more time structuring the music. I can play faster than Rubenstein with the computer, so it [instrumental virtuosity] is no longer relevant. It's getting closer to what music is all about: thinking and hearing."

So technology should be interpreted as a potentially liberating force? "Not necessarily. I don't always find that. Dehumanising things have to be acknowledged. Maybe if you want to be-

KRAFTWERK: VORSPRUNG DURCH TECHNO

1970 **TONE FLOAT** by Organisation. Hütter and Schneider-Esleben with others, produced by Conrad Plank and recorded in a studio in Düsseldorf's Oil Refinery. Includes Silver Forest and Rhythm Salad.

1971 **HIGHRAIL** by Kraftwerk. Hütter and Schneider with Klaus Dinger

and Thomas Homann, who later form Neu. Issued on German Philips label.

1972 **VAR**. Includes first-ever recorded use of a drum-machine.

1972 **KRAFTWERK** (Vertigo 6641-077 2LP) UK edited compilation of earlier Germany-only LPs. Includes Atem,

Strom, and Spule 4.

1973 **RALF UND FLORIAN** (Vertigo) Duo album including strings and woodwind. Tanzmusik, Tongebeinge, and Electrisches Roulette.

Nov 1974 **AUTOBAHN** (Vertigo 6360-620/EMI CD 46153-2) With Wolfgang Flur and Klaus Roeder. Includes

come human, first you have to *be* a showroom dummy, then a robot, and maybe one day..." An expressive wave. "People tend to overestimate themselves. I would never say I am very human. I still have doubts. I can project myself as a semi-god. I can do that. The tools exist for me to achieve that. But I'd rather be more modest about this, about our real function in this society, in these blocks here," indicating out through the plate glass, across the square, to the city towers of finance and global commerce beyond. "People overestimate themselves. They think they are important. They think they are human."

I'm out of synchronisation again. Surely, if people have to extricate themselves from the machinery they have created, to become human, then it's due to the imperfections of the technology — *not* the people. Machines are intended to serve, if they do otherwise, they malfunction. "Not so. They should not be the new slaves. We are going more for friendship and co-operation with machines. Because then, if we treat them nice, then they treat us nice. You know, there are so many people who go in for machines, who when you come to their homes their telephones are falling to pieces, their music centres don't

function, the television set is ruined. But if you take care of your machines then they will live longer. They have a life of their own. They have their own life-span. They have a certain hour of duration. There are certain micro-electronics which work a thousand hours. Then there is a cassette recorder battery which operates ten or twelve hours." The mentality you oppose, then, is that of conspicuous consumption, planned obsolescence, the psychology of 'a spoilt child'? "The energy crisis, the whole thing is a result of thinking that everything is there, we just have to use it, take this, and — *PTOOOOFFF!* — throw it away. But make sure that the neighbours see! This whole attitude of disassociating oneself from machines — humans here and machines over there. When you work so much with machines — as we do — then you know that has to change."

Earlier he'd spoken of growing up 'playing around the bomb-fields and destroyed houses' in the wake of WWII, so this respect for material possessions is perhaps understandable. But he sees beyond this. He sees machines having the potential to free people physically from unnecessary labour, and culturally to create whole new

---

Komet Melody 2, Kristallo and the twenty-two-minute title track ('W'ir fahn fahn fahn auf der autobahn... we're driving driving driving down the Motorway'). Edited down to a three-minute single, the track reaches No 11 in the UK (May 10, 1975; Vertigo 6147-012) and No 25 in the USA (April 12, 1975; Vertigo 203).

Oct 1975 *EXCELLER 8* (Vertigo

6360-629) Compilation. Ruckzack, Kristallo, etc.

Nov 1975 (Ger)/Jan 1976 (UK) *RADIO-AKTIVITÄT/RADIO-ACTIVITY* (Capitol EST 11457 CDP 7-464742 / US Cleopatra CLE CD 58752) First album with Karl Bartos replacing Roeder, now fully electronic and issued on their own Kling Klang label in Germany. Includes Geiger Counter, Antenna, and Ohm

Sweet Ohm.

May 1977 *TRANS-EUROPE EXPRESS* (Capitol EST 11603 CD 7-46473-2) An album of 'eerie empty beauty' (*Mojo*). With Franz Schubert, Europe Endless, and Showroom Dummies — a UK No 25 chart single, February 20, 1982 (EMI 5272). Title track later sampled by Africa Bambaataa's Planet Rock,

an exchange — like we are talking now. I do more of this. You do more writing, perhaps. I do more turning knobs to make music. And this machine [he points at my trusty ITT portable] helps to record the ideas we talk about. So someone should not just come in now and think 'oh — it's only a cassette recorder', and step on it…!"

But its value at facilitating what we do does not make it an equal partner. "Yes, it is an equal partner." Perhaps he's sending me up, demonstrating the absurdist humour he's admitted to? Slipping back into the Kraftwerk image, into role, back behind the mask? I state my position carefully. Connect his music by innate cables back to the primeval. A flute is an inanimate object activated by breath. A synthesiser is an inanimate object activated by electricity, by fingers, and by human intelligence. "Yes. But you could not hear the sound if you did not have the synthesiser."

But it is still a tool. Something to be used. "But terms like the 'tool' and the 'user' imply always that I am top of it. In charge of it. That it is my servant. That if I no longer need it I am justified in throwing it away. And I do not think that whole attitude is correct, because I am nothing without

arts. "I am projecting against the whole attitude in Western society which means exploit this, exploit that — put it together — BOINGGG! — and you don't need it anymore. Goodbye. Auf Wiedersehen.

"Certain aspects of work they do much *better*. They are much better in some areas of music. They can play much better than any human. I can rehearse a thousand hours and still not play some things." Yet they are treated as mere slaves, and "they shouldn't be. There should be

and includes the lyric 'from station to station/back to Düsseldorf city/meet Iggy Pop and David Bowie'. Bowie returns the reference on his V2 Schneider.

May 1978 **MAN-MACHINE** (Ger: **MENSCH MASCHINE**) (Capitol EST 11728 CD 7-46039-2) 'It is the only completely successful visual/ aural fusion Rock has pro-

duced so far' (*NME*). Includes The Robots, Spacelab, and The Model — a UK No 1 chart single, February 6, 1982 (EMI 5207)

May 1981 **COMPUTER WORLD** (EMI EMC 3370 / US Elektra CD 9-3549-2) With Pocket Calculator, Numbers, and Computer Love.

1981 **VIRTU EX MACHINA**

(Klon 1992001) Quality bootleg recorded live from mixing desk in Tokyo, with ad-libbed Autobahn lyrics.

July 1983 *Tour De France* (twelve-inch single EMI 5413) and mixes. A UK No 22 single later featured on the *Breakdance* movie soundtrack.

Nov 1986 *ELECTRIC CAFE* (EMI

my synthesiser. I mean — where is my music without the synthesiser? Where is it?" The music, the intelligence, is in your head. Without that the synth is just…. "Yes, bringing it about! The catalyst. We are partners. We two can together make good music, if we are attuned to each other." But you could operate another instrument. The vehicle you use is incidental. You could walk out this building, buy a new synth here in London, and play it just as well as your own equipment in Düsseldorf. "Yes. That is because I have this relationship with this type of thing."

I'm reproducing this exactly as it happens, and still I'm not exactly sure what he's getting at. Perhaps something is lost in the language gap. Like earlier, he'd said "I would never say I am very human" and I'd accepted it first as role playing — until he'd made it obvious that he equates 'becoming human' with 'achieving freedom'. Humanity is something that has to be earned. You can't be robot *and* human. But this is not a natural conversation. This is an interview. A marketing exercise designed to sell Kraftwerk records by projecting certain consumer-friendly imagery. He is playing games, and this cyber-spiel is what journalists expect from Kraftwerk? But to Ralf Hütter there seems to be more to it than that. He

believes what he is saying. At least on one level. Some impenetrable levels of ambiguity are at work concerning this alleged relationship to technology.

Baffled, I skate around it. What crafty work is afoot for the future? "For me? For Kraftwerk? Well, certain things that I had to remember and memorise and think about are now programmed and stored. So there's no restriction that we have to rehearse manually. There's no physical restriction. I can liberate myself and go into other areas. I function more now as software. I'm not so much into hardware. I'm being much more soft now since I have transferred certain thoughts into hardware. That is why we put those two words together *Software/Hardware* on the album. Because it is like a combination of the two — Man/Machine — otherwise it would not be happening. We can play anything. Our type of set-up — and group, the studio, the computers and everything. Anything."

So with these limitless vistas of techno-tomorrows, Kraftwerk will continue for some time yet? "Yah. Yes." Pause, then the laugh opens up, "… until we fall off the stage!"

Auf Wiedersehen, Ralf…

Eins, Zwei, Drei, Vier…

CDP 7-46416-2) With Techno-Pop, Musique Non-Stop, Boing Boom Tschak, and The Telephone Call. A sequel to projected, then cancelled album, to be called *TECHNO-POP* — scheduled for August 1983 release and designated EMC 3407. Following the release of *ELECTRIC CAFE* Bartos and Flur are replaced by Franz Hijbert and some

robots, while Karl Bartos forms Elektric Music who release the album *ESPERANTO* in August 1993.

June 1991 *THE MIX (DIE KLASSIC WERKS)* (EMI CDP 79-6671-12/CDEM 1408) With new digital mixes of The Robot, Computer Love, Autobahn (nine-minute mix), and Musique Non-Stop.

1991 *HEUTE ABEND* (Deep Records 021) Low-fi live bootleg including twenty-minute Musique Non-Stop.

1993 *THE REMIX* (On It CD 049) Bootleg including studio remixes of Tour De France, plus early demos of Sex Object and Technopop from aborted album sessions.

© Dogger

MOTT THE HOOPLE
IAN HUNTER
IT'S A MIGHTY LONG WAY

IAN HUNTER, *the former voice of* **MOTT THE HOOPLE**, *arrives back in Leeds with a thirty-eight-track 'Greatest Hits & Rarities' double* CD. *So now, from this vantage point where past and present collide, he explains how he once broke into Elvis Presley's Graceland; how he produced hits for Billy Idol ("a pain in the arse"); what it's like to tour with Queen as your support-act... he even finds time to tell tales about Marc Bolan, Mick Ronson, and, incidentally, Mott The Hoople.*

llo."

To be honest, I'd expected to reach his manager. So the single word on the other end of the phone totally throws me. Instantly flashbacking me to the first-groove play-in of the Once Bitten Twice Shy single. It's that same voice. Mr Ian Hunter. And all my carefully contrived cool evaporates. Then it happens again. "Interview?" says the voice on the line. "Sure, we can do it right now if you like! What questions do you want to ask me?"

Okay. The opening line in REM's Man On The Moon is 'Mott the Hoople and a game of chess...' "You what?" comes back Ian eloquently.

I elaborate. REM's song Man On The Moon contains a lyric reference to your old band. "I've *heard* about that, yeah." So did Michael Stipe ever explain to you what that song reference means? A long silence. Then: "What song?" Against the odds, I persevere. REM's Man On The Moon. "Yeah, Somebody told me *abaht* that. But I've never *'eard* it. I've not heard it, y'know."

No. No. This ain't working. I've waited since 1972 (when Ian Hunter charted with the original All The Young Dudes) to interview the voice of

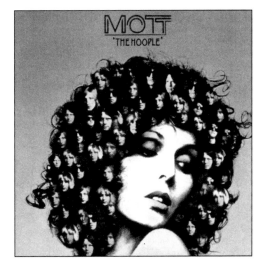

Mott The Hoople, and I'll settle for nothing short of the full pro-active one-to-one interface situation now... Gimme a break!

Three hours later Hunter is spring-heeling up and down the dressing room behind the Leeds Irish Centre. He slurps from a clear tub of Aqua-Pura and picks selectively at the Caribbean Mix laid out for the frazzled musos sprawled out around him. "I 'eard this bloke on the radio last night" he chews around a generous mouthful of nut-blend. "He said 'there's gonna be a meteor

shower tonight'. And all I saw was just one meteor, it went straight across the sky as he did his
introduction. That was the only one I saw. Just
saw this one thing go…" he angles meteorically
through the air with his hand "… like that." Then
he slouches down abruptly hitting the couch more
by luck than premeditation. "Yeah, it was just
one. Bit of a downer actually."

He talks like that. Short sudden statements with
unpredictable switches. A voice like he's been
sucking car-exhausts, shaped into an accent
pitched somewhere between Michael Caine in
Get Carter, or Harry H Corbett from *Steptoe and
Son*. London 'street' perverted by the incongruous All-American alien he's absorbed through
long New York exile. Matey and New Laddish,
boastful and piss-taking by turns as he anecdotes

imaging must have had something of the sleazy
glamour of Ian Hunter's 'you look like a star /
but you're out on parole'. For Ian has written
some of the most perfect crystallisations of Rock's
tacky glory ever committed to vinyl (or CD). His
Rock dreams travel all the way 'from the Liverpool Docks to the Hollywood Bowl', in tour buses
lost 'in the middle of the night / on the open road
/ when the heater don't work / and it's oh-so cold'.
And like he sings it elsewhere on his 'Greatest
Hits & Rarities' album, 'old records never die'.
In fact, its title cut — Once Bitten Twice Shy —
would be a great song for Oasis to cover as one
of their high-profile B-sides. "I have no problem
with Oasis at all" he says, agreeably. "They're a
good band. People say they're very derivative.
But they have a sound of their own. Especially

through the A to Z of Rock from Glam to Punk
and beyond. Names like David Bowie, Bob
Dylan, Elvis Presley, Freddie Mercury, Keith Moon
and Billy Idol occur in high-flying tales. In fact,
it's embarrassing — at one point it strikes me
that I'm neglecting Hunter-ology in favour of
pumping him for stories. He's a fan of Rock from
way back — so am I, so it's a natural. From Marc
Bolan ("I don't think there was ever really much
weight with Marc. Marc never said anything other
than 'buy my records I want to be a fucking star'.
Great singles band though…") and all points beyond, Ian Hunter provides a meteor shower of
verbal shooting stars as spectacular as *anything*
the Perseids can display.

When Noel Gallagher wrote 'in my mind /
my dreams are real' the Rock lifestyle he was

vocally. But I mean, that song's been covered a
lot: Status Quo just did a version. It was a big
No 5 hit in the States in '89 for a heavy metal
band called Great White. Y'know , there's a guy
in France, and he just sent us a list of all these
artists who've done our songs over the years. He's
included everything — Thunder, The Presidents
Of The United States, Hanoi Rocks — there's over
fifty people done 'em!"

Right now *Once Bitten Twice Shy* — the thirty-
eight-track double CD covering Ian's post-Mott
solo career — is the ostensible reason for this
tour. And compilations usually work as a career-
pause, an opportunity for reflection and taking
stock. So let's reflect. "Sure, I left England in 1975
when I quit Mott," Hunter resumes. "So the whole
of my solo career has *not* been in England. And

when you leave, people tend to forget you are actually still alive. I know I did. So a lot of my stuff came out, and it did much better elsewhere than it did here. So in a way, this compilation will be news to a lot of people. There *is* new stuff on it [eighteen previously unissued rare and demo tracks]. But on top of that, a lot of people who bought Mott the Hoople albums here, didn't buy my solo stuff. So this is a chance for them to figure out what I've been doing ever since then." Is there a track you're particularly proud of? "No. Not really." Abruptly and unequivocally. "When something's done, it's done. It's gone as far as I'm concerned. I don't feel a thing. I look back on them with absolutely nothing. When I hear them I tend to remember 'Oh yeah! I was doing *this*, I was doing *that*!' but I don't actually think in terms of the song. I put my heart and soul into the song at the time. But now I'm somewhere else."

In fact, Ian's solo career is strewn with wounded gems of Rock's on-going mythology. It's a mighty long way down Rock'n'Roll, and his albums collect some of its most entertainingly idiosyncratic cul-de-sacs, turn-offs, slip-roads, contraflows and dead-end streets snatched from some stop-over points along the way — albums like *Short Back And Sides* (with Todd Rundgren, plus Mick Jones, Topper Headon and Tymon Dogg of Clash notoriety), *All-American Alien Boy* (with three-quarters of Queen), and *You're Never Alone With A Schizophrenic* (with Mick Ronson and various members of Bruce Springsteen's E Street Band on hand), an album which also features the live stand-out from his Irish Centre show tonight, Cleveland Rocks.

Is there a story behind that track? "I was in upstate New York, a place called Chappaqua — where Bill Clinton lives. I had a house there for about four years. I wrote that song there. I wrote all of the *Schizophrenic* album there. And that song's doing great. One of the biggest TV shows in the States right now is *Drew Carey*. And he picked it up four years ago as the signature tune for his show. It's on syndication, so it's on about ten times a week. That's probably the most successful song I ever wrote if you wanted to talk purely in terms of finance."

While among the newer contributions is the exquisite Michael Picasso, a spine-shivering first-person reminiscence of his long-time friendship with Mick Ronson. Some-time Bowie spider-from-Mars, with a resumé also taking in stints with Bob Dylan, Roger McGuinn, Van Morrison, Lou Reed and Morrissey, Hunter's association with his ex-Mott sparring partner only ceased with Ronson's death from liver cancer in April 1993 — tragically too recent for accurate emotional perspective. Michael Picasso? "Yeah. In a tragic way, they're the easiest ones to write. Because there's true emotion involved, so the words just come straight out. Rather than you having to go out and look for the subject matter. I wrote that really quickly. And I wrote it when he was still alive actually. Because... a couple of things had been said. I was seeing him in the September. He came over for a while. And I was thinking about it then. He died the following April." Their association is further commemorated by the release of *The Hunter-Ronson Band: Live In Concert*, a last souvenir recorded through the good graces of the BBC at the Dominion Theatre in 1989. Ronson contributes a movingly intense instrumental Sweet Dreamer, then they do the matey mic-sharing and grinning laddish camaraderie through Once Bitten Twice Shy and their Hoople hit All The Way From Memphis. But after all, their natural home is the stage. Hunter's voice rips and tears at lyrics with ragged exaggerations and pronunciations, but then it always did. He's the last of the Rock'n'Roll mythmakers, battered by an intrepid courting of toxic danger and nicotine-stained death.

Between 1972 and '74 Mott the Hoople were singles chart fixtures, but with more Rock'n'Roll substance than their Glam contemporaries. As a band, they were seldom reading from the same route-map, always prone to the schismatic disease, and seemed to use their shared iden-

tity as merely the foci for individual contrariness. Yet their ramshackle swagger and loose rolling shambolic sound survives intact through each of its incarnations, bequeathing from that dumb and stupid decade all the contours of human excess, fallibility, and yes, something of its raging glory too. Yet until quite recently, neither Mott's nor Ian's solo stuff was well represented on the re-issue racks at your local mega-store. On his last visit to Britain he spent some time complaining to me about how his back-catalogue was under-represented on CD. Now it's everywhere. "It's absolutely crazy at the moment. In fact — especially with my solo stuff — we're turning down offers of new re-issue projects. Because there's *too much* out there. It should be more, kinda, incremental. All that stuff coming out at the same time is not good. The great thing with Mott *and* me, is you used to have to go out and *find* it. It wasn't just sitting there in front of you. It entailed a little bit of effort. And I kinda liked it that way. Now there's a danger of over-saturation. But it proves that there *is* a market, otherwise people wouldn't keep on doing it."

First up, while other stack-heeled Glam pussies were doing the revival circuit, writing their glitter-memoirs, or doing time for their hardcore hard drives, the excellent Edsel label were res-

SELECTED 'DUDES' ALBUM DISCOGRAPHY

Nov 1969 MOTT THE HOOPLE (Island ILPS 9108/re-issued as Edsel EDCD 361, 1993, a two-on-one double pack with...)

Sept 1970 MAD SHADOWS (Island ILPS 9119)

Feb 1971 WILD LIFE (Island ILPS 9144)

Aug 1971 BRAIN CAPERS (Island ILPS 9174)

Sept 1972 ALL THE YOUNG DUDES (CBS 65184)

Oct 1972 ROCK'N'ROLL QUEEN (Island ILPS 9215/IRSP 7, Sept 1981) Compilation

Jul 1973 MOTT (CBS 69038/ Castle CD CLACD 138, 1993)

Mar 1974 THE HOOPLE (CBS 69062)

Nov 1974 LIVE (CBS 69093)

Jul 1970 BUMPERS (Island IDP1) Various artist compila-

cuing the first two Mott albums and siamesing them into a single two-on-one disc comprising *Mott The Hoople/Mad Shadows* providing a complete hit of Rock'n'Roll outrage in one clean injection. It's a strange mismatch of Rolling Stones instrumentation and hoarse dust-bustin' Dylanesque vocals, the way the group sounded during their failed launch as a 'heavy' album band, before David Bowie gifted them with his All The Young Dudes, and so wrote Hunter into the essential guide to 1970s Rock. Then, for Ian, came this high-charting second-phase of Mott's career when he was doing the obligatory Glam thing on *Top Of The Pops*, and he always felt — in his own words — like a "Bricklayer's labourer in gilt". Noddy Holder, who shared those TV slots, confirms the impression to me in a recent interview: "A 'Bricklayer's labourer in gilt'? Yes, it probably was a bit like that for Ian. He was a bit of a different sort of character to us. He was a bit more intense about it. We looked on it as a lot of fun. Ian wasn't like that. He hadn't got that same sort of outlook on it. He just went along with the Glam flow because that was the thing to do at the time."

Further archaeological evidence emerged with *Mott The Hoople: Friends And Relatives*, an oddities and curios double-pack credited to Mott The Hoople and various spin-offs. It plunders the pre- and post-history of the Hoople, but essentially the value of its tracks lies less in the tracks themselves, but more in the mythology surrounding them, because it takes Mott back to its impoverished Beat-boom origins with the lost 1963 group Silence (made up of Overend Watts and Dale Griffin), and the Rats from Hull (salvaging the first-ever recordings by Mick Ronson and Woody Woodmansey). Then, post-Mott, we get lost group and solo cuts from Steve Hyams, Verden Allen, the British Lions, plus live re-takes on Hymn For The Dudes, Born Late '58, and the Velvet's Sweet Jane. The latter sounds like they're re-stringing their guitars in mid-solo, tweaking raw nerve-endings to screaming point, then sniggering as they suffer. Has Ian heard this simultaneously issued compilation? "No. I haven't. Is it any good?" I'd have preferred a little more Ian Hunter on it personally. "Ah, you know, hur hur hur. I'm not getting drawn into that. Life's too short, you know."

Hunter's book *Diary of a Rock'n'roll Star* — described by Q magazine as 'the greatest music book ever written' — travelogues Mott's chaotic 1973 American tour, including Ian's near-collision with my father: Elvis Presley. The book relates how the band reach Memphis:

tion featuring Mott's **Thunderbuck Ram**

Oct 1975 DRIVE ON (CBS 69154) Post-Hunter Mott

1976 SHOUTING AND POINTING (CBS 81289) Post-Hunter Mott

Mar 1976 **GREATEST HITS (CBS**

81225/CBS 32007, Jun 1981)

1980 **TWO MILES FROM HEAVEN (Island 202429-270 German import/Island IRSP8) Compilation**

Mar 1975 **IAN HUNTER (CBS 80710/Sony Rewind COL 477359-2, Aug 1994) Solo**

June 1976 **ALL-AMERICAN ALIEN BOY (CBS 81310/Sony Rewind COL 491695-2, Aug 1998) Hunter solo**

May 77 **IAN HUNTER'S OVER-NIGHT ANGELS (CBS 81993/ Columbia 474781-2, Dec 93)**

May 1979 **YOU'RE NEVER ALONE WITH A SCHIZO-**

'*By the time we left the gig it must have been 12:30am and by this time we're all a little stoned, and I beg Ike to take us over to Elvis' place. Ike nods and we fly on though the night until we reach the legendary Graceland.*'

They get turned away at the gate, but "in my drunken state I decide this ain't enough". Hunter dodges the guard and breaks in. "It's a wonder we never got killed," he laughs now. "'Cos I actually went into the big 'ouse. So now I'm, like, breaking and entering. The first door opened. I went in. I got to the second door. Second door was locked…"

In the book: '*I'm in the Dude's house. He's somewhere within fifty feet of me now, but I really daren't go further. I felt elated. I felt like a fourteen-year-old groupie.*'

He resumes the narrative: "I met his maid, Alberta. I was banging on the door and Alberta came up to me. She said 'I don't think you want to see *him*. *He's* just seen this movie, and *he did not like it!*' And I said 'f-f-f-f-fine…' So, he'd been to the movies that night, and *he* was in a real bad mood. I could 'ear dogs barking. They could have had me in and bounced me all over the walls. They had everything there. I mean, they coulda killed ya! I'm eternally grateful they didn't. They must have known we weren't actual

Featuring the new single '*The Artful Dodger*' *CIT101CDS* with bonus track '*Fuck It Up*' not available on the album
Meet Ian Hunter at the Virgin Megastore in Oxford Street at 1pm on April 21st when he will be signing copies of '*The Artful Dodger*' & '*Diary of a Rock 'n Roll Star*'

thieves. They must have known we were just idiots. But it was all scary — I mean, when the beer started wearing off, or whatever it was I'd been doing, I began to get a little shaky."

Mr 'Unter chomps at a wedge of brie as I delve further into his book. So what about *this* section, the one where he writes thusly about drugs?: '*Take a bit of advice. I've been through it. It's a fucking mug's game. Use your loaf. Nobody ever made it stoned.*' "Well, that just goes to show you, don't it! Can't believe a word I say, can you?" He munch-munches through eruptions of explosive laughter. "I probably thought that at the time. 'Cos I mean, with Mott the Hoople we never used to get stoned. And when we went over there none of us would even have a joint. None of us. One of the first ever American gigs I remember us doing was with Quicksilver Messenger Service and Blue Cheer at the Fillmore West. And people were sorta saying 'what do you want?'. The *name* of the band was kinda strange, and they thought we *were* kinda strange. But we were only strange in a small-time kind of way, and they mistook it for 'they're on this weird shit'. I always remember this black girl sitting there and she went through all these abbreviations for illicit substances, trying to find out what we were 'on', and I kept saying 'nah, nah, nah', and her eyes were getting wider and wider. She thought we had this *greeeaaat* stuff that nobody had heard of. And we were just sitting there, terrified…"

Hippie excess — *WOW!* But after the Glam Rock chart hits, unlike most of their contemporaries, the Mott legacy was not spat upon by Punk. In fact Ian went on to produce the Generation X album *Valley Of The Dolls*, which spawned their biggest hit single, King Rocker. What was the young Billy Idol like to work with? "A pain in the arse!" he guffaws. "At the time he was trying to sing high. But he was out of tune all the time so there was a lot of dropping-in to do, and he would get, like, *very* frustrated. I don't blame him,

'cos no-one likes dropping-in all the time. But that was the way it had to be. So he was rather difficult. But y'know, we did it, and it was alright. Also Billy wasn't singing his own words at that time. He was singing Tony James' words, and Tony's idea of lyric writing was to pick up a TV guide, get a bunch of movie quotes and bang 'em together. And that's what Billy was singing. Later, when Billy began writing his own stuff he started coming out a bit, lyrically. Then he went on with Keith Forsey and started singing low."

Now, where past and present collide, Ian's using this tour as a dry run for some new songs. "I've been writing material for the last five years. So it's good to get out now and again and play. Otherwise you can find you've been writing music that doesn't really work live, when you get out there in front of people. Songs come in all ways. The best ones come together. The music with the words. And it's lovely. Because it's quick. But you know, sometimes songs can be so frustrating, you get something like Ships [covered by no less a performer than Barry Manilow!]: I had two-thirds of that song for six years, then all of a sudden somebody said something one night and I had the whole song. So it took six years — but it did well for me too. So, y'know, you can't really generalise. I wrote Once Bitten round

ONES ARE TAKEN (CBS 35379/ Columbia 474780-2, Dec 1993) Hunter solo

Feb 1985 **TEACHERS (Capitol EJ240247-1) Movie soundtrack with one Hunter solo track, (I'm) The Teacher**

May 1986 **FRIGHT NIGHT (Epic EPC 70270) Movie soundtrack**

with one Hunter track, Good Man In A Bad Time

Jan 1990 **YUI ORTA (Mercury 838 973-2) Ian Hunter & Mick Ronson**

July 1990 **MOTT THE HOOPLE: WALKING WITH A MOUNTAIN (Island IMCD87) Includes rarities and out-takes**

1990 **MOTT THE HOOPLE: THE COLLECTION (Castle CCSCD 174)**

Aug 1991 **IAN HUNTER: THE COLLECTION (Castle Communications CCSCD 290) Sixteen post-Mott tracks**

1992 **ALL THE WAY FROM MEMPHIS: MOTT THE HOOPLE (Hallmark/Pickwick SHM 3055)**

Ronson's place, at the back of the Albert Hall. And I wrote it all in ten hours, with Suzy just coming in and bringing me coffee as I was writing it.

"Then there's another song I do called Now Is The Time, which is a comment about Fred — Freddie Mercury — who was another mate of mine." He explains it with some real perplexity. "*That's a good song too.*" An unaccustomed pause of uncertainty. "It's difficult. I'd thought about doing that and the Ronson song — Michael Picasso — together, in a row, but thought better of it."

It's embarrassing. But I have to ask. Freddie Mercury? "Fred? He was outrageous. Total loony." His mood switches back onto anecdote mode, and all uncertainty evaporates. "Queen are old mates from way back. They opened for us on an early tour, or we closed for them, whichever way you want to put it. We did an English tour and then an American tour together. Queen were just getting started, and Fred would be pacing up and down the dressing room going 'why don't the silly bastards understand, for fuck's sake?' And I'd say 'well, y'know, it takes a while; America's a big country'. Much later on I used to go sometimes with them on gigs when they had their own Lear jet. I always remember one concert they played in Toronto. I see Brian [May]'s in trouble while Fred's playing piano. There's all this farting going on from the amps, y'know. Fred's not singing so his mic is supposed to be off. But his mic is still on. So you hear Brian go over right in the middle of all this drama, and Brian's going 'Fred, Fred'. And Fred goes 'what? what?' And he says 'me amp's off!' Fred goes 'oh, just fuckin' dance around a bit, the silly bastards won't know the difference'. And the whole 20,000 people went ape-shit. It was greeeaat!"

Ian Hunter, a mighty long way down Rock'n'Roll, and then some... but "no, I never look back. To look back and do all that bullshit is alright when you're seventy-five or something, then you can go 'ah, we weren't too bad after all'". For this line he adopts a frail geriatric quaver, then reverts to "but no, I'm not in the slightest bit interested in looking back. Neither was Mick. We never sat around listening to old records like people seem to think you do. I like doing what I'm doing now. I enjoy myself doing the gigs, and really enjoy myself writing the songs. It's a lot of fun. I feel fuckin' great. Pays well too. I still feel I'm a viable proposition, and I'm still happening... "

1993 **MOTT THE HOOPLE** (See For Miles SAECD7) Six rare and previously unreleased post-Hunter tracks, featuring Steve Hyams

Feb 15, 1989 **BBC: THE HUNTER-RONSON BAND LIVE IN CONCERT** (Windsong/ Strange Fruit WINCD 078, Sept 1995 & Feb 98) Hunter-Ronson Band live at Dominion Theatre

Mar 1995 **IAN HUNTER'S DIRTY LAUNDRY** (Norsk Plateproduksjon IDCD/Cleveland Int CIR 1001-2, Oct 1995)

Sept 1996 **THE ARTFUL DODGER** (Polydor Europe 531 794-2/Citadel UK CD1, Apr 1997) Ian Hunter solo

2000 **MOTT THE HOOPLE: FRIENDS & RELATIVES** (Eagle EDGD 104) Various pre- and post-Mott groups featuring several Mott members

2000 **ROCK'N'ROLL CIRCUS** (Angel Air SJPCD 061) Mott the Hoople live in Wolverhampton April 6, 1972

2000 **ONCE BITTEN TWICE SHY** (Columbia) Ian Hunter double CD featuring demos

© Dogger

CAN
HOLGER CZUKAY ON
THE WAY TO THE PEAK
OF THE HYPER-NORMAL

CAN, *the link between Stockhausen and Hip Hop, were Germany's most seminal subversive sonic engineers of the 1970s — and their influence lives on, from Radiohead to Leftfield and beyond...*

'm time-sliding with a German of militant tendency and a name like an anagram clue to a cryptic crossword.

Holger Czukay is seven-years-old, ensnared in the wind-down of WWII. He's a refugee from Danzig where his family had been close neighbours of novelist Günter Grass. Their Red Cross train gets bombed, caught up as the Americans come in across the Elbe and snarled up in the Soviet advance from the East — and everywhere there are discarded arms, guns, uniforms, helmets, jettisoned by the disintegrating troops of the Reich. "I had some friends, some children, I put everybody under arms, I put helmets on them, and guns. I had a white flag. I didn't know what it represented. We found a white flag, that was all. And we marched on the schoolyard which was occupied by the Russians." Soviet sentries watch the crazy kids coming in across the street playing at soldiers, aping the march of the armies they see all around them. The sentries smile benignly and make indecipherable jokes, and before they know it — *KA-WHAAAAAAM!* — the munitions dump ignites, set off accidentally by the games of Czukay's war-gypsy children. "Kids, okay, ya? But the kids have

blown the whole thing up, nothing was left standing. I know the next day when I was passing by there was a little part of the wall left, and a sign: 'BEWARE THAT THE WALL FALLS DOWN!' I was very pleased, but so afraid at the same time, knowing how powerful I can be in destroying something..."

In Manchester Square directly below us and about a million miles away, a Honda Accord whispers past, hangs a sharp right turn and phases out of sight. Czukay has that effect on things. He communicates telepathically with plants. He schemes of record albums that will make the entire medical profession redundant overnight. He hurls people across rooms with the sheer energy projected by his stare. He dreams of being Defence Minister of Germany. He manipulates time — shrinks two years down into just eighteen minutes. He's made an album with Jah Wobble using a hundred hands. He was once an integral part of Can, Germany's finest and most megaton-heavy band. He studied sound subversion with the visionary avant garde composer Karlheinz Stockhausen; made music for a porno movie, and, and, and...

His walrus moustache is neatly clipped. His black suit slept in, his frill-front shirt stained and his right shoe coming apart. He digs into the biscuit tin and retrieves a shortcake, then uses it to poke in my direction as he denounces the entire medical profession. "In Germany the doctors are all very rich," he explains. "Extremely rich, and therefore I say I HATE ALL DOCTORS!" His emotional intensity is such that the shortcake explodes, sending fragments spinning into the air and cartwheeling across the carpet. No matter, we're time-sliding again. "In my childhood I

once made a decision. *No doctors*. And it happened when I came to be checked for Military Service. With the Doctor, I would not allow him to check my body at all. So they fired me. They said 'he is not able to be a good warrior'." An image snatched straight out of the draft-dodging *Alice's Restaurant* movie. And like that movie's counter culture hero, Arlo Guthrie, I'd consider it a compliment to be judged a bad soldier — but not Holger. "I said 'I *want* to be a good warrior!" His voice ascends a clutch of octaves. "I want to become Defence Minister of Germany! And I was very militant. I can be extremely militant. But that was too dangerous for them, so they didn't want me." He shrugs his whole body from the shoulders down. "Okay, I said. If *that* is the armies of the world, then I *am* no soldier. But I think, if you *really* want to start a war, just take me...", and he breaks out into a series of laughs that register on the calm like seismic shocks, that slam me down firmly into 1982, confused.

So let's slow things down. Take things step by step. Like, the reason we are here is an album called *On The Way To The Peak Of The Normal*, a complex work made up piece-by-piece out of strands of treated tape woven together into a texture lush as an aural tapestry. An all-purpose vinyl you can treat on a variety of levels. Its main theme — Ode To Perfume — can get you lost in a shifting morass of sound multiverses until your brain cells get cross-eyed. Or you can treat it subliminally, like functional muzak, a soundtrack for your living that you can step into or slide out of at your discretion. Yet it refuses to lie down and be slotted into anyone's preconceptions. Czukay is a one-off. A unique. An eccentric.

It must be nice to be in a position where you can earn a living out of chasing your own obsessions, I suggest. Cat-stalking him onto more mundane terrain. "Ya. It's a luxury," his eyes gloat. "Especially under the eyes of the Kremlin, the grey administration." He repeatedly uses the word 'Kremlin' to denote any form of faceless authority, the grey 'walking weed' of bureaucracy. Even his record company fall under its mercilessly contemptuous condemnation.

But to what extent is such music premeditated, I probe. Was it complete in his head before the recording commenced, or did it 'evolve' in a haphazard fashion? The answer lies somewhere between. He lives in Cologne, and still uses the Inner Space studios that spawned the eleven Can albums spread across the seventies. But for the kind of work he now envisages "you must have more than a hundred hands. And that's where this medium makes sense — it actually *gives* you the hundred hands. But you must have the brain which makes them work in a harmonic and corresponding way, otherwise these are just effects and nice gimmicks."

The first building block towards *On The Way To The Peak Of The Normal* was technological. He bought a "new professional amplification system, everything included. But I found so many mistakes in it. And I was extreme. I said 'isn't there anything in the world, even for the highest money, that I can buy without getting fucked up, without there being some kind of unprofessionalism in it?' And I decided to make all the repairs and corrections myself. I didn't have the calibrating instruments, so I found all kinds of tricks to be precise. Because I want, in whatever I do, to be accurate. If I can't do it, then I learn. Anyone who works with me is getting unemployed in a very short time, because I learn so much. I am like a microprocessor. When you make yourself so small you can fit into every screw of your mixing desk, then you become totally aware of it. That's one of the reasons why I construct my studio myself."

After three months of solid construction, di-

rectly contrasting strategies are brought to bear on the actual music. "Somehow you have something in your mind but you don't know what it is. And you make decision after decision — like a dog who runs out into the street, he smells here and he smells there, then makes a decision to go... over *there*." So it's like a bringing together of two elements: the intense precision, attention to detail, and the intuitive part where you start with a vague idea and gradually it comes together? "With *no* idea. That is the thing really — with *no* idea. I can't play good guitar, really not. But I make a random chord and it sounds a vibration. So you follow this vibration, and it sounds almost like a ballad. I really thought it sounded like a ballad, a slow piece, like jazz musicians used to play. The idea of the ballad has completely gone today. A piece that is quite calm and retiring — retiring is maybe the wrong word, but relaxing in a way. People seem to be very loud and nervous these days, and so excited. So let them feel the quality of ballads. And I say to that concept 'you will do', and I work two years on it. Two years constantly, and only and fully dedicating myself to it. I would like to do something which survives for a long time. Growing too fast is poison for me. I want to go slowly, but constantly and definitely. Something which is worth listening to even after twenty years..."

CANNIBALISM

'Relaxing' — or 'retiring' for that matter — are not words that readily suggest themselves to describe the music of Can. Czukay gleefully relates how they appeared on *Top Of The Pops* to promote their surprise (Dave Gilmour-penned) hit, I Want More — and his delight with the charade of miming to tapes, a game that allowed him freedom to use his double bass as a visual prop, spinning it, dancing it, using it like he remembers Rudy Pompelli using it way back with Bill Haley's Comets. But — back at the narrative — Can had an intensity, a tension that seems to be removed on this solo work.

"Is it removed, or *transformed*," he side-steps. "I don't feel myself that it is just removed. Somehow you would feel it, and you wouldn't go on for two years just for nothing. No, the intensity just goes into different — a technical word, parameters. It goes into different places. For example, take editing and splicing. It is a work which takes a lot of time and requires very strong musical decisions, otherwise you destroy the natural flow of the music." Flippantly, to fill the gap, I suggest that promotion-wise it would be a very difficult album to play live. "No. I would never do it. No. I would never try" he berates me. "Can you ask Elizabeth Taylor when she is appearing in her next movie 'live'? It is impossible to ask this question...!"

Suitably chastened I clutch at straws. Salvaging what remains of my dignity, and my humour, I refer back to his tale about *Top Of The Pops*. Perhaps he could make a video in which he mimes Ode To Perfume to pre-recorded tapes, playing the whole multi-tracked phantasmagoria on Bill Haley's double bass? I guess that earns me a reprieve. He grins broadly.

INCANTATIONS

The movie preoccupation is strong with Holger Czukay. Ode To Perfume is not unlike a soundtrack for a movie they haven't got around to filming yet. And his previous solo shot was called simply *Movies*, featuring a long complex Hollywood Symphony. (There was an even earlier Czukay album — *Cannexis 5* — with Buddhist chants and tape-looped Cambodian songs, but it was originally intended as a Germany-only release.) While, predictably the movie angle runs

like celluloid thread through the Can story, too. Can's 1973 *Soundtracks* album collected their film music, drawing on their contributions to Roland Klicks' *Deadlock*, Roger Fritz' controversial *Mädchen Mit Gewalt*, Thomas Schamoni's *Bottom*, and their most accomplished score written for Jerzy Skolimonski's *Deep End*. But if such a background suggests a fascination with New Wave European directors — no. Instead, Holger zones in on earlier periods. Mentions Charlie Chaplin and WC Fields. The thirties — before the rise of the Big Studio 'Kremlins' — and the forties when the medium, he claims, was technically "not highly developed". A time when — although "unperfect" — the movie was "not just simply photographed or filmed, it was painted onto the celluloid".

He sees this process as directly analogous to his own attitude to recording. "People take their instruments, they play something, it is photographed onto tape by a microphone, and is put on a record." This inter-relationship between the two different disciplines is something he learned from keyboard-player Irmin Schmidt. "Irmin was the guy in Can who was best experienced. He had a very good talent to feel the common aspect between picture and sound. He sees moving pictures in the rhythm of music. For him these things are not different: a good movie is a good music, a visual music. That's what I learned from Irmin."

Can came together in a converted cinema, and grew out of this interaction of forms. Holger himself "was a clerk before I was a musician. I was also a teacher, and I became only very slowly independent." He'd first met Schmidt in 1965, midpoint in this process of self-liberation, while both of them were attending seminars in Darmstadt's Kranischrein Institute, under Germany's enfant terrible of avant garde electronic music, Karlheinz Stockhausen. And even as we talk — Stockhausen is in London delivering lectures at the Lyttleton Theatre and playing recitals with his son, Markus. While Cornelius Cardew, another of his erstwhile pupils and figurehead of radical improvisational music in England, had died just prior to Christmas in an autowreck — an incident shamefully ignored by the majority of the music press. Czukay tells me about the teacher they shared. "Stockhausen is somehow a prophet" he enthuses. A prophet who also "shows himself being a real musician when he takes everything into his own hands; his fingers are the concentrating points. But he's always thinking in terms of music — never just effects. When he makes electronic music — like *Kontakte* — he controls just everything. This is where he comes together with Charlie Chaplin, he has total control over his art. He is the man with the hundred hands."

Czukay was playing bass in an R&B group, the Jetliner Trio. While Schmidt had conducted a Symphony Orchestra, and had worked with modern classical composer Luciano Berio. But, drawn together by Stockhausen's idea of 'balance in the compositional concept' they began their own experiments in sound, recruiting guitarist Michael Karoli, and drummer Jacki

Liebezeit. Jacki's experience with the jazz groups of Gunther Hampel and Manfred Schoof fed another component into this embryonic Can mix. Until the final element was provided by the spontaneously invented lyrics and scat passages of black American Malcolm Mooney, the 'Syd Barrett' of the group, a fountainhead of too much weirdness to regurgitate here.

Mounds of tape followed: some early experiments, later salvaged on the historical retrospective *Un/Limited Edition*, some fed into *Soundtracks*. But more significantly there was their privately pressed and distributed *Monster Movie* album. It created a growing underground notoriety that soon led to a distribution deal with United Artists (significantly, the label spin-off from the movie production company founded by Charlie Chaplin!), and it opened the floodgates internationally for the contagious virus of Deutsche Rock. A daunting experience even today, the album's effect in 1969 was totally disorientating, prompting vague comparisons with the Velvet Underground. The most immediate effect is rhythmic — a compulsive, hypnotic drums/bass pulse that provides bedrock for spaced keyboard and spatterings of fragmented guitar. Their approach to recording, according to Czukay, was deceptively simple. "You take your instrument. Somebody throws the first stone. And you follow it. You go on. And that's the experience." So a random chord becomes the first chronicler of new-born ideas for which no vocabulary yet exists. Holger's own playing was sparse and minimalist. "When we started with Can, I was playing thousands of bass notes. And Jacki once said 'why are you playing so many notes?' I said 'it must make interesting music with many notes, ya?' He says 'if you play so many notes it means you haven't yet found the right one!' Simplicity can be a real serious musical quality."

It was a vastly productive period for Can, based on the internal tensions thrown up by the conflict in styles and ideas, and the compression necessary to unite them. "Can's only chance was that everybody would reduce themselves as far as they could with what they did, ya? Otherwise it would just be a group of four egos, and no-one likes to listen to that." And through the destruction of preconceptions and musical barriers, came creation. "To destroy something is the beginning of building up something. If you put these two aspects together, then you make an interesting act, ya? That is exactly the quality of Can in those early days. We have a big archive out of that time. We have recordings we never dared to offer a record company. But today, times have changed. And now it makes sense."

He pauses and stands up, produces a cassette with a casual flourish. "I have here something Can will bring out on a new album which is provisionally called 1968. During that year Can were on full power, and this gives some indication of what the live quality of the group was." He slots the tape face-up into the EMI music centre and punches the key sharply. Green

lights behind the dials glow and the volume needles snag into alert. The fade-in drone swells to multi-megaton overkill and the cross-rhythm shocks begin. "Being somehow heavy," he commentates. "Very heavy. They could destroy just everything." The violent electrical storms of aggression and barbaric sophistication are unmistakable, as startling and challenging now as they were then. The comparison with John Lydon's Public Image Ltd is inevitable, and as inadequate now as those with Velvet Underground in 1969.

"The rhythms were holy. Jacki was strict about it."

With international tours, the albums that followed were carried on a seemingly limitless momentum, and came fast. *Tago Mago* in 1972, features Can's second vocalist, the Japanese Kenji Damo Suzuki. Its focal point is a long drifting track called Aumgn, an early recipient of Czukay's tape-splicing and mixing down. Described as a passage of 'modal improvisation' it spread clear across the double pack's third side. During those years they also supplied incidental music for Leonidas Capitano's soft porn movie *Cream*, and for a television sci-fi programme called *Gomorrha*. Their only German No1 single, Spoon, came from a similarly visual source. It was the theme for TV's detective thriller series *Francis Durbridge*!

Ege Bamyasi came next, then *Future Days* with its twenty-minute Bel Air, dedicated to screen siren Hedy Lamarr. *Soon Over Babaluma* arrived in 1974 by which time Damo had discovered the Lord, become a Jesus-Freak, and quit Can. A trilogy of albums — *Landed, Flow Motion* and *Saw Delight* — came through a new pact with Virgin, displaying a conspicuous disintegration of the band's collective vision. The line-up was briefly expanded by the addition of some ex-Traffic musicians, freeing Holger from on-stage bass-duties and allowing him to concentrate on electronic sequencing and short-wave radio interference — an idea pioneered by Stockhausen in his *Kurzwellen*. But "it happened at the end, when I felt I was somehow a clerk again." The end of Can was a "cellular division. A group one day gets born. It is an organism where one hand works with the other hand. But the group grows, and gets old, and after a while it dies. There's a certain kind of life and age a group can have. Can got about ten years. Then everybody is getting out. You have to survive. So after the division you go on, and go on..."

Since the final product — *Out Of Reach* in 1978 — the association has remained flexible

with ex-Can members guesting on each other's solo projects. Schmidt made an album called *Film Musik*. Czukay made *Movies*. Czukay and Liebezeit with Kraftwerk-producer Conny Plank worked on a very strange and very impressive Japan-only LP by singer Phew. While in Germany, for new bands, "Can has a certain good reputation." One of them — SYPH — has even "got fascinated with the way Can worked", and Czukay has been in the studio with them.

But the last two years he's compressed down into the eighteen minutes of Ode To Perfume...

CANDID CAMERAS

"I've become more and more sensitive towards everything which lives" he confides softly. "Until eventually I found out about the telepathy of plants, and it means I can speak with plants." Can were always a band who seeded mythologies — from the beginning bizarre tales and gaudy legends sprang apparently unprompted in their turbulent wake. I'd previously put it down to over-zealous press exaggeration, to gullible or stoned journalism. Now I'm not so sure. For example, what do *you* make of this story? A tale he relates straight-faced and in absolute seriousness:

"It was two or three years ago" he commences thoughtfully. "I was going in the evening to a café, I sat down and wanted a cup of coffee. A woman was working in the kitchen, she was dancing to the music on the radio and suddenly she grips my hand, she wants that I should go with her and dance, and I can't help it, I don't want to dance. Perhaps I'm tired, perhaps I'm preoccupied with something else. I can't really explain how it was. But at that moment I look at her and I can feel a really warm stream of energy. And it's like the whole energy of your body goes out through your eyes. We were standing together — and she was pushed back *just by the power of my eyes* for ten metres! And she crashed against the kitchen wall! She didn't touch me again, *ever*, and I felt what kind of destroying power I could have. What it is in me if it really comes to the point that YOU CAN KILL PEOPLE WITH YOUR EYES!" He shakes his shaggy head ruminatively. "The next day I was talking to her — but at a distance, ya? With respect. The person who was most surprised about this was myself. I'd discovered again this kind of energy. Like when I was the child who blew up the munitions dump..."

Now I've read my Stephen King, and I've

watched *The X-Files* with the rest of them. I even watched the *Omen* films. I enjoy the whole fiction of demonic possession, but exactly how do you interpret a story like that? And he intends it to be taken literally, not figuratively! I dodge the issue by suggesting that this kind of emotional violence can be translated into musical terms. He nods enthusiastically. But this evasive action brings us into his 'telepathic' relationship with

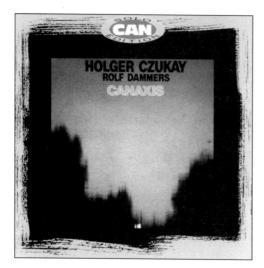

Jah Wobble, with whom he's worked. So is he a good musician? "He's extremely good. One of the best musicians I can imagine, because he gets this quality that he reads your mind without you speaking it out. And that means music — having a telepathy towards the other musicians." Which brings us directly back to psionics! Like — when he speaks of this 'telepathy' does he mean a very heightened sense of rapport, something that becomes so exact and finely developed that it *appears* to be telepathy? That I can buy, but an actual touching of minds...?

But by now impressions are gravitating together in my head, then separating out like chemicals in a retort. About six months ago, in this very room, I met and talked to Ralf Hütter of Kraftwerk. Hütter is very much the new-image

German: impeccably polite, smart, precise, even the business suit is right. Czukay is different. It's difficult to pin down and impossible to write, but he is very much the old-image German. The Wagnerian mystic. The Bavarian craftsman. Even the walrus moustache is right.

Meanwhile, he's still spieling on about Wobble. "One of the most sensitive persons I have ever known. And a person who has a very strong identity when he plays. That's what he has. You see, there are thousands and thousands of bass players, and they all play fantastic. On albums and records all bass players play good. But if you listen to him you know after the second tone that this is Jah Wobble. And that means something. To have only such a little note, and to put everything into it, to show his whole personality through it. That means, for me, that he has got the secret. He has found it. He is young, and he will learn how to take the secret out into all kinds of dimensions to make music. He will grow those hundred hands." I point out the coincidence that the first Public Image Ltd albums — on which Wobble plays — were immediately compared to early Can. "I love to listen to Public Image" he claims. "My attitude is very similar to theirs. And Jacki became fascinated by them more and more. The first album — *Metal Box* — he didn't like so much, but the next one flipped him out. He said 'fantastic how they use the drums'. They were very strict in their way; uncompromising, like Can. And I think there is something true about it. A real listening quality. They were being not so helpful with people somehow, ya? That means they make no 'oily' music." But beyond that, the connection is accidental. "They found out later" he explains. "They just went on doing what they did, and found out later what it was. The same thing happened to me with Lee 'Scratch' Perry. I finished my first album and some friends from England showed me. Brian Eno, he was the first one, he said 'listen to Lee Perry, listen to this one', and I found out — my goodness! — there's somebody who's going a similar path to you. That's a good experience."

On more familiar ground now, we get to comparing notes on Dub producers, me pushing Augustus Pablo, and Holger explaining the superiority of Lee Perry: "Just listen to the rhythms. To what happens there. Jacki has a good word for that: 'infrasound'! It describes a musician who makes music in different shades, but with a subharmonic continuity. Not just a series of disconnected sounds or effects. Lee Perry has exactly this quality. Take somebody else who makes exactly the same kind of Dub rhythms, who works in a similar way — but the difference is like day and night. That shows me that he's highly spiritual, and definitely a high musician. Not a musical materialist."

Listening to Ode To Perfume his meaning comes clear. Despite its changes, there is continuity. Something more than just a periodically resurfacing motif. It's a cohesive quality, a natural flow. He concurs. "That's the thing — what is natural. You listen to something which is not worth listening to and it causes cancer of the brain. We say *earworm*, ya? The 'Earworm' is something which is a hit, a melody which doesn't go out of your head, but if it is rubbish it makes you sick after a while. Music is a medicine to me — *really* a medicine. And so you have to treat all the ingredients right, and let them work in a good way. I know people suffering from depression who use music as a drug, and become not depressed. I am really very much interested in using music and recognising music as a form of medicine. If I can manage to invent a kind of music — a kind of acoustic vibration — and bring out a record which is sheer medicine, which will heal people! I know that these experiments are being done in Germany. I know there's a

professor who has made fantastic results with fish. To make fish die — and then getting them healed again! It is amazing to see these possibilities." I can almost see the next statement looming huge on his tongue. Hear his brain working inexorably towards its only possible conclusion — "and if that makes doctors unemployed right away, then THANK GOD THAT IS POSSIBLE! This would be a fantastic invention." He beckons me forward into a conspiratorial huddle, and informs me "I'm working on it!"

I'm just thinking of Albert Ayler's beautiful album *Music Is The Healing Force Of The Universe*, when the Can demo tape on the EMI system snaps suddenly shut like an emphatic punctuation. Holger slopes up to flip the cassette over. The silence becomes unnatural, unnerving. It's like coming awake. Like I've been mesmerised into his tantalising illogics, caught up in his ca-

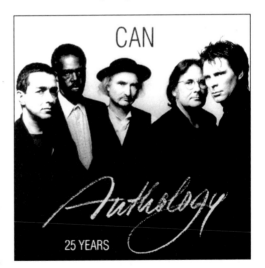

dences and persuasive intonations until I'm believing him, and now it's left me stranded, attention disconnected and drifting. I'm watching a box of Holger Czukay freebie T-shirts across the floor just off left to a particularly interesting formation of cigarette burns in the carpet. Then the cassette snags into side two and there's a rush of tape hiss washing like surrealistic tide across the room. It slots me back into synchronisation. Thoughts — temporarily interrupted — slither smoothly now, lubricated on fresh sound. Holger Czukay has that effect on people.

The conversational connection presents itself easily — a bridge between medical innovation, and the fad gadgets of musical innovation. I launch a new initiative, my voice dubbed onto the Can soundtrack. In the field of electronic music, I tell him, Holger Czukay is a trained musician. He studied music and can apply a musician's mind to new electronic technology. But how, I wonder, does he react to new innovations that *remove* the skill element from making music? For example, there's an oscillator that uses a laser to replace the keyboard, it operates like playing a harp in a beam of light, each break translated into patterns of sound. Actions that require no strict musical disciplines or knowledge. Anyone can play it intuitively.

"That's an interesting point" he concedes, and considers for a moment. "Conny Plank — he's a good friend of mine — is developing a concept. He says 'I would like to see a dancer in a field of light'. Yes, you can say lasers, but I think he has something else in mind. All the dancer's movements are somehow registered by a computer and transformed into music. Really — into music. And this is possible. He's talking with computer specialists about it and they consider it a viable idea. Conny wants to create this kind of disco to make the people somehow…"

Create the music through their dancing?

"Ya, ya. Be more creative in what they do, instead of wasting their time because they feel bored all the time, waiting until the ceiling falls on their heads! There are good aspects to modern technology, besides so many disadvantages. Everything which dies somehow gets born again. Things seem to be getting more and more primitive, but somehow things get born again out of that 'primitivity'. So in this way the two things come together. Dying, and being born again."

Like a bad dancer would produce bad music? It develops new skills to replace those that are lost?

Czukay nods energetically. It's only later I get to wondering what kind of music would be produced in this laser-disco of the imagination at the height of fighting…

Holger Czukay is a strange, and a strangely wise man.

© Dogger

SIOUXSIE
& THE BANSHEES
MAD-EYED SCREAMERS
IN THE TWILIGHT ZONE!

For a Creature like **SIOUXSIE SIOUX***, where does persona end and person begin? But while trying to discover the girl behind the mask, we wind up talking about hugely inflated breasts and spooky doppelgängers from* THE TWILIGHT ZONE...

Let's examine closely this dangerously evil creation. This 'New Breed', encased and contained within the supple skin of woman, the softness is there, the unmistakable smell of female, the surface shiny and silken, the body yielding yet wanton, but a word of caution — handle with care, and don't drop your guard…
—Russ Meyer's
Faster Pussycat, Kill! Kill! (1966)

e are sat in the Mountbatten Suite of the Covent Garden Hotel, slumped deep into the yielding comfort of futon-draped rattan chairs. Mozart is busy piddling baroque-muzak softly in the background, and across from our alcove there's the 'Mountbatten Exhibition' sealed behind clinical glass — an imperial red uniform, some faded newspaper headlines, and a scattering of sepia photographs of strange figures come adrift in time and space.

A uniformed bellboy with a label identifying him as Chester brings us a dark cafetiere of rich coffee with a silver tray of individually hand-crafted biscuits.

"Mountbatten? Wasn't he the royal who got himself blown up in his boat by the IRA?" The collective grasp of the minutia of Royal history is slight. "And all the forensic experts were able to determine was what brand of shampoo he'd used. Yes, they found his Head & Shoulders washed up on the beach." Shit — I wish I hadn't said that. But all this establishment regalia *does* create a deliciously apt counterpoint to Punk priestess Siouxsie. She sits forward, face as close

THE CREATURES

as this, hair in a jet-black bob, eyes deep and intimate beneath eye-brows precise as scalpel-cuts. But you notice these things because it's Siouxsie. In every other way she's dressed unexceptionally enough: sparkle nail-varnish, zip-suede boots with black slacks, soft gauze top with wine jacket, dark ruffs around neck and cuffs. People walking by on their way to the reception desk don't glance twice. Unaware that this is the woman who once outraged the nation on the Sex Pistols vs Bill Grundy TV confrontation.

In the file of press cuttings back at her hyper-compressed and mega-hyperactive PR company office there's a quote about Siouxsie 'not liking to do interviews'. "I don't think *anyone* does" she admits sharply. "Depends on the interview, really. I haven't done one for a long time. And it's hard doing your first interview when you've not done any for a while. It's something you need to remember how to do."

Suitably chastened and fore-warned ('handle with care, *don't* drop your guard') I meekly venture to ask about her dates at the Dublin Temple Bar Music Centre. "We haven't played Ireland for a long time" she admits. "'Cos the last Banshees tour we did didn't go to Ireland. This time it's the Creatures. The Creatures only ever toured once. So I don't even know if they *ever* played Ireland before. So, it's exciting because the audience won't know what to expect. They haven't a clue. And it's good not to have any preconceptions. I remember we tried to play the Belfast Hall in Ulster around the time of *Peepshow* (1988), but we were still banned from some incident that occurred there in the late seventies. Which is funny."

It must be nice to know you're still considered dangerous, though? "Yeah! Well, y'know." The new Creatures' album is as subversively stimulating as we've come to expect. Metal Burundi rhythms. Cool electronics. No intrusive guitars. Just suggestive ventures into Portishead zones with the shimmering stasis and ticking contra-puntal rhythms of Don't Go To Sleep Without Me. The album is called *Anima Animus*. That means male/female, right? "It's the woman within the man, and the man within the woman," she says carefully. "There are both elements in both sexes. Interchangeable. It's certainly something that exists within a lot of popular music. But there's still a lot of stereotype-playing too. This sort of macho Rock bullshit. I've never liked it — *and I*

never will [done in a gruff, comedy old codger voice]. The roles that females are supposed to play within music is usually as something ornamental — it used to be really bad, and maybe it still is really bad. I always found that really insulting." But you've never accepted such restrictions. "Nooooo! No, no! And I was considered difficult because of that. That's how narrow it was. People are now very scared of being accused of sexism, so they're no longer *openly* like that. But it's still there."

But aren't boy-bands marketed in exactly the same way — as decorative sex-objects? "I know. And I find that just as totally vacuous. It seems to me that more and more and more the industry is grooming acts visually. That seems to be much more the criteria. When I was growing up, if we saw Pop stars that were a bit different — they looked that way because they dressed *themselves* that way. But now it's gangs of stylists, y'know, even for a lot of people who are so-called credited with being highly individual and weird and freaky. There are teams of stylists and make-up artists there. You're talking *armies!*"

But there's always been homoerotic elements to the way male Pop stars have been presented. Even Elvis. "Oh yeah… he wore makeup and dyed his hair, didn't he?"

Ladies and Gentlemen, welcome to violence. *The word and the act. While violence cloaks itself in a plethora of disguises, its favourite mantle remains sex!*
—Russ Meyer's *Faster Pussycat, Kill! Kill!*

For a Creature like Siouxsie Sioux, where does the persona end and the person start? Her story begins about a million kilometres sunwards of Mars where Susan Dallion was born on May 27, 1957. That same week Andy Williams was No 1 with Butterfly, and Lonnie Donegan, Elvis, and the Chas McDevitt Skiffle Group (!) were all in

Siouxsie's a punk shocker

ex Pistols are sent packing

handle orders for the disc, Anarchy in the UK.

As the fury grew, the group's planned concert tour was hit by a spate of cancellations.

Bookings made for Bournemouth, Preston, Lancaster and Newcastle were scrubbed by anxious organisers.

A spokesman for Rank Leisure Services, who had arranged the Bournemouth show said: "It is not the type of presentation with which we wish to be associated."

Preston entertainments chief Mike Smith said: "If anything like the TV programme happened here parents would be up in arms."

Bill Grundy banned for a fortnight

the Top Ten. From the start she was the girl who liked the kind of outfits that girls in magazine stories never wore. Then I imagine her practising misspelling her name on the covers of her school-books during particularly boring algebra sessions (*Sue = Sioux?*). And which Pop stars would Susan Dallion have stuck up on her bedroom wall when she was fourteen? "Mick Ronson. Bowie. Bolan. David Cassidy even. But that was when I was eleven! And pictures of horses. I think it was horses I was *really* into. But actually I loved Mick Ronson, he had such a pretty face." Personally, I never saw Mick Ronson as a glamorous figure. He always looked more like a bricklayer. "*No! No!*" she protests in animated shock-horror. "That picture on the cover of his *Slaughter On Tenth Avenue* album? He wasn't at all like a *brickie!* No — some of the others [in David Bowie's Spiders From Mars] were: Trevor Bolder, and Woody Woodmansey with the *huge* sideboards — *gross*, gawd they were *horrible! They* were brickies in Glam-rags. And I hated Sweet as well. I really wasn't fooled by the likes of Sweet. But no, Mick Ronson had a sweet pretty face."

After that, I guess, would come the difficult dysfunctional adolescence? "When adolescence hits you and you're feeling vulnerable, particularly when you don't have a skin like a rhino, you either shrivel up and go hide in the corner, or you deal with it by finding some really good armour. By standing in the middle of the road and screaming at the top of your voice. And... that's the way I went [she laughs]. And that's *really* what's underneath. It's something that takes a long time for you to actually understand and feel confident with. But that's part of just growing up. They're very hard lessons. But you learn from them, and you end up toughening the exterior. But there's a price to pay for over-protecting yourself — you harden yourself to everything, and lose what's really precious. People think that

cynicism is the modern attitude. And yes, there is a veneer, and yes, being sensitive and stumbling at every stone that's thrown at you can be destructive — you're not going to survive it. But hopefully you can toughen without becoming totally cynical and losing that innocence. I find it really ugly when people lose the ability to look at things as a child. Because you are killing a part of you off when that hardness penetrates the centre."

After that, I see an untidy set of preconceptions galloping ahead of her. "During my first excursions up to London around my late teens, my first sort of pals were always gay. It was only within the gay community that I felt any kind of lack of pressure from the clichés that girls of that age go through. And being in a gay club or whatever was the first *sane* place I felt I was in. And as far as anyone being homophobic — I've *never* understood that, in the same way that I could never understand racism. Or *any* kind of 'ism'. But you can tell that in society in general, even in the law, that it's still there. They've grudgingly passed a law that you can now have a gay relationship at the age of sixteen. While it was *always* been legal for someone to be pregnant and married at that age. So that's how backward things still are."

Then there was Punk. To Julie Burchill it was 'shit in safety pins'. It was also the last gasp of vinyl-based humanity. It was running around hyper and making things happen. And it was an extreme hazard-sport acted out in shit-pits and grot-holes. Oh, Brave New World! Now, it's like trying to remember that month you spent on Mars. A world of beautiful mutations, genetically modified humans, and sounds that scream till they retch and eat through metal like a virus. Perhaps it's just the definition, re-definition and de-definition of what Rock is, might be, and can never hope to achieve? One damned thing after another. One thing damned after another. But at its centre there's the Banshees: John McKay's jagged unorthodox chording pinned down by the deep precise rhythm section, perfectly counterpointing Siouxsie's taut vocal, austere ambi-

ence and compellingly monstrous presence — while she seems to be singing incantations in languages no human being has spoken before or since, a spitting visceral darkness implying levels of abuse, self-disgust, and menstruation, all teetering on the brink of mental breakdown.

You look for the slash-marks on the wrists. The Banshees collectively spit blood and tangible malevolence for their vitriolic illogics. But if you fuel your creativity on negativity, don't the fumes it kicks off make you sick? Not quite. She relates to extremes. And feeds them accordingly. And that involves elements of shape-shifting metamorphosis. Her penchant for incisive lyrics soon transcends the hollow outrage, proving that it *is* possible to exceed the speed of light, fucking $E=MC^2$ to Alpha Centauri and back again. Punk? "I feel like I gate-crashed my way into the music world" she laughs. "I certainly wasn't invited. And it was only supposed to last ten or fifteen minutes. Turned into *bloody twenty years!*"

In the 'Heaven-Knows-We're-Miserablist-Now' Punk aftermath, Siouxsie is the Goth it's okay to like, creating worlds like a novelist, art like a painter, and intrigue like a riddler, sucking in elements of nineteenth-century Symbolism, *fin de siècle* Decadence and Surrealism, then exhaling it all streamlined with a futuristic fascistic fetishistic edge. Not Goth — but using the potency of Goth semantics. Now the brutally smudged black hair is not Statement Black, or Sexy Black… but Fetish Black, S&M Black. While the palely vampiric complexion comes with a new neurotic realism shot full of all the puerile tics and neuroses of Greta Garbo prematurely buried alive in *Fall Of The House Of Usher*, and only now disinterred. In the sex-war, she is the new camp kommandant. And if it sometimes seems that hers is a dysfunctional confused femininity, revelling in the electricity of that unsettled, molten state, then if you generate electricity, you might as well *use* it. Pretty fly for a whiter-than-white girl!

But when she puts that Banshee stage make-up on, 'the surface shiny and silken', is she putting 'Siouxsie' on over Susan Dallion? Is 'Siouxsie' another shell of carefully contrived 'armour'?

"No. That's a very cartoony idea of what my 'image' is. It's not like that. I've *never* worn white pan-stick make-up. And I don't *just* wear black, that's a real misnomer. And if the external attraction is all there is then I find it quite worthless. There's got to be more than that." But the make-up *is* an important part of the spectacle. "Oh yes. It's almost a ritual. And part of the ritual is the preparation. It's like any drug culture — it's not *just* the drug, it's the whole paraphernalia that goes with it. As with any fetish or obsession, it's not just the end result, it's the build-up, the preparation, the lead-up and the whole ritualising of it."

And there's always been that pronounced fetishistic element to Siouxsie's stage persona. "I certainly *hope* so. I suppose there's a lot of fetishism within the performer/voyeur relationship. *That's* what it's all about really. People watching something happening. And obviously, the performer is responding to the voyeur. It's two-way. It's interactive. That's not a *bad* thing. But you can't claim that it *isn't* that." So performing provides a sexual buzz? "I suppose, yes, it's got an element of that to it. But having the time of your life isn't always — 'Yeeeaaahhh!' — like that, y'know. That's not the *only* expression of having the time of your life. It can be frightening. But it can also be very emotional, or very uplifting. I think to be *uplifted* is the *real* hooked drug of it. That kind of... elevation, getting over frail human weakness and limitations. That's the thing that makes it so appealing and mesmerising. It gives it that addiction quality. It keeps you coming back for more."

It's an adrenaline high? "That as well. But you know, there's a down-side too, when you're failing, when you're not quite making it in your own terms. You can come off-stage and everyone says 'great gig, great gig', but you *cannot* be consoled. *You* know IT WAS FUCKING SHIT! And that's

the worst feeling in the world."

So why did the Banshees come to an end? "As a band evolves and grows together, the characters in the band become more defined and developed. It's inevitable. It happens with all bands that last for a long time. It's not *normal* for a band to last that long. The Banshees were very much a working band. Very much a live band. Four people. A democracy of sorts. It had its way of doing things. And it had its baggage that came with it. But because you know each other so well, the intuition and the spark of things *just happening* doesn't happen the same. There seems to be less surprises".

While simultaneously, there was The Creatures — initially as a side project. "The first time we did the Creatures it happened as a mistake. It wasn't by any kind of design. It was whilst writing for the *Ju Ju* (1981) sessions that me and Budgie just did something together while the other two were out of the room. And it was John McGeogh who actually said 'This track doesn't *need* anything else doing to it'. And that was a song called But Not Them, which subsequently ended up on an EP. It was drums and voice, just using those varied primal elements, and as a result it was sonically very unique. Almost like using just primary colours. It really had a sound, and an approach of its own, very simple and basic. It was a lot more visceral. A very different dynamic. There's a lot more air. A lot more space. And because of that combination of elements it was very immediate. Once we'd done something like that we said 'God, it'd be nice to keep it separate'. So, then we did an album, but The Creatures only happened when there was a break or some kind of window in The Banshees schedule. Until around about the time of the final Banshees album I found I was actually looking forward to doing the Creatures. I was actually longing for a kind of 'back to basics'. A real simplicity, generally. It coincided with a lot of real changes in my life."

And now, in truth, Siouxsie seems very much like a woman at peace with herself, and her career. Released from the commercial expectations imposed on her by the Banshees 'baggage', and revelling in the artistic freedoms provided by the DIY-or-die operation through which the Creatures operate, things are looking good for Siouxsie Sioux. But "I haven't mellowed out. I feel pretty much the same. *Inside* of me, I pretty much feel the same. I've just done a few more things, that's all. I hate this horrible cliché of people reaching this thirty-ish number, getting married, having kids, and like — giving up on life. 'I've done my wild bit.' I find that really sad. It doesn't *have* to be like that. Nobody's *forced* to live that lifestyle. I like extremes. I *do* like things that refuse to sit in the middle ground. I like people to be bold about what they do. I don't see the point of tip-toeing around an issue. I just find that really… 'cowardly' is the word."

Everywhere that I go, I see me,
in a life that I had not long ago,
I'm not recognised or heard
but I swear I was me, I was me, I was me!
—The Creatures, I Was Me

"America has got a big problem with sex" says Siouxsie suddenly. "England is repressed sexually. But in America it's the *hypocrisy* — the acceptance of certain things, and the *un*-acceptance of other things. It's acceptable so long as you're not caught doing it. Do you know what I mean?"

Mountbatten drew a line — any line — arbitrarily across the post-colonial Indian sub-continent triggering religious massacres in which thousands died. Now he regards *us* with aristocratic contempt from behind his clinical glass exhibi-

tion case. Me, and Siouxsie — this 'dangerously evil creation' whose worst sin was to swear on TV, say 'fuck' on stage, and claim the right to be 'difficult' by demanding equal treatment within the music industry. He watches with dead eyes as Siouxsie warms to the subject. "In America you can't see a film without huge inflated breasts

— you know what I mean? Then they'll have someone else who's relatively small and whose nipples you can see and they have to be airbrushed out. It's like — what the *fuck's* going on? They'd be so happy if the woman's breasts didn't have nipples. I just find it ridiculous. It's all *about* sexuality, it's overt, but it's all really distanced. It's not at all *tactile*. For instance, it's fine if it's a cartoon, or if it's phone-sex, because that's all about distance. It's nothing to do with connecting with people. It's not about getting close. It's superficial. It *seems* so explicit and up-front, but it's not. It's very clinical. A friend of mine — well, not a friend, an acquaintance — she had the boob-job, and the irony is that afterwards she couldn't bear to be touched. 'Cos it was too painful. I find it really bizarre. I don't find hugely inflated breasts attractive at all…"

Perhaps it's an identity thing? There's a very lyrically strange track on *Anima Animus* called I Was Me. It seems to be about a confusion of identity; about other people assuming or taking over *your* identity. Like 'Siouxsie' taking over Susan? Or Siouxsie's reactions to seeing a 'Siouxsie-clone'? Is there a story behind that track? "I didn't write it purely from that angle. But there could be that element about it. It's got lots of different levels. This album is a lot more personal. Not confessional. That's not the way I write. But I like things that have an ambiguity to them. I don't tend to write from just a flat one-way point-of-view. I like to look at things from a number of angles. And that song has elements of an early *Twilight Zone* story to it. And there was also a film called *The Double Life Of Veronique*. I don't know if you saw it? No, you didn't. But it's kind of a spooky story about — I suppose, not quite meeting your doppelgänger, but traces of that person having been there before you. An impostor, you think, of yourself. And I remember the *Twilight Zone* story. [The episode she's referring to is Mirror Image, with Vera Miles as doppelgänger victim 'Millicent Barnes'. First broadcast February 26, 1960.] It was one of the old black-and-white ones, and it's about somebody arriving at a bus station where people keep ignoring her, saying 'you've already checked that bag in', and things get really confusing as she protests, "but I've only just got here!' Then she's running outside and sees the bus pulling away and there's a guy saying to her "but you just left on that bus...", and she sees the face in the window pulling away as well. And it's side-face, but it seems to be her!" Siouxsie acts out the role, squirming around in her rattan chair to give the tantalising effect of a half-glimpsed half-face head-and-shoulders in a receding greyhound coach window. In doing so she screws her hu-

man-hair ear-ring out of its immaculate alignment

"Then," she resumes, "on a more frivolous throw-away level, I *have* been seen in places that I couldn't physically have been. In clubs where they say 'oh, but you come here every week. I always put you on the door'. And I'm thinking 'somebody's out there impersonating me'. And of course there was a time in the 1980s when even shop windows were dressing their dummies up to look like me. And that could be quite a double-take when you're walking down the street, and something that once repelled people is actually there looking out of C&A's shop window at you. It's quite a bizarre sensation."

An alternative interpretation that occurred to me was that perhaps it was about your reactions to watching old videos of yourself, and seeing a person there that you no longer quite recognised. "Er... possibly. I mean, subconsciously. That's a very weird idea." She pauses to consider it for a long moment, while concentrating on screwing her ear-ring back into its correct alignment. "It *is* very strange to think that you are there, on film, as you were, and that it is never going to age. It's that kind of *Sunset Boulevard* thing... Yes, that's a very weird idea."

Meanwhile, Rock Me Amadeus drifts invisibly around us. And that's weird too — Mozart, the Punk-genius upstart of Vienna, coming adrift in time and space. Ending up here in a form *he* would no longer recognise either, as lift muzak.

...obscure metaphysical explanation to cover a phenomenon, reason dredged out of the shadows to explain away that which cannot be explained. Call it parallel planes or just insanity. Whatever it is, you find it in the Twilight Zone...
—Rod Serling's final voice-over to 'Mirror Image'

© Dogger

THE FALL
MARK E SMITH THE MAN WHOSE HEAD EXPANDED?

*I can't recall exactly when I first interviewed **THE FALL**. But this is the full text of the encounter, and, judging by references to album titles, it must have been around the middle of 1987. Yet the issues dealt with here — the problems of being a 'Career Punk', an 'Establishment Outsider' — remain as valid today.*

*I saw The Fall most recently at a festival in August 2000. **MARK E SMITH** had collaborated on some tracks with Elastica, who played the same festival. Same tent. Same day. But they didn't guest with The Fall. And he didn't appear with them. Instead, he prowled the stage in a kind of unpredictable edginess, vanishing behind the amps for long stretches of the set as the riffs continued, then — to the consternation of the drummer — becoming preoccupied with dismantling the drum-kit, the annoyed stage crew hastily re-assembling it as he wandered off to seek new toys.*

The Fall may have added years and albums to their history, but they are still not fully assimilated into the mainstream. As 'Career Outsiders' they've succeeded better than most...

false colour photos from the dark side of Uranus. A switch-back of black rings no unlensed eyes have yet seen, a dance of ten new unpaced black moons in lost frigid orbits, beautiful and complex... but what the hell *for*? For whose benefit? If those moons, those rings, didn't exist would it *really* upset some vast eternal cosmic plan? The system runs in total impersonal isolation, according to its own illogics and for the apparent benefit of no-one.

A wonderful and frightening world... like The Fall. Ring-systems of black vinyl noise across some ten albums, a spatchcock of LPs with tracks not so much posed or even composed — more decomposed. A more extensive back-catalogue than that racked up by either the Velvet Underground or the Doors. But a band hermetically sealed off in its own space-time continuum run on its own devious motives. As real, and as irrelevant as Uranus, The Fall are something of an enigma, and one worth probing.

"Shall we go for a drink, and do the interview there?" leers Mr Hip Priest. "I've always enjoyed the idea of a Yorkshireman buying me drinks!" I'm working out the logistics of cross-town traffic between here — the Leeds Metropolitan Univer-

sity — and the local hostelry most conducive to civilised discourse over a cassette machine, and decide on the close shot: The Cobourg. We go down a cascade of ferroconcrete stairs and out into that vinyl-black night. People recognise the hunched-up guy by my side: "Hello Mark E!" they yell matily, and he replies to each and every one of them in an affable and equally matey way. And so, across the flesh-pale argon-lit tarmac to The Cobourg. They used to have live Trad Jazz here (the Ed O'Donnel Band) before they lowered the ceiling. Poet Jeff Nuttall, who wrote the excellent book *Bomb Culture*, was oft to be found sprawled semi-sober over these very beer pumps. And I was once savaged by an alsatian dog just there, I bear the scars to this day...

A pint of Stones' bitter for Mr Fall, slouched in behind the black intricately wrought-iron lacings of the table set in the scuffed mock-Victorian decor. A theatrically quick grin, artificially cheerful, and "Well, Andy, what do you want to ask me?" You've probably read a lot of Fall interviews, right? and you therefore know they conform to a set pattern: writers set up a topic which Mark E then demolishes with scornful contra-think wit, before setting up the next target. It's a mutually supportive game that reinforces the roles of the awkward sod bugger-all dour Mancunian, versus the scribe's post-Watergate journalistic delusions of probe/controversy/significant-statements and the like. This interview is not like that. I don't want knee-jerk blanket-negativity. That's been done to death and *then* screwed some more. This probe wants to orbit Mark E's *enthusiasms*. Find out what excites his *interest*. The *positivism* side of it all.

Gene Vincent. The Fall don't usually do cover versions, so why choose Gene Vincent's Rolling Danny — why that particular track, as an A-side single a year-or-more ago? "That's the first one we did, yeah" he concedes. "The first cover version. Gene Vincent. I've always been into him [or he might have said 'interested in him' — I'm still getting adjusted to the rise and fall of the Mancunian drone]. I think he's great. I like him 'cos he used to... er... do you ever listen to his records?" Nod. "He *never* used to have *any* production on them, or lyrics, or anything ready — it's all noise'n'stuff. *Really*. And if you read up on him you'll see that, apparently, when he used to go in the studio, like — nobody knew what they were recording. So Gene Vincent just used to

make up lyrics. That's why I've always liked him, y'know. There's a lot of *noise* on his records, which phased down some to the latter end of the fifties. Y'know what I'm saying? I think a lot of it was unconscious — but it was *really* good. I like all his stuff. I don't play it all the time — but I played it last night when I got in."

Did you ever see Gene Vincent in the Jayne Mansfield/Tom Ewell movie *The Girl Can't Help It* [1958]?

Enthusiasm? Mark E Smith? This one near scores on the Richter scale. "Good film that, innit? Ridiculous script. [Frank Tashlin take a bow.] It's all innuendoes, the script — it's all double entendres. And you know the guy who made it was a Marxist? He was a Marxist, right? And that was the last film he made, 'cos he was subsequently banned. Senator McCarthy got him right after that film." And in that film Gene Vincent & The Bluecaps perform Bee-Bop A-Lula upstairs in the Beaux Arts Rehearsal Rooms — and it completely epitomises the vital brat-energy spirit of what Rock is supposed to be. "Yeah, it's brilliant." Then he adds, more conspiratorially, "You know in that film-clip they've got those pictures of Beethoven and that, on the wall? Well, apparently in the out-takes, when he hits the climax of Be-Bop A-Lula *they all fell off*, 'cos the band was playing too loud! All the pictures in the room fell off, but they didn't put it in the film. Sounds great that. You know where they go *DANG-DANG-DANG-DANGDANG-KRRRRRANG!* — all the pictures of Beethoven on the wall go *pwoo pwooo* — all smashed! They never used that take."

Perhaps we'll see it on one of the TV out-take shows — *It'll Be Alright On The Night No 126*? Mark E don't seem impressed by my attempted humour. "I very much doubt it," delivered with withering scorn.

PHOTOS FROM THE FALL-GUISE

The Fall: a wonderful and frightening world...?

In the battle for the hearts, minds, and wallets of the Indie consumer, the Fall are old stagers. In his twenty-plus years of radio babble, DJ John Peel has consistently championed just three names — The Undertones, Captain Beefheart... and The Fall. The Fall are the only band to record a full ten studio sessions for his programme. Yet Peel himself confesses confusion. While describing them as 'my favourite band since the Undertones ceased trading' he goes on to add that 'my enduring admiration for their unwholesome racket is not something that can be sensibly analysed' (*Observer*, August 24, 1986). And still into tens — The Fall capped their decade's career with an integral slot on Factory's G-Mex 'Tenth Summer' celebration of Manchester's glorious musical heritage. And isn't *Bend Sinister* their tenth (or, if you count the *Slates* twelve-inch EP — eleventh) album? That's a l-o-n-g time. What exactly *is* the Fall?

"It's Punk," chirps Brix (aka Mrs Smith) pre-gig by way of definition, emphasising her asser-

tion by stubbing her cigarette into the plush maroon Students' Union upholstery she's decorously draped over. I point out what she's doing: is that the last residue of Punk disrespect? She smiles delightfully, "using the back of the chair as an ash-tray?", and drowns it out in a gush of naughty sniggers so delightful it near-derails my investigative train of thought. Billy Idol comes to mind — he was Punk too, wasn't he? I was watching a Billy Idol interview on TV... "I saw that" burbles Brix. "Oh, he's *adorable!*" He's very stylised Punk. He's exaggerated Punk into Showbiz. "Yeah, exactly. But in America *that's* what Punk is, you see?"

And isn't it true that Rod Stewart used to play The Fall's 1980 single Totally Wired over the PA prior to a gig — as warm-up? "I didn't hear about that. That's *really...*" Brix is probably totally mystified — *bamboozled* — now by my line of enquiry. So into the punchline: don't you think the punter on the street would see Billy Idol and Rod Stewart in a similar light. Both of them in the same category, both of them big Rock stars removed from reality by their celebrity? "I don't think so because, see — Rod Stewart is like old school Rock'n'Roll. Do you know what I mean? Like Led Zeppelin, like those kind of *men* who strut and prance, right? But Billy Idol is young — Punk, New Generation, the New Kids coming up, you know what I mean? So it's sort of very different. But they are both big business, big money — I see what you're saying there. But to a kid, he'd think Billy Idol was cool, and Rod Stewart was for his mam, y'know?"

But my point is that The Fall are now into their tenth (or eleventh if you count...) album, and that same kid on the street is going to look at the Fall and think — wow! — eleven albums, that's really something to achieve. "It is," agrees Brix, "mmmmmm." So The Fall must now have something of that kind of Star mystique. Not quite Rod

Stewart, or even Billy Idol, but that same kind of logic applies. You're a career musician because The Fall have been an established part of the scene for ten years. So how do *you* think that kid on the street would look at The Fall? She sits back carefully. "It's like a contradiction, really. The only reason we've released so many albums is that we've got a lot of songs. We're prolific. And the fact that we *do* sell them. But we've only been going the same amount of time as Siouxsie & The Banshees or whatever!"

Craig Scanlon (lead guitar) shrugs as I shift attention in his direction. "I don't know. I missed the first section of your l–o–n–g question!" And the whole intricately constructed thesis falls apart in three-way waves of laughter. Conversation collapsing like a ton of brix.

"I don't know," he resumes. "I mean, I can't judge anymore what the audience see and hear, 'cos we're on stage. It doesn't matter. If they like us that's great. Each person's got a different idea about what The Fall is — including the people in the band! Basically I don't try to analyse it or do a MORI poll thing on it..."

MORE PSYCHE-SPIEL FROM THE WORD-SMITH

This is a cool group
Here are your Wedding pictures
they are black...

Before voyaging out tonight I'm watching TV *Wipe-Out*, a Doublevision video compilation with extensive live footage of Fall at the Venue, blurry figures in streaky darkness, "good evening, we are The Fall, and these are the words of expectation / these are the words of success, expectation / every now and then I would like to do something like this..." Fast-cut to Mark E Smith sat on a floral-print couch. He toys ab-

stractly with a cigarette, stub-stub-stubbing at the ash-tray resting precariously on the couch-arm. There's a stereo speaker cabinet behind his head, level with his left ear. His left leg arches up over his right knee. He's saying "...'cos I, in my sort of... dreamlike world", uncrosses his legs, stub-stubs his cigarette absently. "I sort of see myself as a writer, and The Fall is a very good vehicle... and it's the only vehicle that allows me to do it."

Now we're sitting face-to-face in The Cobourg, this low-rent Leeds hostelry. His hair's hacked back from the video mop-top. Such hair as remains is as multi-directional and as style-less as a Fall guitar solo. He seems more re-laxed too. Is this man deep?

Tell me, Mr Smith — how do you feel about being asked banal questions? And is the name 'Fall' used in the Catholic sense of the 'Fall from Grace'? Is that a deliberate reference? "Well, that's the idea of the name, yes. But there's loads of connotations you can pick." Religious conno-tations? "All sorts of connotations. There's loads of things it means. If you go to America the name Fall means 'fuck all'. [F all?] All it means is bloody autumn. So everybody thinks you're called the fucking Autumns! So sometimes you lose out, y'know. Or in Germany, the Fall means making an idiot out of yourself. It means you walk down the street and you can't bloody walk — in German. So you're 'Das Fall', and it means you come a cropper."

Fall-guy Stephen Hanley (bass) was born in Dublin in 1959 — just two years after Jackie Wil-son's Reet Petite was in the Top Twenty for the first time. He joins The Fall twenty years later, following a stint with a gospel/religious outfit called Staff Nine.

John S Woolstencroft replaces drummer Karl Burns in August 1986, in time to play on the ga-rage-acid Mr Pharmacist single which scores The

Fall's highest Top Forty placing. Meanwhile, Burns was last reported to be in Geneva rehearsing with Iggy Pop.

Simon Rogers (bass/DX7) is also a recent Fall additive. Classically trained, he was scoring a Mark E piece called The Classical for Michael Clarke's Ballet Ramba, and was subsequently requisitioned into The Fall full-time. There's also Craig and Brix in the current line-up, while ex-Fall Mike Leigh was last heard doing cabaret, and Mark (Creepers) Riley is scripting 'Harry The Head' for IPC's juvenile zine *Oink!*

Then there's Mark E Smith from Prestwich, 'a name which inspires dread and respect' (a self-blurb from Channel 4's Teletext), the only member left from The Fall's 1977 inception. So The Fall is not static. The irresistible rise and rise of Fall has taken them into a niche midway between upwardly mobile and horizontally frozen. Each album giving both Fallophiles and Fallophobes pretty much what they've come to expect — some further conjugations of the verb 'to Fall' (in which everything is delivered, and nothing much is revealed). Same as it ever was... same as it ever was... But as a band of ten years standing (and Fall-ing), is it still *going* anywhere? Is

there a conscious progression? Are The Fall evolving in any particular direction? "I think so, yeah" admits Mark E grudgingly. "A lot of people think it's just the same old stuff all over again" — staring me out, challenging me to argue. Well, a *Melody Maker* review *did* say that album-wise you've re-recorded Captain Beefheart's *Safe As Milk* ten times over! "Yeah, right. That's rubbish," mouthed around a sneer. "But I thought it was quite funny really. It's all horse shit, innit?" A long pause. "But I find that an *amazing* viewpoint. I think everything's very, very different. Different people. Different attitudes. Every time. In fact, I think that's what a lot of people *don't* like about it! They try and pretend that they don't like the fact that we're just the same — when it's the fact that we *do* actually change that they don't like. They always want you to come up with an album that sounds like the one before, so they can classify you. It's always been the case. I mean, the easiest thing you can do — the best thing for us to do — would have been to make *Bend Sinister* another album like *This Nation's Saving Grace*. We'd clean up. I've always known this. People think you're stupid. They talk to you like you've not quite cracked it, they talk to you like... [the repetition of the phrase is delivered with all the derisive vehemence of his stage-diatribes]... they say 'why don't you stick to this?', and you go 'well, you know, don't you think that's *really teeeeedious?*'"

"You take something like U2 or Echo & The Bunnymen or — I'm not knocking them groups" he hastily adds, "they're... talented," and he coughs round the words in a way that might imply his Stones' bitter has got re-routed the wrong way, or may signify a certain choking on the word itself, I dunno. "But their second and third albums! There's not much you can see between them is there? There's *no* difference! And the fourth and fifth... it goes on like that for fuckin'

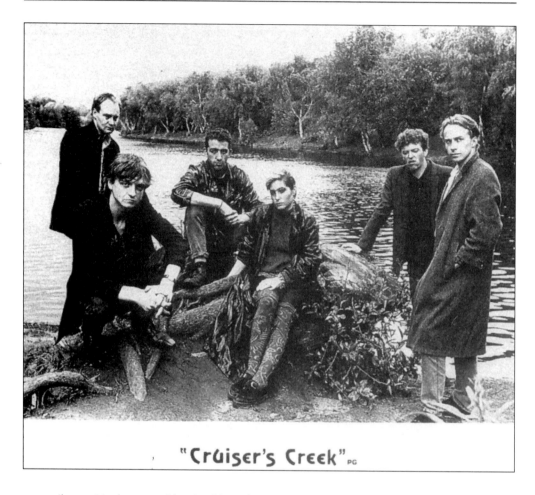

"Cruiser's Creek" PG

ever, y'know. It's the same bloody old..." the word gets lost — it's probably 'treatment', but might be something stronger. "All that's happening is that they're spending more money on it as they go along. Maybe the album after next has an orchestra on it. But it's the same fuckin' album really. And I've always thought that was pretty obvious and pretty insulting. So I think it's very *ironic* that people charge *us* with just doing the same thing for y–e–a–r–s. I think that's very odd. And very interesting."

How do you define what is good Fall and what is bad Fall? "There's a lot of our early stuff that I don't really like... if I listen to it. But I don't knock it, y'know."

I always thought *Hex Induction Hour* — the fifth album, from 1982 — was quintessential Fall: eleven tracks, one hour's playing time, cuts like Iceland and Hip Priest. "Exactly. *Hex Induction Hour* went down very well." And there's quite a contrast between that and *Room To Live*, which followed it, in October of the same year — featuring the consciously art-house Papal Visit, the twinned guitars of Scanlon and Riley on Marquis Cha Cha and Detective Instinct. "Right. It's deliberate. If we'd done *Hex Induction Hour II* — even though *Room To Live* was very heavy and noisy — if we'd followed that up with something really similar, people would really love you, 'cos they're getting used to you. Which is not the point. I mean, once you're doing something you should do it for the fun of it. You should do it for the *creativity* of it. You shouldn't go round repeating what you've done. That's why The Fall lasts a long time."

Journalist Colin Irwin describes how The Fall recorded the Iceland track during a tour of that country:

'Iceland's rich history of legends and folklore fired Smith's already rampant imagination, and he'd jotted down a series of scattered thoughts, fantasies and genuine incidents surrounding the visit, while the rest of the band concocted a weirdly haunting tune in the studio. The track, opening with a cassette recording of the wind blowing outside Smith's hotel window, was done first-take with the band and their leader having only the vaguest idea of what the other would be doing.' (*Melody Maker*, March 6, 1982.)

That 'inspired accident' method of working seems to imply that you rely to a degree on intuition? "Yes, sometimes. Not all the time. It'll be about half'n'half. Half of our stuff is very, very worked on. But I like that 'accidental' aspect, I like that, yes. It's not good to go into the studio with songs that you know backwards, y'know? — and just get 'em down. I don't want to do that because I just don't want to be stale. I don't want to go on tour and practice a load of songs and then go in the studio and just recreate them. You end up not even feeling what you're singing."

So do you have tapes of failed Fall experiments? "No, not really. My experiments never fail. No, I'm just saying, y'know... there's a lot of groups who have an odd attitude to experimentation. They think they'll put brilliant improvisation on their records, so they just do it and it comes out like dosh. Like Public Image or something like that. They think their every utterance is

brilliant art. We're very conscious of getting away from that. You can't *plan* anything really. You can't *plan* improvisation, which is what a lot of people *try* to do. That's just a contradiction."

Do you consider that you're working inside the Rock tradition? "No. I'm just saying there's a lot more things here than people give us credit for. The trouble with Rock music is that it's too easy for a lot of idiots to play it." A pause. "But that's also its greatest beauty." But don't you think there's any cross-over in attitude between what you're saying about the value of spontaneity, and the way that Gene Vincent worked? "I don't think so, no. I just think that the way he worked is great." No continuity in that use of pure noise? "I don't know. I just like the fact that there's *no lyric sheets* with Gene Vincent for sure. It's all like 'wirr wirr WHIRR! — what what WHAT! — uh-huh uh UH-HUH!'. You know what I mean? I like it... with The Fall we can get very literal a lot of the time."

PERVERTED BY LANGUAGE

Uranus is 18.181843 astronomical units from Earth, and has a surface temperature of 57 kelvin. With its stubbornly inverted poles and oceans of methane gasses, the system runs in total impersonal isolation, according to its own illogics, and for the apparent benefit of no-one.

A wonderful and frightening world... like The Fall.

Brix: "I would hate for The Fall to be like the Damned. That's my worst fear. To just evolve into a 'Rock' band and not have anything really unique about us, or stop the experimentation — that is my *worst* fear. That will never happen."

Craig: "That'd be just like doing the cabaret circuit, doing that. We *need* to play. We do get rusty if we don't play. It helps us a lot."

Brix: "We need to play to *eat*! To play to live, you know? That's what keeps us vital. Within ourselves we *have* to do it."

The Fall tend to engender fierce extremes of reaction, from uncritical devotion to vociferous revulsion. Me? I've always found them consistently 'interesting'. That's the kind of smug word people use as a patronising put-down, but in the case of The Fall it's used fairly accurately. They are a band who suggest and imply all manner of intriguing possibilities while masking it all in what looks to be webs of deliberate obfuscation. Can it be that it's all just prick-teasing? Perhaps the blurry definition is an essential part of The Fall's Working Class Prole-Art conception? It is

ideologically uncool — as well as flash — to wear your culture too conspicuously. Hints and nudges are all that's necessary. Audience suss will do the rest. But then — catalysed by Brix' more Pop-attack orientation — *Bend Sinister* is not only their most invigoratingly direct and accessible album, but also their most commercially successful seller to date. I like it a lot. It provides evidence that — even after ten years — The Fall *are* still evolving.

But do you see a point where The Fall will exhaust the permutations of their style? A long silence. *Bend Sinister is* your eleventh album? "Yeah, so what? I don't see anything wrong with that! It's just that... a–w–w–w–w–w–w... I always take it day-by-day. I always have. I don't look more that three months into the future. I never 'ave. There's endless possibilities with lyrics. There's endless possibilities with music. You can go on forever, really. The danger is that you don't become ridiculous, or start taking yourself seriously'n'stuff!"

Another thoughtful pause. Then: "Is that it then, Andy? Is that it, now? You finished then?"

No. Not really. The Fall are still something of an enigma, but they remain one worth probing. But I guess it will do to be going on with.

Until the next time...

When The Fall recorded I Am Damo Suzuki they were name-referencing Can's highly unconventional vocalist, and thereby neatly linking back to an earlier chapter. Now — as the interview winds down into small-talk — Mark E accommodatingly provides a bridge to the next one. Cabaret Voltaire? "They're clever lads, yeah. I remember seeing Cabaret Voltaire in 1982, and it was like the best live show I'd ever fuckin' seen. It was intimidating, loud, and a real experiment on its own."

Once again, he's not wrong....

© Dogger

CABARET VOLTAIRE
DESPATCHES FROM THE
SILICON VALLEY

If Blues was a coded message that went around the planet (as suggested by Dave Davies of The Kinks), electronics is another code. On another frequency. A different sequence encrypted into a different language. But just as rural Blues got electrified into R&B, got psychedelic-ised into a kind of anarchist futurism, so now it goes elsewhere...

... splice yourself in with the Newscasters, Prime Ministers, Presidents.
Why stop there? Why stop anywhere? Everybody splice himself in with everybody else. Loudspeaker voices mutter through corridors and rooms... words visible as a haze... tape recorders in the gardens answer each other like barking dogs...

—William Burroughs
The Invisible Generation (1966)

ou hear the latest Club Mix from the post-Rave/Acid House Dance culture, pulsing with sequenced sound-bite samples and relentlessly programmed drums and you go *yeah*, great — but Cabaret Voltaire were doing this *at least* ten years ago. Before William Gibson wrote *Neuromancer*, Stephen 'Mal' Mallinder and Richard H Kirk were *already* living the cybohemia of high-tech squalor his groundbreaking novel would envisage, sucking in cultural influences from past visionaries and projecting them into futures sheened black and shiny as vinyl. Theirs were tactile futures you could smell and experience as well as see and hear. And the gleaming edge of their noirishly imagistic futurism has never rusted or biodegraded. They laid the conceptual foundation for the real-world growth of all those Electro-Dance digital confections. Without them the world would be different. And now the Cabs are no more, but their influence is everywhere... and you think back to the summer of '84...

A nervy subtlety. A sound like biting steel nails. The shock of the newer. Mal takes a bass-line for a walk, a low-rider in a contraflow of rhythms

with a low, low drag factor. He's leaving afterimages of nervous shock and mind-games of terminal disorder hanging in the air, doing wheelies over your brain cell tissue — ideas sometimes disguised as sound, sometimes as a geometry of moving pictures. Watch the sounds. Listen to the pictures. Mal's face is made up of vertical, planes and angles, sparse and economical.

Richard's is made up of curves, flourishes, and flowing lines. Richard chain-smokes and watches the wrap-around screens. Extracts from Japanese

TV. Aerial shots of the Toyota/Xerox buildings. The screens overlap, overlay. A Harrison Marks nude housewife comes down the stairs… comes down the stairs… comes down the stairs, trapped in trick-frame repetition. A Blue Thunder whirlybird slides out behind skyscrapers into the sun. Over and over. Over and over.

Cabaret Voltaire is a multipack of projects. Better. By lack of design.

FROM REEL LIFE TO REAL LIFE

Heat vibrates. My watch reads 02:45. I'm pacing Portobello street, Sheffield, Yorkshire, England. Past a long prowl of sweltering Bengali restaurants and Italian pizza takeaways, round the corner from the live music Beehive bar, to where 'Western Works' stands across the road from a freshly sandblasted church clad in scaffolding. Hot to the touch. A late-teen with a tastefully precise crimson flame crawling his right temple, watches me go up with my ITT portable. Later he'll watch me come down. All the while he sits on the church's dry-stone perimeter wall, heel pecking out the private sounds of his Sony Walkman in absurd intensity.

Western Works — where dark, dark blueprints were evolved and Xeroxed into a plague of electronic corruption — is old. Late-industrial. It has chickweed and grass in the guttering and its name picked out in sandstone relief lettering. The building is sub-let into split-level units: 'Bard Electrical,' 'Industrial Trade Scissors & Shears' and 'VDS Transforming'. Cabaret Voltaire inhabit two rooms in its uppermost level, three flights up, all the way is far enough. An echoey stairwell of worn reds, blacks, and faded creams with cast-iron balustrades. A faint tepid echo. Their control room previously belonged to the Young Socialists. It is homely unkempt, as in lived-in. It's dominated by the well-thumbed mixing desk bequeathed them through the good graces of Rough Trade when they signed on the dotted line, a record-by-record deal circa *The Voice Of America*, their second album. There's a 'Fiftieth Anniversary of the Russian Revolution' poster on the wall in violent splashes of red and black. Uncage the colours, unfurl the flags. There's also a Patti Smith poster. The heat is sticky.

"Suppose we'd better get back and rehearse," asserts Mal, to no noticeable reaction. Rehearsals, Richard explains at me, in preparation for a string of live dates, including Manchester's Haçienda. But, as a delaying tactic, to avoid resuming work, he hunts half-heartedly across the console for cigarettes. "We're having trouble finding a decent venue here in Sheffield" he continues. "The Lyceum's shut down; the Top Rank's shut down; the Leadmill's fine as a venue, but it's just too small for us. It only holds 800. We need at least 1,000. We usually pull about 1,200–1,300, when we play home ground."

Mal tackles the work-evasion problem from a slightly different angle. "It just keeps getting hotter and hotter," he self-justifies. "The hotter it gets the worse the sound becomes."

"You got my lighter?" asks Richard of no-one

in particular. He stands up and crosses to the window. Separates the lattice of Japanese cane-blinds. When he stands against the window I almost expect the sun to refract through him. Instead, his eyes do a slow tour-route of factory roofs. A shimmering urban desert. An interminable chain of megalithic post-industrial archaeology sleeping towards extinction in the sun. There should be riots here. Instead the disaffected get Electro-Convulsive Therapy passed through their frontal lobes via the Cabs. From this city, Human League first wired the world's ears, tuned in its eyeballs, then flooded both sensory channels. In this city, ABC now lie where New Romance lies (and lies, and lies) — but this Cab-ish duo would look bad in gold lame suits.

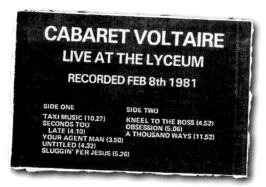

Richard's shirt at first seems to be a garishly tasteless Technicolor Hawaiian job. Then like some elaborate abstract Expressionist silk-screen print. A shirt that bags untidily loose over his slack belt, so he keeps shoving it back in place irritably. It's that shirt, above all, that belies any pretensions to Pop star posing.

A trimphone purrs. Alan Fish gets it. Something about mini-bus hire for a low-key wind-up gig in Bedford? Mal's girlfriend Karen, in deep maroon, hair immaculately crimped, ignores it all. Sits to one side concentrating all her attention on the Panther edition of Henry Miller's *Sexus*.

In a token concession to interview roles I make

some inept comment to the effect that, if Sheffield has/had a 'sound' (which every band I've talked to denies), then if that hypothetical sound has a centre (which it obviously can't have), then this place — Western Works — must be it. "A few people have drifted through, shall we say" answers Richard in a phrase that effortlessly encompasses the likes of New Order, Eric Random, Hula, Test Department ("do you know them? They play 'metal'. As in bits of metal objects"), Clock DVA, The Fall, and UV Pop. "I suppose it's because we were the only people who had a studio apart from anything else. But it's always interested us, working with other people. It's something that's always, kind of, appealed. To be able to steam in there and play around with other people's material. Provided they're into the idea, of course."

Yes. I'll buy that, Richard. Just one thing I don't understand, why the Russian Revolution poster? "Oh that? It's a legacy. The place used to be the Young Socialists' headquarters in the sixties. Before we had it. We left all their posters up." And where does Patti Smith fit in? "Patti Smith? Oh yeah. Somebody sent me that from Italy. I used to like some of Patti Smith's earlier work, I must admit." Mal laughs, maliciously low. "She was alright. Till she woke up one morning and thought she was God!"

STAY ON THIS CHANNEL — THIS IS AN EMERGENCY!

… everybody is seized by an indefinable intoxication. The [Cabaret Voltaire] is about to come apart at the seams, and is getting to be a playground for crazy emotions…
—Hugo Ball writing of the first Cabaret Voltaire at Meierei Café, Zurich, March 5, 1916

Andy: "The original Cabaret Voltaire was a

Dada Theatre caught up in the middle of WWI, enacted by absurdist artists like Kurt Schwitters, Tristan Tzara, and Jean Arp. You also did a track called Dada Man on an early Industrial-label tape."

Mal: "Yes. we were influenced by the Dadaist spirit and feeling."

There's 70 Billion People Out There,
  Where Are They Hiding?
There's 70 Billion People Out There,
  Where Are They Hiding?
There's 70 Billion People Out There,
  Where Are They Hiding?
There's 70 Billion People Out There,
  Where Are They Hiding?
—Tape-loop on Yashar, from *2x45*

Operating on a dream ticket dual-key control system, Richard and Mal have already done a near ten-stretch as Cabs, kick-starting the project when they were "about seventeen or eighteen". That was around 1974 — not exactly a classic year for Rock. It was Osmonds. It was the Chinn-Chapman hit-machine. It was Abba winning Eurovision. In retrospect the most intriguing event of the year had to have happened in the Sheffield attic-room that birthed this experimental recording studio group of uncertain input and unlimited output. "The band didn't form. It just started playing around with ideas," Kirk told an early fanzine interviewer. At that point it was Stephen 'Mal' Mallinder (bass/vocals), tall, lean, dour, and intense in appearance; serious, direct, and positive in conversation, voice pitched in largely inflectionless monotone. It was also Richard H Kirk (guitar/sax/FX) who carries the edge of humour, a rise and fall of intonation to his speech, a slight rounding lilt to his vowels and a more obtuse orbiting around his subject-matter. I get impressions that Mal is more inner-directed.

Kirk, to a greater degree, outer-directed. Although I could be wrong. Alan Fish denies it, but doesn't offer a corrective viewpoint beyond suggesting an internal 'fluidity' of roles within the group. In the beginning, and until April '82, there was also Chris R Watson (Vox Continental synthesiser/tape sequencing), but he's since relocated to Tyne Tees television. He's not been replaced — but Alan Fish (of Sheffield's Hula) is now an added component member, in care of drums/percussion on stage, screen and record.

With the treatment of conventional sound sources by electronic processes, and by secondary treatments such as splicing, loops, and fast-cut tape montage, they made howling rippling impressionistic torrents of noise — try-outs and try-ons scored for Dalek voices. Soundtracks for

the half-life of technological decay in this former 'Workshop of the World'. Canvasses of incongruous and unexpected juxtapositions that meticulously cancel each other out. A nag-nag-nagging accumulative power that near assumes psychokinetic properties. Sounds infused with burbling snatches of short-wave radio and TV conversations feeding in and out of audibility by splicing and repetition. Sounds, according to the *Sunday Times*, taking them 'on a trip without a destination'. Ideas assembled like Jean Arp's 1916 collages, 'according to the laws of chance.' Better. By lack of design. Games less with the art of noise, more the noise of art. Sounds like Rorschach inkblot tests — random, but with metagenic implications that confuse sound and meaning to mess minds. In this way, initially using little more than an Akai two-track with overdub facility, they predated the 'Sheffield Sound', the Industrial avant garde, Electro-Pop, Garageland Experimentalists, Acid House, Trip-Hop, Rave, and the cassette DIY underground, by a clutch of years. Ushering in a time for entrancing discord. All the way is far enough.

Their first Rough Trade single was Nag Nag Nag c/w Finding Someone At The Door Again, a bizarrely compulsive chain-saw psychedelic-punk artefact produced in June '79 in collusion with Red Crayola's Mayo Thompson. But long before that they'd begun working with mail-order cassettes. Their first issue done in a batch of twenty! Later, following the Cabs groundwork throughout the late seventies/early eighties, in an average week the Pop papers would get twenty such C60s in every post, by bands operating similar types of material — electronic drones of severe structures and colours; doctored or sublingual vocals as near the boredom threshold as enthusiasm will allow. "In a lot of ways that's one of the reasons why we decided to change" concedes Mal. "Because that approach to it became a bit worn in some ways. We're just trying to use a little bit more subtlety. To try and keep one jump ahead of what everyone else is doing."

Kirk orbits in supportively. Picks up Mal's thread, and takes it back to roots. "The point was that a lot of people latched onto the fact that the way we made music, and the things we used to make music, were very instant. Were very

available." Martyn Ware, I think, said that his impatience to create/to become a musician, was so urgent that he didn't have time to learn an instrument. So he took to electronics as a short cut, and formed Human League. "Maybe it was a similar case with us" nods Richard over his Technicolor shoulder. "I think that was it. Nobody could play anything — nobody really can. It was a case of just using electronics and using instruments purely for the sounds we could get out of them rather than any musical thing."

"Cabaret Voltaire is so diverse because we draw from a really wide catchment area" explains Mal. He warms to the subject of origins and inputs. Adding that contemporary musics, in the beginning, were less of an influence than "looking back on what had been done in the past. Taking a little bit of inspiration from the German groups who worked around '69/70. Can in particular. They were quite an influence because of their rhythms. They were very rhythm-orientated. They weren't doing just pure abstract stuff — it was their rhythms that always appealed. We really respect Can, and particularly Holger Czukay's stuff."

There's a rustle of matches as Richard fumbles for a cigarette. "Can used to use old radio sets on stage, too. I remember seeing Holger Czukay playing — in Doncaster, of all places. That was when he'd actually gone beyond just playing bass with them. Instead, he was surrounded by a mass of tape recorders and radio receivers, and he was just standing there in the middle of all this equipment. It was quite nice to see somebody using that solely as their instrument. We'd been doing it, so it was really great to find out that someone else was doing it as well."

"That European connection, and the Velvets, were like the two link-points. We've always been pretty keen on the Velvet Underground" emphasises Mal. "Plus some of the stuff that Eno was doing. They were probably the only things we saw as parallels. The only places where we could see similarities to what we were doing." The Velvet Underground connection took flesh in October 1978 when Cabaret Voltaire issued the Lou Reed song Here She Comes Now as part of their very first vinyl release — the Rough Trade EP *Extended Play*. And the link survived at least until the classic '81 *Three Mantras*, which was "just the idea of doing two longer numbers — one very much in a Velvets Sister Ray vein."

Although it "wasn't a case of just listening to them and copying" insists Richard. "We were doing what we were doing. *Then* we found out that other people were doing similar sorts of things. So obviously you're bound to feed off it a little bit." But the Cabs methodology has always subsumed a 'collage' technique that's not found in any of those 'admitted' influences. They've always used trinkets of found-sound, tape-loops and cut-ups. "That's always been so, even now. A lot of that is perhaps like an audio version of what [Dada-ist] Marcel Duchamp was doing. What Brion Gysin, and what William Burroughs [Beat generation author of *Junkie* and *Naked Lunch*] were doing. I must admit that's where the principle lies, only we did it with sound. In principle it lies a lot closer to that than it does to any groups or musical influences. The original link was Duchamp. Only it wasn't a conscious effort to do what he'd done. It was more a case of, it fitted the needs if the time. When we first started we were aware of Burroughs, but we didn't know *everything* about him. It's only over the years that we've learned a lot more about Burroughs."

The William Burroughs connection extends clear through to Cabaret Voltaire's involvement with the 1982 Final Academy events. "We did one of the nights there" recalls Richard. "We did the video and film show for that, and provided

low-key improvised music as a soundtrack. It was a good event. I only saw one night — the one we were involved in, but it was quite a feat to get all those people together for four days in London. I know Burroughs doesn't move unless he's guaranteed a certain amount of money these days. He needs it to keep his habit together! He's quite a nice old guy. We first met him in October 1979 in the Brussels PLAN-K club. A similar sort of thing. We played there with Joy Division, he was there and Gysin was there. We just met him briefly. He probably never remembered meet-

ing us then anyway. He must meet loads and loads of people who come up to him and say 'I think your books are brilliant, pal'. There's not much you can say beyond that. It's a case of being a little bit in awe of someone who's done so much work that you respect... Plus the fact that his only contact with people is through his books."

... a three-ring psychosis that assaults the senses with the sights and sounds of the total environment syndrome... discordant music, throbbing cadences, pulsating tempo...

—*Variety* magazine reviewing Velvet Underground in Andy Warhol's Exploding Plastic Inevitable, 1967

To a certain extent I think we were fascinated by certain aspects of psychedelia in the sixties, especially the multi-media aspects and the darker more evil side of the music...

—Richard H Kirk, *Flowmotion* fanzine, 1980

TIME: MUCH LATER
LOCATION: HACIENDA CLUB, MANCHESTER

Peter Hope, vocalist for Sheffield's Box, sits catatonic with concentration. Like some Bhikku or Bodhisattva. He's razored bald but for tyre-tread shading up the back and a truncated quiff at the front, he's hunched forward, impassive, watching...

For a start, there's *Doublevision* triple-screened... two videos on closed circuit relay overhead, suspended between lightbooms and girders, and one more screen panning across the backstage backdrop. They're synchronised — if not always exactly to the same colour setting or degree of focal blur — into festive junkfood for the eyes and ears, a fun fair Coney Island of the mind. Eye-Wire. A Skinhead gets naked in a bare concrete yard, wraps himself in petrol-soaked blanket and torches himself. William Burroughs crosses a city street all wasted and cadaver-thin, enters a phone-booth, lights a cigarette beneath a ripped collage of French-language hoardings. Riot Police (like on the *Voice Of America* sleeve or some Kent State University documentary) advance through tear-gas with

night-sticks erect. There are outtakes from the adult movie *Jungle Burger*, replete with galloping penises. Poorly animated UFOs big and bright in black-and-white coming in low over Hollywood (the CBS building in the background). Flying Saucers like '57 Chevrolet hub-caps from Ed Wood Jr's trash classic *Plan 9 From Outer Space*. A Harrison Marks nude housewife comes down the stairs... comes down the stairs... comes down the stairs. Geisha Boys and Temple Girls. Aerial shots of Tokyo, sodium streetlights, auto factories. They all fall into and out of place. Capitalism + Electronics. The Power of Technology + the Technology of Power. 'Toyota City' — you get the picture? Yes, we see.

And all the while, "someone, sometimes, *cracksdown!*"

An insistently solid pagan repetition of Funk bass strips Western music back to its primal roots, the natural-magic triggers of the race-consciousness. Mal mouths lyrics that are vocal rhythms in chant. His white guitar, brown C&A sweatshirt and red neckerchief concede no flash or showbizzy projections — yet Cabaret Voltaire is all around you. I've heard the *Crackdown* set on a domestic sound centre, seen the Doublevision video on small-screen, met the personae dramatis at Western Works. Yet, experienced *en masse*, collectively, in toto, it's stunning. A multi-sensory circus for all senses — and then some. An organic unity only glimpsed at when its constituent elements are ingested in plural forms. Live, with added perspective-effect and depth-of-field, it's an incomparable spectacle. The only remotely suitable analogy I can come up with is the magnificent Clock DVA stage ritual.

Richard chain-smokes throughout. He's in leopard-skin top, leather pants, hennaed (?) hair shimmering and slip-slithering over his forehead. He feeds in a squiff of synth, some silver metallic sax passages, some guitar as required by whim or premeditation. He sequences the infiltration of taped voices burbling beneath the mix and filling the twixt-number silences. Alan Fish squats behind a Berlin Wall barrage of Perspex drums, hexagon synth-drums, and percussion, meticulously laying down anchor-chains of beat around which all else swirls. He's in red, a single aquatic-turquoise earstud, a frontal bush of clean hair black against the shifting colour-filtered videos.

"Twenty-four, twenty-four, twenty-four hours a day," intoned into a web of sound dense enough to make neutrons dance in different formations. Real notes, real solid drop-beat riffs and kicks plentifully jived up by a grafting of taped voices that decode all those messages programmed into the conventional syntax of 'conventional' musics. Normal service may never be resumed. Cabaret Voltaire is about as old as Atari Electronics Inc — but it's getting younger every day. You'll see nothing quite like it on any British stage this year.

Pete Hope, vocalist for Sheffield's Box, is sat hunched in introverted isolation, scarcely blinking. Impassive. Watching…

FROM THE INNER MIND
TO THE OUTER LIMITS

… turn off the soundtrack on your television set and substitute an arbitrary soundtrack pre-recorded on your tape-recorder, street sounds, music, conversation, recordings of other television programmes. You will find that the arbitrary soundtrack seems to be appropriate…

—William Burroughs, The Invisible Generation

So, with superficials thus disposed of, we can get down to specific vinyl issues, and chase up some ghosts of meaning through verbal therapy preserved on a packed C90 spool. I tap into the

Cabaret Voltaire logic-functions as follows: I point out Clock DVA's fixation with 'pornographic blackness', Genesis P Orridge's Aleister Crowley flirtations, then add that Cabaret Voltaire have never been on that Dark Side Of The Force. "Well, we've had our moments," says Kirk. "But it's something that we never want to make too much of."

Talking time is democratically distributed. Mal: "There's a danger of people picking up on that, and also the danger of doing it as a pose. With us it's more a case of considering if it fits into the perspective of everything else we do. But sure, there's a few things. A few blow-jobs in the video… but nothing that merits too much attention. Our concern is to keep everything on a similar level. We don't want to make too big a play of any one particular thing."

But this pitching for the middle-ground twixt light and dark can seem a little evasive. They've scrupulously avoided any kind of political connections to the extent that (promoter/label-boss maverick) Marcus Featherby issued their *Live In Sheffield* album under the Pressure Company pseudonym to avoid the 'Solidarity' implications of that project. "Yeah" agrees Mal, as though unable to see any problem, Lenin and Marx uncaging the colours on the wall behind him. "That's true. We never wanted to use the name Cabaret Voltaire for any political motives. Not that we're not aware of politics. Obviously we have certain political beliefs, but we always thought it was a bit out of order to use the group as a political mouthpiece. It's something we've always had strong feelings about."

"We never knock anybody for doing it" qualifies Mal. "It's just a case of, we don't want to do it ourselves. Whenever you start using the group and the music as some sort of soapbox, establishing some sort of morality and set of principles for yourself, then the danger of hypocrisy becomes greater. The danger is, once you set up 'these principles' then by pure rationale you've got to see them through everything you do — the way you live, the way you eat, the way you speak. Once you start you have to moralise and break down every single thing you do. And we don't want that responsibility falling on *us*. We don't want to *be* something, or stand up for something in that way. It's better to keep it to yourself rather that run the risk of becoming a complete hypocrite. It's human nature to be slightly illogical and not to be totally rational. So we felt we were right in being amoral about a lot of things we did."

"Another reason is — I've never come across a political party that I've ever felt any kind of affinity for. I think they all suck, personally. My politics are probably the politics of individuality. I don't see the need to be part of any organisation like that. I've got a lot of respect for what [extreme anarchist Punks] Crass do. I don't particularly listen to the music, but they do tend to stick to their ideals. Which is really good. I mean, they're totally independent of everybody, which is great… But then again, the sense behind what they do is to use that medium to reach the main number of people. For them to do anything other than Punk-orientated music would be — almost — Middle Class. It wouldn't be reaching the people they want to reach. They have to go to the base level of communication which is very angry, instant Punk music. Which doesn't mean anything at all to me."

Their message shapes their medium, right? Which seems like a fitting point to mention the Cabs own Sluggin' Fer Jesus. A tape of mad American orator 'Doctor' Eugene Scott's demented evangelising, used as raw material for some compulsive rhythm overlays and tricksy improvisation. Was the original tape merely a slate of interesting grain offering itself up for constructive chalking? It's voice presenting a series of audible contours and wave-forms with sound possibilities? Perhaps its quirkiness made it a polarity, an irresistible base to work from? Or was there any deliberate anti-religious slant? Richard furrows a shock of fringe hanging around his off-centre parting. It then falls meticulously and precisely back into its shock. "I hate religions personally," he offers amiably. "But I don't think it was an anti-religious record. It was more, not a joke, but… it was just, like — the way we were confronted with that kind of thing on American television. Probably an American would regard it as normal, but for us, it was something that obviously inspired us. We were out playing gigs in San Francisco and when we got back afterwards there'd be this crazy bloke on TV ranting on. It was a totally strange situation."

"If it *was* a statement of anything it was, like, a statement on the state of American TV. It was a complete and utterly ludicrous waste of time. It was like a 'Catch 22' situation. He was on TV. He had his own TV station. To get your own TV station you need money. And the only way he got money was to ask for it over the TV! So therefore he had a channel which was basically just asking for money to keep that channel on the air. He didn't actually *say* anything apart from a few religious quotes he'd slip in while he was begging for money. But basically he was just asking for money to keep him on the air to ask for more money. It just went on and on. It was really funny." There's the ghost of a sneer on Mal's thin lips.

"You could never tell whether he was live or whether he was pre-recorded" Richard resumes, hunting the mixing desk for matches. "But he was saying 'we gotta get $100,000', and this little clock was counting up all the money people were donating. Then, every now and again they'd wheel out a load of reformed alcoholics — who all looked like Ronald Reagan — to sing Gospel songs."

"He's in prison now, I think" muses Mal in tones of delicious contempt. "He used to wear a pair of cowboy boots as well, didn't he?" Richard offers, looking out over a heated Sheffield. Mal grins ludicrously. "He looked just like Jimmy Saville."

And all the while, across the road from Western Works, is a freshly sandblasted church clad in scaffolding. Hot to the touch.

There is no such thing as a hit or a miss,
only good or bad.

—Some Bizarre label boss, Stevo

CHANCE VERSUS CAUSALITY

From somewhere comes the faintest strumming of an electric guitar… a whisper as soft as a revving motorcycle… as gentle as the screams of a victim in pain!

—Stan Lee presents The Fantastic Four in *Spiderman and his Amazing Friends* No 555

It's a month or so later. Jet-lagged and strung-out I step off a Manchester pavement, duck under an up-and-over sliding door, and into the abandoned Haçienda. It seems Cathedral-vast and atmospherically cool in the unsympathetic wash of afternoon.

Cabaret Voltaire is a multi-pack of projects. Cut-ups, Mix-ups, disinformation, information-scrambling. Mal is on stage submerged in murky monitor echoes, a drizzling ugly leaden pulse, like out-of-synch rough cuts for a bootleg snared on a Sony Walkman. He's playing to disinterested roadies and soundmen. The screens are expanses of whiteness. The sound spectrum tilts and modifies in fragments and fractures around

the constant tonal core of Mal's guitar. Noise annoys. The bass-line emerges gradually as Why Kill Time (When You Can Kill Yourself), a hypnotic and probably meaningless lyrical repetition from the *Crackdown* album — side one track three. Later it will be illuminated by flickering slides of burning tanks. There will be strident strip-cartoon montages of monochrome, Kodachrome, and film noir. There will be Richard Nixon and Arab voices, a time-lapse Rayographed hand, mug-shots of Dylan (Isle of Wight festival phase), the Ku Klux Klan… and Kennedy. But now it's all shaved back to voice and bass, and a slight dissolving rill of feedback that goes nag-nag-nag.

Now, across that stage/audience interface of snaking black cables, luminous green digital numbers and inflamed cherry-red flicker-bulbs I'm descending into the guts of the Haçienda. Down a square black Meccano-style metal staircase that Test Department could probably make an album out of playing. Down level one there's a projection cell strewn with film-cans and equipment. Down level two there's the polite and well-modulated pre-gig warm-up, sans decadence or the usual related Rockist fripperies (or sans *most* of them anyway!). The assembled cast goes something like this: first up is Charlie Collins, hirsute saxist from the magnificent Clock DVA/Box, crumpled low against one wall. Pete Hope's there too, along for the ride. Claude Bessy, club vee-jay, cat-paces up and down between them, slouched in stylishly relaxed Gallic charm and a green flack-jacket. He sequences and co-ordinates the screens, mixing culls from Kenneth Anger's *Scorpio Rising* with 1940s RKO musicals, James Brown with Laurel & Hardy, Hong Kong martial arts with the Cab's Yashar (Dance Mix). There's a side-table of salads and cold-cuts, an hospitable ice-box of Pils and Coke. Mal is deep in conversation with Karen. She's stunning and aloof, effortlessly decorous in abbreviated white shorts and dark tan.

Alan squats beside me, completely unthrown when at first I fail to recognise him. But then, he carries absolutely no affectations. He even confesses to stage-fright. It emerges that, career-wise he's now going in three simultaneous directions. He's studying architecture at Sheffield Polytechnic. He's a playing member of the inventive Hula with a Red Rhino mini-album (*Cut From Inside*) to promote. And he's drumming with Cabaret Voltaire. He got sucked into the Cabs on an enthusiasm-high around the time of the *2x45* package, and he's still here. Still high on enthusiasm. Still suffering pre-gig nerves.

Richard Kirk zones in. Did I get the album off Virgin press? Did I like it? "Yes, and yes." I come back with comments about catching the naked soundcheck. The set stripped down sparse and

CABARET VOLTAIRE

6

THE ART OF THE SIXTH SENSE

200 PAGES OF INTERVIEWS / HISTORY / OPINIONS.

58 PHOTOGRAPHS. FULL DISCOGRAPHY. DOUBLEVISION CATALOGUE.

amputated from the sound/vision dialogue of the lightshow. Were the slides and films always an integral part of the Voltaire masterplan? "Yes" he states emphatically. "From our very first live performance we've used slides. I mean, they're not there to detract from the fact that we don't particularly move around much. It's more a case of trying to maintain some kind of standard whereby we always present something other than just a couple of people on stage. It's more a case of creating an atmosphere to go with the music, so it's like you get a total sense of being surrounded by the whole thing — as opposed to just being stood watching it."

It's an obvious step to extend from there into other areas of visual media. The overlaps that first led from 8mm projections, into devising the soundtrack for Pete Care's unique movie *Johnny Yes/No* (for UK Channel 4 screening). Now it's gone as far as launching their own DIY video label — Doublevision. "Video is an obvious way of linking the two aspects" agrees Mal. "We've never seen ourselves as purely a *'group'* that's only able to express itself in sound. It's quite nice that now — through Doublevision — we can utilise the visual side in a more concrete way, instead of just when we play live. We've found a home for what visual stuff we wanted to do."

"When we first started doing things we were pretty naïve about it," Richard resumes. "It showed in the freshness of what we did. We just steamed straight in there with very little technical knowledge... There's a case for saying that the less you know the better it is, because the less you're restricted by formality, by regulations and things like that. We've since picked up a lot by actually *using* that technology. By working in proper editing suites and things."

"The more you know, the more useful it is. You can bring the best out in all the things that you're doing. It's quite nice because now we're in a position where we're getting there with video *and* with sound." Product thus far includes a Cabaret Voltaire ninety-minute self-history. A compilation of pieces in flashing narrative, from Nag Nag Nag (filmed in colour negative), into Eddie's Out and This Is Entertainment (illustrated by computer graphics). From Photophobia, through the blurred landscapes and the smudged prints of Moscow. Fading out in neon. There's also been a video magazine — "a video programme," corrects Kirk. "It's about two hours long, something that you're not really meant to watch all the way through. Just in small doses. Something you can put on at any point and absorb to whatever degree you feel like. Its got a very wide cross-section of material on it, ranging from clips of underground films that have yet to be released, interviews with various people [including David Bowie], and the odd promotional video that we managed to acquire [like Clock DVA's one for Resistance]. As far as the technicalities are concerned, we did two-thirds of the work ourselves, the other third of it was done by St John Walker from the Art College. We supplied a lot of the stock footage for him to use but he actually edited it. That third of it was done on more up-market equipment than we've got. We also managed to secure distribution through Virgin. The release of our first video did quite well. So they took it up for their shops. But we want to keep control of Doublevision, mainly because we want to make our videos available at a price that people can afford, rather than £30 or £40 or something."

As it originally emerged the Cabs video-programme cost just £17. With further releases, including footage of 23 Skidoo and the complete *Johnny Yes/No* movie, slated to follow.

INCONCLUSIVE CONCLUSIONS IN TIME HIGH FICTION

The Cabaret Voltaire fostered a unity which resulted from no act of will, an enthusiasm based on mutual inspiration which started things moving — although no-one could tell what direction they would take.

—Hans Richter writing in *Dada: Art And Anti-Art*

This is entertainment. This is fun.

Life has been getting dull in the solar system. Fashion is out of fashion. The record industry is dying the death of a thousand cults. Perhaps it's time to catch that Cab, make it flavour of the month? But unlike Philip Oakey's telegenics, Heaven 17's paramilitary Disco or ABC's meticulously contrived consumer paradise — all of which relate to exteriors, to audiences — Cabaret Voltaire always remained a hermetically-sealed self-contained unit. All their characteristics are self-referential, all their messages are channelled through a closed-circuit of internal lines. This becomes clear as I come down out of Western Works watched by a late-teen with a tastefully precise crimson flame crawling his right temple. This becomes clear as I duck under an up-and-over sliding door and step from the Haçienda into a Manchester street in the early hours of morning. This becomes clear as I sit at home and watch the *Doublevision* video. A trip-movie of time-lapse rippling blackness, a slow-motion maelstrom systematically and purposefully destroying the context of the events it snares. It deliberately offers no consistent argument, and intends to present no rolling accumulative point of view. It is *not* a sum of its parts. It is instead a demonstration of its motivations. It betrays Just Fascination with its mode of conceptual logic, and no more. The reason it exists is to celebrate the techniques of its construction. The reaction of observers is of peripheral concern, and occurs after the event anyway.

Once that is understood the rest follows easily. Sluggin' Fer Jesus is *not* an attack on religion. That conclusion doesn't mean that attitudes to religion don't exist. Just as Cabaret Voltaire's scrupulous self-exclusion from political stance doesn't mean that those attitudes are absent. Merely that they lie outside Cabaret Voltaire's essential area of concern. What Mal defines as "the Dada-ist spirit and feeling". Within that spirit all images exist to be used. To be abused. To be cut up and disfigured. Motivations reveal themselves through the random juxtapositions so revealed. Their music is not 'about' something. It *is* that something itself. Firm conclusions and exact statements detract from the mystique of that elemental process. Recording is discovery, not performance. Of course, conclusions can be drawn from that. But like Dada, it is no fixed idea — it is attitude. It deals more in the intuitive than the rational.

But that was then, this is now. And now the Cabs are no more. The mass-market breakthrough into mainstream-consciousness never really happened. But their legacy is everywhere. You hear the latest Club Mix from the post-Rave/ Acid House Dance culture, pulsing with sequenced sound-bite samples and relentlessly programmed drums and you go — *yeah*, great, but Cabaret Voltaire were doing this *at least* ten years ago. It was they who laid the conceptual foundation for the real-world growth of all those Electro-Dance digital confections. Without them the world would be different. Current bands I speak to — Leftfield, Moloko, Prodigy, Erasure — speak of them with awed reverence. While CD reissues, compilations and occasional albums of previously unreleased radio sessions help maintain their profile. Richard Kirk is still in Sheffield. Still making challenging electro-based music through a number of aka's, through the good graces of the still-challenging Warp

records. Mal, on the other hand, is rumoured to be perhaps as far away as New Zealand.

I've still got the Doublevision videos. Unfortunately, they're on Betamax.

The biorhythms of the record industry depend on hits at regular intervals. The Cabs' sense of (mis)adventure always resisted that. Listening to each new Cabaret Voltaire vinyl was like walking downstairs in the dark and missing the last step. They never became just another picture in the Pop Exhibition. Instead, they existed in a walled garden of their own devices and strategies. 1983 saw Stevo offering the real deal that locked their new-consciousness industry into the mainframe of Some Bizarre marketing, a slice of Virgin-ity on the side. For their first single through the hook-up they went twenty-four-track and recruited Johnny Luongo, a producer notorious for work with chart confections Blancmange, Michael Jackson, and KC's Sunshine Band. They came up with Just Fascination c/w Crackdown, a neat concise three-minutes-a-side twelve-inch that refused to budge from my sound centre deck for solid weeks. While simultaneously the album track Talking Time instructs 'lesson one / you clap your hands', and the suggestion is hard to resist as they dance, blipping jabs of fizzy electric washes over fast popping mechanical percussion augmented by Alan's planish sheet-metal drumming.

But wait. This was *still* state-of-the-art electric music for the mind and body. And any slight recidivist preferences on my part for the vintage violence of *Red Mecca* or *2x45* should be politely ignored. Despite wildly exaggerated claims to the contrary their changes in 'approach' were essentially cosmetic, more concerned with packaging than product. After all, cynical pundits had been eagerly howling 'sell out' at the Cabs with monotonous and premature regularity for the best part of their career, every time they put some more jive in their stride or some Funk bass lines in their mix. So suddenly you can dance to their albums? So suddenly you can buy them at your local Top Forty store instead of the Indie specialist ghetto? They continue to make highly unlikely Pop stars: from the disruptively worrying spilt music and provocatively dismembered flickerings of their very first live event, through to their single Dream Ticket c/w Safety Zone — cloaked in scratching — and beyond. With commendations from hip technoheads like Steve 'Silk' Hurley, through *Groovy, Laid Back And Nasty* (1990 Parlophone), from House collaborations with Marshall Jefferson into virtually their final real-time product, *Conversations* (1994) — those characteristics stayed constant. And constantly intriguing. Theirs were tactile futures you can smell and experience as well as see and hear. And the gleaming edge of their noirishly imagistic futurism has never rusted or biodegraded. So if they remain household names only in their own households, then that's a situation that probably suits them fine.

Yet you think back to the summer of '84... and Hey, Tristan Tzara — thou shouldst be here at this hour...

© Dogger

THE STONE ROSES
INTO THE NEW
STONE AGE

The planet Mars is paradise... Me? I sold up and moved to Madchester. The rest, as they say, is hysteria.

I'm here, driving up Portland Street. An urban canyon of vertigo-high cliffs; Piccadilly Radio to the left, Britannia Hotel to the right. When WHAAAAMM!!! — my foot slams down hard on the brake, stripping tyre-tread through multiple-G deceleration to a gut-canting dead-halt. A sudden wave of nubiles mass across the lanes, weaving through the traffic-snarl — a torrent of yelling girls rippling with tides of high-decibel shrieks lifted directly from the HARD DAY'S NIGHT soundtrack. A pure-white tour-bus hunched beneath Piccadilly Radio's neon awning, rocked by girls, besieged by girls, crushed on all sides by girls...

I'm impressed. Grab parking space. Up a waterfall of concrete steps. Uniformed doorman yanks the double-doors open. Inside, the Britannia is like the Mothership interior from CLOSE ENCOUNTERS (SPECIAL EDITION). Triple-floor chandeliers downhanging miles of curved stairwells. A guy in tails playing chintzy piano muzak that drifts through the lounge like expensive perfume.

I sit with press liaison man Philip Hill, who drinks a long tall Grolsch lager. He deals a straight handful of bands: Beats International, Deacon Blue, Beautiful South... and **THE STONE ROSES**. *"I'm impressed," I tell him. "Stone Roses must be really huge here in their home town. The girls!" "Naw. They're not here for Stone Roses," he says. "New Kids On The Block are doing a radio promo shot from Piccadilly. The girls are here for them, not us."*

*The past was yours,
but the future's mine,
you're all out of time...*

—The Stone Roses, She Bangs The Drum

 eet the Stone Roses. Another year — another music sensation. Another not-so-much a band, more an attitude. Another earboggling head-butting mindbend of an album to change your life by. Another bid to boost the fine art of consumer spending.

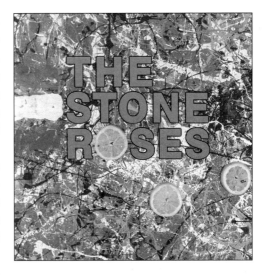

Finding a quality record on the pop chart is still like finding an American flag in Iraq. In commercial terms — who sucks wins, while Indie bands ('HEY DJ, WHERE'S THE TUNE?') are now the losers who set themselves low, low standards and then fail to live up to them.

So why should the Stone Roses be any different? Yet they've made it across the board: in *Smash Hits* teeny town because they give good face, in the NME because they have cult credibility, while the Q magazine mindset can relate to their sweet high-gloss harmonies through race-memories of Love, Byrds, Buffalo Springfield, Rain Parade, Long Ryders...

"Yes, the more the merrier." Ian George Brown. Born February 20, 1966. A stoned immaculate glaze to his eyes of deepest brown. Soft black barbs of basin-cut hair styling a surly Morrisonesque petulance. "Satisfied? Not really, no. Reasonably unsatisfied. 'Cos the album's not No1, is it?"

The album fades in with deep bass, a tinsel of guitar, solid 4/4 drums, and this man intoning "I wanna be adored... you adore me, you adore me", repeated like a mantra, a post-hypnotic suggestion, a subliminal command. So is getting to No1 important? "Getting to No1's good. 'Cos that means you're the top selling record of the week, yes. No-one can take that away from you. But we're not *trying* to get into the charts. We're just trying to make good records." Ian is currently reading *Lipstick Traces* by Greil Marcus.

John Squires plays guitar, a Stratocaster with a big clean sound ("I wash it every day"). He also paints the record sleeves. He speaks carefully and with premeditation. "Being heard, by people — by a lot of people — that's important. 'Course it is, yes. We never wanted to be elitist, or be a cult group. We don't aim at any particular audience. If you aim at something you limit yourself. We're not writing for other people. We're writing for ourselves. But we want as many people to like what we do as possible. Whether it's a fourteen-year-old girl, or a thirty-five-year-old man. If someone's going to appreciate the music then that's enough." John is reading Joseph Heller's *Catch 22*, which he thinks is "really close to the film," adding that "most Penguin Books are good — those Orange Classic ones."

"… And there is a small element of exhibitionism in what we do as well," concedes Reni (drums and backing vocals). Reni is currently reading "glossy men's magazines", and has a fetish for odd floppy hats.

Gary Mounfield plays bass. Signs his autographs 'MANI', decorated with an Acid House Smiley. He drinks Guinness, wears his hair scratched back tight into a tuft of pony tail, and sometimes goes to the Hacienda club. "I saw Vera Duckworth there one Wednesday night. She was singing and what-have-you. She was fucking excellent. A right hit." So can I mention *Coronation Street*'s Soap Opera star as an influence on Stone Roses music? "Yeah. On me personally." Mani is the slum-boy of the group. He's probably reading *The Beano*.

*I'm throwing stones at you
and I want you black and blue,
I'm gonna make you bleed,
gonna bring you down to your knees
… submission ends it all*
—The Stone Roses, Bye Bye Badman

The Stone Roses have come here direct from Wolverhampton crown court. It's not that they're *bad*, it's just that they're drawn that way. And I'm apprehensive — if the hearing has gone badly for the band, perhaps they'll take it out on journalists? "Naw. We won't do that. It's too easy, innit?"

The album charted high. A single from it, She Bangs The Drum, reaches No 36 (July 1989). The loose naggingly repetitive Fool's Gold follows it in December that same year, hits No 8 and sells 200,000 copies. As Made Of Stone and Elephant Stone hike their profile onto a higher plane, their former label FM/Revolver re-issue their years-back Sally Cinnamon to catch the wave. "It's not so much the record itself that we're bothered about" drawls Ian. "It's the video they made to go with it. The video, and the man himself."

"There's nothing wrong with him putting an old record out, 'cos we made it, and we made it for his label. So — fair enough" John elaborates. "But doing a video two years later without consulting us, and making one that we thought was offensive to us as people… 'cos it was, wasn't it?"

"It was really patronising. It was all shots of Manchester, Moss Side, women holding babies, Cola cans, dandelions, people at fruit stalls, Stone Roses T-shirts, the Arndale Centre, the front cover of *The Face*, things like that. It was wrong. So we went down there and told him that we thought it was wrong. But he didn't agree. He thought he was in the right."

"If you'd been there on the night you'd have seen why we fuckin' did what we did. 'Cos the guy was being a completely obnoxious character," Mani cuts through to essentials.

"He's making more money now that he's ever made before, out of us! And we were saying 'what's going on, you're making money out of us', and he's yelling 'MAKE AN APPOINTMENT! MAKE AN APPOINTMENT!' and we, we... decorated him!" Paint cans are famously involved, resulting in a kind of walking example of John Squires splash-art.

"We subsequently got charged with Criminal Damage, and got fined £23,000. But we're contesting that amount. We don't think we caused that much damage. It's just him, trying to do us over again. It was *him* that publicised it all. We didn't intend doing anything further about it. It was just a matter between us and him as far as we were concerned. But ten minutes after he's phoned the police he puts out a press release to the papers, the music magazines, everyone."

"'Cos his record of our Sally Cinnamon was still just outside the Top Forty then. He was hoping to capitalise on it, hoping that the publicity would make that critical difference. That's the sort of tosser he is."

It's the Roses' second hearing on the case. The first — fanwise — was like a New Kids On The Block radio promo. Two girls carved 'STONE ROSES' into the paintwork of a police van parked alongside the court. Today, says Ian, it was "short and sweet inside. Only ten minutes long. The Courtroom was cleared, with only a few people there. We were sent up for further proceedings at Dudley Crown Court in September." Two girl fans appeared later the same day charged with malicious damage to a police vehicle.

I suggest that it's no bad thing for a band to be just a little notorious. "Well, yes, we know that. But we didn't expect all this to happen." And what do you do if a journalist gives you bad press? Do you come round and redecorate *him*? "Naw.

What for? You're entitled to your opinions." Just thought I'd get that sorted out before I reach the contentious questions. Mani leers generously. "No. Call us what you want."

THE SECOND COMING

In the beginning... was the weird. Me? I sold up and came to Madchester.

Manchester is the Hollies. Freddie & The Dreamers. The Dakotas (but not Billy J Kramer). Wayne Fontana & The Mindbenders. Some of 10cc. Buzzcocks. Fall. A third of Crosby Stills & Nash. Slaughter & The Dogs. Magazine. Joy Division. A Certain Ratio. Smiths. The Savoy Holman Hunt African Orchestra. New Order. James. Happy Mondays. Inspiral Carpets. Oasis. A Guy Named Gerald... Candyflip. The Stone Roses are (largely) from Manchester's Chorlton suburb, "two of us from the Southside, one from the North, and one from the East."

Were there other bands before this one? Ian: "No. First one." John: "First and last."

Did you start out doing cover versions of other people's material? Mani: "We don't have any time for doing cover versions." Ian: "It's best to make your own up. More fun, innit? We've always tried to make our own songs, 'cos we couldn't play very good, so we couldn't even learn any of the songs we liked anyway." Reni: "It's very difficult drumming like another drummer. I'm not good enough to play like someone else."

"The first gig we ever played was in London" adds Ian. "We didn't play Manchester for ages. We didn't want to play any of the venues round here. We didn't like them. So we did warehouse parties in London. Hired big places underneath railway arches. Built our own stage. Hung out around clubs, or got our mates to hang outside clubs giving out leaflets with the location where this warehouse party was to be. Then we'd just turn up on-stage at three in the morning. That was 1985 or '86. We did that for a while, then graduated to playing other venues."

Did you do support spots for other bands? Ian: "We *never* support. You're joking, why support? That's a no-ambition to want to support somebody else, to want to warm-up for somebody else. It's a waste of time. We supported some people when we started: That Petrol Emotion at the Riverside in '86, a group called Mercenary Skank — first few times we ever played we supported them in London. But history doesn't dictate that everybody has to start out doing support spots. It's prostituting yourself. Because we'd done it, we realised we hated it. So we stopped. People just nip out of the bar to have a quick look at the support band, then nip back into the bar again. So why do it? We did a lot less gigs because of that decision, but you don't really *have* to do *anything* that appals you. We don't do *anything* that appals us. You do what you think is right."

Even Guns N' Roses play support (to the Rolling Stones on their 'Steel Wheels' tour). Reni: "That just shows you the limit of their am-fuckin'-bition, dunnit?"

The album was recorded at Rockfield in Wales, and The Battery in London. Why not use a Manchester studio, like Strawberry? Reni: "We don't like the chippies near there. Yeah, that's important. Battery is good because they've got a great Afro-Caribbean food place nearby."

"And Rockfield was good because it got us out of the city for a while. A bit of fresh air," says Ian. "You can lie on the hills and watch jet-fighters training. Waiting for one to crash. That's the only distraction." Was producer John Leckie important in realising the album's sound? Reni: "He made sure we all got up at the same time." Mani: "He brought an element of discipline to it. But

he's not a Phil Spector." Ian: "No, he's not into that. He's into getting the best out of what we're giving. He did the knob-twiddling. We didn't like any of the other groups he'd done. We didn't know enough about music to even know whether he'd done a good production job on them or not. He maybe suggested things, and we said no. The songs were already there. On this album everything was put together before we went into the studio. We did them pretty much the same as the demos we'd given him. Who wants to sit around in the studio all day pissing about? All that's not trying to take anything away from what John Leckie did. He did put his own thing on it."

You played Europe early on. Mani: "We did Sweden when we started. That was pretty good. We played to three people one night, four people another night. We go back there soon. This time it'll be a bit better." Reni: "Yes. This time we're aiming for double figures."

"We did Belfast too," comments Ian. "We did six gigs in Northern Ireland. Belfast was excellent. Then we played Dublin, at a place called McGonagles. It was Heavy Rock night. We walked in the place, they were playing Deep Purple's Smoke On The Water, and there were all these Rockers on the floor. Then we came on stage. People were throwing things. People were running up to the stage and going 'Fuck off home, go home'. We couldn't even get into McDonald's later on 'cos we had ear-rings in…" John takes up the narrative, "but our stage sound is pretty good though. Was it in Cologne four people walked out? They said they were disappointed that we were miming to a CD. So I think we do it alright."

Mani: "But drugs and shagging tour stories. Is that what you're after?" Reni: "I cut my finger once shaving, in Paris. I fell over a bottle of beer from the night before, too. Almost banged my head… but not quite! Bruised the palm of my

hand on the radiator as I fell though. But hey —
that's Rock'n'Roll for you!"

STONE ROSES · SO YOUNG / TELL ME

I'll not rest till she's lost her throne,
my aim is true, my message is clear,
it's curtains for you, Elizabeth my dear...
—The Stone Roses, Elizabeth My Dear

Space Fleet Biog notes that sci-fi comic hero Dan
Dare was born in Manchester in 1967.

My friend Eddie describes the Stone Roses
album as being as good, and as important in
its way, as The Beatles and The Stones. (Perhaps
he just means as good and as important as the
single of that title by the House Of Love?)

TV endlessly recycles the past, from *I Love
Lucy* and *Mr Ed* to *The Invaders*. While the charts
are dense with theft — direct sampled steals,
cover versions, remixed reissues, or at the very
least, stylistic recreations of the past. The Stone
Roses reinforce the consistent power of Trad Rock,
the guitar-bass-drums triad that's been around
since the dawn of time, since years BC (Before
Cassettes). The Roses sound doesn't challenge,
affront or startle, it pleasurably soothes and re-
assures. No iconoclasts they. Solid cascades and
glittering flourishes of crashing guitars are laced

in tight by bass figures of immaculate symmetry
and flickering ghosts of colour. The light high
harmonies are as insubstantial as cumulus, as
warm as the summer of love. Class without struggle. How can the mums and dads of sixteen-year-
old Roses fans feign the outrage expected of their
parental role when they have Little Richard, the
Kinks, Hendrix, Jefferson Airplane and probably
the Sex Pistols, all sonically wilder and more extreme, in their own private vinyl stash?

"People always look to the past with every
group. They're always going to do that" argues
Ian, draped decorously across the duvet of the
hotel bed, Room 163. "They said the Pistols were
like The Who or the Small Faces. It's only later
on that people start thinking 'well, maybe they
were originals'. I was never that much into the
Byrds or any of those other bands they compare
us with. I've only really heard their singles on the
radio" (that must explain the lyric to I Am The
Resurrection, which runs 'Turn Turn / I wish you'd
burn / there's a time and place for everything',
right?)

Wrapped in John Squires' Jackson Pollock
splash-art (Pollock's *No 5* also gets as name-
check in their Going Down), the Stone Roses debut album is richly melodic, intelligently mature
mainstream Rock with depth, light and shade.
But — musically at least — it's hardly innovative. "It could be. In two or three years it could
be seen as innovative, 'cos you don't know
what's going to happen. To be innovative it has
to 'innovate' something. And those things are
happening now. There are groups now being
influenced by what we're doing. I'm not saying
it *is* innovative, I'm just saying that it's too early
to say..." John looks out over the vertigo-high
New York skyline, ablaze with fierce constellations of light — there's no window, but surreal
curtains part to reveal this photographic mock-
panorama impression of a window.

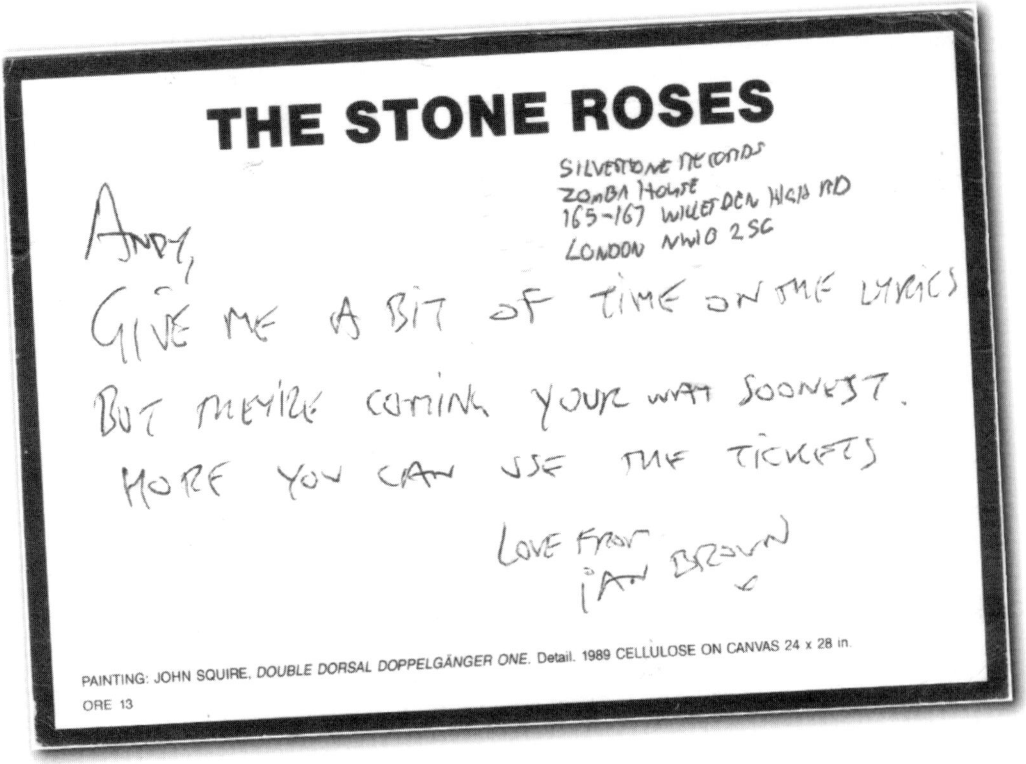

THE STONE ROSES

Andy,

Give me a bit of time on the lyrics but they're coming your way soonest. Hope you can use the tickets

Love from
Ian Brown

SILVERTONE RECORDS
ZOMBA HOUSE
165-167 WILLESDEN HIGH RD
LONDON NW10 2SG

PAINTING: JOHN SQUIRE. *DOUBLE DORSAL DOPPELGÄNGER ONE.* Detail. 1989 CELLULOSE ON CANVAS 24 x 28 in.

ORE 13

I persist, suggesting that Jesus And Mary Chain, for example, also take elements from the past. But they mutate it, disfigure it. I don't see that confrontational ingredient in what the Stone Roses do. "We don't want it," retorts John. But for the creation of Stone Roses product, all the wonders of post-futurist technology are ignored too. (Song For My) Sugar Spun Sister opens with the Pretty Flamingo/Angel Of Harlem guitar riff (prompting NME's Jack Barron to playfully dub them 'U2 on E'). While the album peaks on the 8:12 minute I Am The Resurrection, which opens with a sharp Rolling Stones' drum run, then goes into a long fluid instrumental orgasm which busts Punk's minimalist fatwa while simultaneously basing itself around the Jam's Start bass-figure, building through chakk-chakka percussive dances and polite guitar distortion that runs from a fine spray to a torrent. Exquisite — but trad. Nothing to identify it as happening *now*, no high-

tech, no sampling. "There *are* bits of high-tech stuff in everything we do," says John, "it depends. We utilise it to the extent that you wouldn't notice it was there. And all sampling means is digital recording…" "And anyway — sampling is hardly innovative, is it? It's last year's thing," grins Reni.

But instead they requisition psychedelia's most sacred totem, the most effectively used hail of reverse-tapes since *Revolver*. Mani shrugs. "Some sounds really *surge* and sound excellent, if you can use them properly." There's a Zen sparseness to the room. A TV plays newscasts soundlessly: Strangeways prison in post-riot ruins. Dave Britton's shock-confrontational novel *Lord Horror* on trial for obscenity. Manchester's anti-gay Police Chief James Anderton communing with God.

"Yes. We did use backward tapes on Don't Stop. We were listening to the instrumental tapes of Waterfall over and over again, but they didn't sound quite right. Until we thought 'let's hear it backwards'. So about eight in the morning we put the tape on backwards and thought 'Oh yeah! Let's go home and write some new words for this'. It sounded so good. The result was Don't Stop."

(Elsewhere, their track Full Fathom Five is actually just Elephant Stone played backwards!)

One of John's paintings illustrates Waterfall on the CD liner booklet. A kind of stars'n'daub on the Union Jack (from an original oil on canvas painting 30x26). "You can't always say that a riot of colour illustrates a particular song. But the flag one for Waterfall does, it's about Americanisation. American cultural imperialism." John's vivid visualisation also extends to Sugar Spun Sister which becomes a Miró-red sun slashed by comets and vapour-trail squiffs (32x32), while the front cover — Bye Bye Badman — is citrus rings on blue dribble (31x26.5). The lyrics to that one bathe in 'citrus-sucking sunshine', but the track is also a very pointed attack on... someone in particular? ('I've got bad intentions, / I intend to knock you down'). "No. No-one in particular. Forces of authority in general. Bye Bye Badman — the Lemon Song. That's the one that's to do with CS gas. It's nothing to do with 'squeezing my lemon till the juice runs down my leg'." John's Led Zeppelin misquote deftly shifts attention from the precise relevance of the CS gas reference.

But Ian warms to it. "We met an old man in Paris who told us that if you suck lemons it stops the tears when CS riot gas is sprayed at you. He'd been on the student riots in '68, in fact, in 1970 too. But he was still looking forward to change on the street. And so that he could do something towards that he had this lemon in his pocket at all times. He was older, but he could see longer that way, and he could carry messages back from the barricades through the CS gas without tears — by sucking this lemon. That's the story. It was a unique experience in how to go about

changing the world." And a handy tip for the next Reclaim The Street or G7 World Trade riots!

There are long silences clipping away the seconds. There are armed police in lines of Perspex shields across the TV. The Stone Roses conspicuously lack a gob-on-legs. There's no hypospeak, no talking the band up. Stone Roses don't usually write about issues either. "We do write about issues. It's just the way we put the words together that makes that not so obvious. We don't write rubbish. Sometimes there's maybe ten different things all going on in the same song. We write about everything that we see, and everything that we wanna see. The imagery that comes from the words pieces together in the listener's mind, that's what is important, not the ideas that I'm trying to give you by talking about it afterwards. It's the total thing. It's not a poem written on a piece of paper. It has sounds and feelings too. The imagery might just as well come from the guitar. It spoils it to break it down and describe what each line is supposed to mean. If it's unclear then I'd prefer it to remain unclear. When I like a song, but maybe I'm not too clear on the words, and I hear the group saying that it's about the time they did this and this and this — or maybe even ten years after they've written the song they trivialise it by explaining it's about 'this' — it ruins the mystique for me. It makes it less personal."

Reni agrees. "Maybe sometimes the best way of describing what you feel is already there in the song, so to go outside the boundaries of the lyric is to cheapen the song." But you don't appear to deal with social or political issues. "We do. The whole LP is full of them."

I didn't make those connections. "You missed out, then." What exactly did I miss? "The social issue connections. Freedom is an issue. That's what they say to me. They're all 'freedom' songs. Every one of them." But 'freedom' is just another word from a hit record by George Michael! "We don't sing about the Labour Party. Billy Bragg and Clash have done that already. Writing a political manifesto within the music seems pretty shallow to me. It's like chest-beating. I don't think there's a place for it in music."

"A lot of people have got a lot of different ideas about what a lot of our songs are about" volunteers Mani. I see them more as abstract. Like a Jackson Pollock splatter-painting. "Life's abstract" says John with Zen-like sparseness. "It's only abstract if you don't understand it" challenges Reni.

I like the hard urban poetry of Made Of Stone. I quote the lyrics, 'sometimes I, fantasise / when the streets are cold and lonely / and the cars they burn below me / are you all alone? Is anybody home?' Then the line 'I'm standing warm against the cold / now that the flames have taken hold' — it works as powerful imagery. But what does it *mean*? "It means what it says." A long silence in which a car explodes in a rage of flame on cue on the TV. Beirut? Belfast? "It's a death-wish." A longer silence. "Sometimes it's good if you're not sure what the lyrics are. Some of them are fiction. Some of them aren't. Elizabeth My Dear is pretty direct. Most of them aren't as direct as that one." Yes. The Royal Assassination song, side two track one on the vinyl edition. A sweet fifty-nine-second rewrite of Scarborough Fair that closes with 'it's curtains for you / Elizabeth my dear', followed by a soft gunshot in the fade. "The sneaky sniper shot from behind the curtains, yes."

Monarchy has been one of the Stone Roses' main points of media contention, thus far. Anti-Royalist comments in an earlier interview provoke a storm of righteously indignant tabloid *Sun* hacks to besiege Chorlton. "You can't really be in trouble with *The Sun* though, can you?" reasons Mani reasonably. "They'd have to have an intellect to trouble you with in the first place."

"Yeah — yes," yawns Ian. "They were round my Mum's, bugging her, knocking on her windows. But the press thing is inevitable in a way, that's what we're here for, for people like them to have a go at. The more you go up, the more they want to cut you down. But no, I'd say mine were 'mild' opinions as far as I'm concerned. I just said what I thought, that Royalty are the lynch-pins of most things wrong with this country. They are the 'symbol for a nation'. The Royal Family is the symbol of health for the nation, the mum-

and-the-dad and the kids. And it's all hypocrisy. That's the sad thing. The lies have been pumped into people so long that they don't know what the truth is any more." Already I'm warming to this band. Of course it *is* insulting that monarchy should still exist. They should get back into the history books and fairy tales where they belong. I'm with the Bolshevik policy on this issue.

Mani cuts to essentials. "They should get straight to fucking Strangeways. To what's left of Strangeways after the riot!"

"They've got the backlog of history against them" says Reni, by way of summing up. "That's the Royals for ya, wrong 'uns!"

ONE LOVE

Manchester. As I expected, the trip was no picnic. Stone Roses: another year — another music sensation. The rest is hysteria.

Top Of The Pops dribbles anaemically onto the TV screen. "Who's the token Indie band this week?" "Oh no, it's Pat & Mick!" (a PWL duo who hit No 9 in March 1989 with I Haven't Stopped Dancing Yet, fact fans.) "I love Pat, he's great. Not so sure about Mick, he's a bit dodgy."

It's not so long since Stone Roses were miming Fool's Gold on this very show, vamping the cameras, giving good face, hair shimmering and slip-slithering telegenically. Success has been a seamless glide thus far. Even Shaun Ryder (of Happy Mondays) concedes "the Roses are a top band. Their album is brilliant. I play it at home all the time. I wish we'd made it" (NME, April 21, 1990). But Madchester…? "We don't feel part of no scene" protests Reni. "'Scenes' are created by lazy bastards who try to contain everything inside one term. It's just a strange coincidence when lots of different creative things start happening in the same city."

"I don't feel a common spirit with them. But we respect them for what they do" adds Ian. "We feel a lot of rivalry between us and everyone else. And between each other." So does the media create 'Scenes'? "No. They're usually trailing six months behind what's happening." But the press have been good to you, with Stone Roses splash covers everywhere. "No. *We've* been good to *them*. We allowed them to put us on their covers. Anyway — Phil Collins never gets good press. But he does pretty well."

I've never interviewed Phil Collins. What questions would you ask him? "Ask him why he's such a prat." "Ask him why he doesn't give the royalties from Another Day In Paradise to the homeless." "Tell him he looks shorter than he does on television." "Ask to borrow his comb…?" But writing about Phil Collins from the point of view of follicle-loss and receding hairlines is like basing a critique of the Stone Roses around their use of flared trousers. Cheap trend journalism. "Yes. You're right. It's juvenile."

And trends are like drugs. When you're vertigo-high, you can only come down. What happens in six months when Manchester is no longer news? "Ambient Skiffle" says Mani, unfazed by the prospect. "The great Skiffle revival. Lonnie Donegan. Derek Guyler on washboard. It could happen!"

"We'll go on for as long as it's good. Could be three years. Could be thirty. We could be Francis Rossi. The Status Quo of the year 2012. I want to live till I'm a hundred…"

THE STONE ROSES was the perfect sixties album. As luminously era-defining as, say, Love's FOREVER CHANGES but stripped of its sugary strings, with a harder healthily anti-monarchist edge. A harder softness. But where do you go from the perfect album? You don't. For no matter how good the next one is — and make no mistake, SECOND COMING is better than good — and despite Seahorses and Primal Scream, that moment is never going to come again.

This moment. Now.

*But they were right and I was wrong. I admit it. The Stone Roses —
if not exactly innovative — were influential. For here we're talking
cusps. And that day in Manchester was situated precisely on several
of them. Without the Roses, chances are there would have been no
Oasis, and hence no Brit Pop — the century's (and probably Pop
music's) final flirtation with guitar bands.*

*But New Kids on the Block were there, too. And without them there
would probably not have been the Boy-Band phenomenon... but that's
another argument to do with consumerism and merchandising. Personally, I'm with Beck on the Boy-Band thing. It would be nice if
one of them eventually aspired to create a PET SOUNDS. After all,
vacuous posterboys with sub-Presley quiffs and cloned sneers were
hardly uncommon in the 1950s, and the mind-numbing dullness of
glitter-pretty early seventies teeth'n'grins were legion. And conveyer-
belt Pop? Larry Parnes and Joe Meek knew something about that. As
did Howard-Blaikley later in the sixties. And Chinn-Chapman. And
Stock Aitken Waterman... but that's another book entirely.*

*In the meantime I watch Ian Brown in the 'Radio One: Evening
Sessions' tent at the Leeds 2000 Festival doing a cover of Michael
Jackson's Billie Jean, and I watch Mani on the main stage with Primal Scream, and I remember them sat in that hotel room taking the
piss out of Morrissey on TOP OF THE POPS. "November Spawned A
Monster... a monster what?... A monster FART!" Delivered to collective hilarity.*

© Dogger

SKUNK ANANSIE
STOOSH...
AND ANTI-STOOSH!

"I think it's a black girl! With a mohican!!" He's (almost) right. It's the back of the Indie tent at the Carling Festival, Leeds. The taller of the two is leaping up and down for a better view over the undulating crowd at the inaccessible mosh pit, and the stage beyond that. Passing commentary down to the smaller of the two. What he can see over the mass of heads is **SKUNK ANANSIE***, and Skin, a girl with a confrontational stylee that goes from vowel movements to bowel movements and back again. You can taste the difference. The Skunks are the Damien Hirsts of Brit Pop, taking the dead sheep of Metal, R&B and Soul, and suspending it all in a formaldehyde of angry energies. For example: Don't Want Your Charity runs a Funk groove of Soul vocal across Ace's spine-shivering Steve Cropper-esque guitar, followed by the metallic assault of Here I Stand (built around what I swear is the T Rex Children Of The Revolution riff). "Yeah. Nice one," says Skin. Twice. Then, during the Dance and combat Rock fusion of I Can Dream, she exudes confidence, radiates attack and itches with mischief. She pogos up and down, enabling the guy at the back to see her single-striped shaven head. Voluptuously stuttering rhythms lurch and tweak around uncontrolled lyrical substances clear on through the anthemic Intellectualise My Blackness, a blood-and-guts voodoo manifesto so different you can taste it. She goes "we only know one more song". They encore with Just A Cliché, and then kick the drums over. For the guy at the back who can't quite see over the mass of heads: imagine something a little like an animated* TANK GIRL*, but with a better soundtrack.*

Now, a year and some later, my back's up against the wall. The door shut tight. Just me, a complimentary bottle of tequila, and four Skunk Anansies deep beneath the Leeds Town & Country club. "What did HOT PRESS *say about us then? THE BASTARDS!" demands Skin. I'm here to interview the band. Coincidentally, the current issue of the magazine commissioning the piece is mercilessly slagging off their album. I breathe deep, and quote from the review phrases like 'flash-bastard fretwork... poodle-headed plank-spankers... piss-weak polemics...' Cass leans forward, dreads tumbling around his face, smiling with sinister menace. "Let's go and KNIFE 'im! YEAH!"*

Then we get to specifics. We're talking STOOSH*, the second Skunk Anansie album. The first —* PARANOID AND SUNBURNT *— had a certain rough clit-Rock charm, and shifted 200,000 units in the UK alone.* STOOSH *by comparison, according to Peter Murphy's* HOT PRESS *review, is nothing 'more magical than four musos licking their chops in an overpriced recording studio'. "Oh, I see — EXCUSE ME!" protests Cass, coming as close as it's possible to get to vocalising italics. "We're supposed to stay in the gutter where we come from. I GET IT! We're only REALLY credible when we're suffering — LOOK, you can see every one of their ribs. LOOK AT THAT!"*

I feel it's safe to exhale around about the time the guffaws begin.

ame planet. Different dimension. Actually, I quite like *Stoosh*. It's not perfect. But by nature Skunk Anansie are spiky, combative, unpredictable and adventurous. With those kind of pluses I can take a little imperfection. The soundcheck comes at a playful 'if it ain't hurting, it ain't working' volume. While between the walls of noise guitarist Ace plaintively quips "two pints of lager and a packet of crisps please" in twisted tribute to the time-lost Splodgenessabounds.

They prowl through most of the scheduled set, then throw in some extras. From the storming aggro-Rock of Yes It's Fucking Political, through the Top Twenty hit All I Want, to its follow-up Twisted (Everyday Hurts). There's also the twiddly delicacy of Infidelity, with the seductive absurdity of a holographically simulated string quartet hovering somewhere in cyberspace around us, and Hedonism which they don't actually do live — yet ("we're just warming that one up. Just practising. Getting it ready"). Quizzed elsewhere about its hidden lyrical meaning Cass attributes it to oral sex — as in 'head-on-is-*mmmmmmm*!' Political? You could say that it is to serious political analysis what Paul Gascoigne is to Mar-

riage Guidance (more about that later). Call it divine inspiration, strategic sound-balancing, or call it luck, but here at Leeds butts get righteously kicked and knickers get well-twisted.

Skin's a charismatic and unlikely sex symbol. She contorts each song into a documentary of her life and hormones, as though she's assumed the curious responsibility of living through the extremes of our time, to record exactly how they ache. It is the mission of amiable bassist Cass, drummer Mark (this is his first album as a Skunk), and guitarist Ace, to give her crazed kookerama a metallic and richly narcotic undertow. And occasionally they achieve brilliance together.

Theirs is an Indie Houdini genre-straddling sound. For example, on the *ITV Chart Show*, their videos figure confusingly in the upper regions of both the Rock and the Indie Top Tens. "That's because we're on an Indie label [One Little Indian], but we're a Rock band," explains Cass patiently, "so that forces us into both situations." "But we write Pop songs," adds Skin brightly.

"So we get on *Top Of The Pops*, too. Hooray! But that could be our saving grace. Because once you fit within a category then it's very easy to dismiss that category, isn't it? That happens with *any* category, from Heavy Metal to Brit-Pop." "So that's it. The Music Industry has a short life-span. And if it's just a small period of hard work — *let's do it!*" "You've got plenty of time to rest when you're sixty-five," Mark switches to a quavery old man voice.

Stoosh is an album of sonic sleaze that enters and inhabits madness, overloaded with toad-licking weirdness to the point of collapsing under the strain. But Skunk Anansie are a band who remember Splodgenessabounds. Punk is their history. And there's a strong vein of agitprop Punk-by-numbers mischievousness underlying it all. Fitting, therefore, that they should tour Australia supporting the reanimated Sex Pistols. "The Pistols tour? It was pretty good actually," admits Cass. "We were touring with a band three-quarters cool, and one-quarter cunt." No more specific than that? Which Pistol is the Neurotic Outsider? "Use your imagination!"

Stoosh ends in loops of manic laughter.

SKIN GAMES

If men come from Mars (as novelist John Gray claims they do), and women come from Venus, then Skin probably comes from Saturn — via

Brixton. Cocooned here in the virtual reality oddness of this hall we can construct whatever illusion we want. She's catwalk skinny. Pectorally challenged. Allegedly bisexual. And she wears tight leather trousers. She has a woollen hat pulled so low that the focus is not so much the confrontationally polished smoothness of her cranium, as the finely defined features of her face. In fact, she's deceptively attractive up close.

She talks tight, fast, and unexpectedly low.

Track one is a four-way band composition called Yes It's Fucking Political. A noses-front, soak-up-the-pressure, apply the killer instinct howl of snot-and-visceral-volume. Peter Murphy complains of its 'gratuitous over-use of the F-word', but then — *excuse me* — the song *is* dealing with the infinitely greater obscenities of political injustice. So what's the big deal about a few strategic expletives?

In the Leeds drizzle outside the club a cluster of band-stalkers yell loudly over the PA fade for Skin. She can't resist stalking across the hall's vast emptiness to talk to them, clasp hands and sign the various things they thrust at her. There's an Amnesty International stand here too. She pauses to read the neat stacks of atrocity leaflets, and signs posters of the band in support of their cause. Of course it's fucking political. Everything's political. But there's more to Skunk Anansie than just full-on stuff. "It would probably get a bit linear after a while doing it just that way" explains Cass. "That's our *real* ace. The *potential* of Skunk Anansie".

"We do get lots and lots of negative response because of the politics in our music, and because of that first song on the album [Yes It's Fucking Political]," says Skin. "But I wouldn't say that — as a band — we're *that* political. There are many, many more bands around who are more overtly political than we are. But they don't have a front-person that looks like *ME*. Some people have a problem getting around that."

Cass: "They assume that the make-up of the band has more of a political inclination than it has. D'y'know? Even if we're not singing something political, or even if we're not saying anything political. It's just the way that the band's made up. It has political ramifications." Skin: "But we're just four people who are on the same vibe. Into music. We didn't set out to look like... oh, we've got to have a black person and a white person and..." Cass: "Yeah, yeah, do you know anyone with a Mohican? We need a Mohican in the band! I mean, if we'd operated from that angle we'd have a Chinese person in the band, too. We would."

"Or we'd call ourselves Chessboard. Alternating black and white, y'know!"

But let's get to specifics: there's something here I can't get a line on. There's a song on *Stoosh* called She's My Heroine ('for her lies, she's calling / she's crawling, smashed you in the face / up against the wall / still your secret's safe'). Is that about anyone I should know? "It's about a situation. A personal situation." Skin comes over suddenly reticent. "There's nothing political in the song whatever. It's like on the first album there were lots of songs that are not political. It's just a song about a person who... y'know, who you crave for. That craving can also destroy."

"It's about Wonder Woman, innit?" suggests Ace.

"That's the double-edged sword song" adds Cass mysteriously. "The one that says 'She's my Heroine' because 'she's my saviour' or 'she's my downfall'. That's the mark of a good song anyway, because it has that ambiguity to it. It can relate in a million-or-one different kinds of situations. It doesn't *have* to be read as happening in the same situation that it was written about. You can take it out of context and it still makes sense. 'Genius' I think they call it!"

I persevere. But is it a particular person? "Yes" from Ace, "but we're not gonna tell you who." "Well, okay," concedes Cass grudgingly, "it's about *Virginia Bottomley*?" I attempt to ape the spirit of the jest in the interests of interview-continuity. So do Virginia Bottomley's policies influence any of the other tracks — Pickin On Me, for example, the semi-acoustic school bully song which Skin wrote with Len Arran? There's various current affairs angles on that about disruptive pupils, Conservative party moral panics, and the possible reintroduction of corporal punishment to discipline unruly youth.

"No. We won't talk about Virginia Bottomley," sulks Skin. "It was a *joke!*" stresses Cass, "and now you're killin' it. Are you Swedish?"

So Skin, were you a disruptive pupil? "I was for a couple of years. I wasn't a bully or anything — just the person who disrupted the class. But that didn't really last a long amount of time. I just did that, then I knuckled down on my studies and forgot about all that rubbish. The song is about a boy I was at school with who was the kind of person who got pleasure out of treating all the other little kids badly. I had lots of fights with him, taking up other people's causes. And it was just like looking ahead ten years from that. He's going to be a politician, or a policeman, or he'll join the army or something. It's that kind of mentality. And it's just about where that kind of mentality comes from."

It's a theme that in some ways shocks back to the very first Skunk Anansie controversy, when Radio One picked up on My Little Swastikkka, about the way racists indoctrinate children ('who put the little baby Swastika on the wall? / it's not very high / couldn't be more than four-years-old'). " The other context is that if you see other kids picking on someone and you don't help them out, when that person gets *you* in their power they're going to be beating on you next. It happens all the time. They 'picked on' people with Clause 28, so later on we had the Criminal Justice Act, right? We had all this information about Clause 28 — how it was picking on gay minority groups — but lots of people didn't get behind that situation. So then they thought they could just 'pick on' youth in general. And the Criminal Justice Act came along. It's like — yeah, they're able to pick on you now because earlier you didn't support someone else. But if you kind of just stand on stage and shout that kind of cliché at people it doesn't work. We won't do that. Because we don't like that being done to us. We won't listen. It's just like chanting 'BLACK AND WHITE UNITE' — it's like, yeah, but what does that actually *mean*? How are you going to achieve it?"

"It's more real to say blacks and whites *come together*," suggests Mark, putting the letch into intellectual. "Haw haw haw haw!"

OF COURSE IT'S FUCKING POLITICAL

Tonight we discuss the phenomenon of hooliganism. Armed gangs of youths have taken to the streets, looting shops…
—Media sample fade-in to *Stoosh*

Rock'n'Roll is the nation's favourite blood-sport.

Skunk Anansie do more than most to unsettle its complacency. The first album includes Funk-Metal assaults like Blood And Guts ('it takes blood and guts to be this cool / but I'm still just a cliché'), Intellectualise My Blackness and Nigga Rage, which Skin aims at "the Anglo-Saxon Old Boys Network whose worst nightmare is an intellectual nigger". To those who accuse Skunk Anansie of being to serious political analysis what Paul Gascoigne is to Marriage Guidance, it's this kind of material that says Yes It's Fucking Political. And in this light, do journalistic attacks — accusations of 'Stratocaster circle-jerks' and 'irritating ads for Anadin-Extra' — have an effect?

"Erm, no. Not really" says Skin. "When we did this album we were very kind of happy about it. We think it's a brilliant album, y'know. But we knew that after a while people were going to discredit it, because that's what happened with our first album. It's like, 'yeah yeah, it's really a great record', but then after a while everyone kinda goes 'ah, but it's not *that* great'. But then it eventually reaches a yet further stage of 'oh shit, it's really great after all'. And that's one of the reasons why we can't take the press too seriously. Because if you believe, or if you run your life, or if you think you're as *bad* as the press sometimes say you are, you won't last very long. The press are very fickle. We just go in and out of fashion. When we did our first album we tried to make it sound the best we could at the time. But we made lots and lots of mistakes, so it cost more. This album was actually cheaper to make, which just goes to show that what looks and sounds expensive can be deceiving, and we just love it a lot. I mean, you just learn how to get better sounds in the right way. We know more what we're doing now."

"The truth of the matter" adds Cass, "is you don't want to sound like greenhorn novices, or sound like you're at the beginning stage of your career *all* your life. That's rubbish. Because then you won't progress."

"Also, you're being dishonest really. It's that kind of 'make it sound shit so the critics will like it' thing, isn't it? It's good if people don't expect us to do the same album over again. Because we haven't. Perhaps it's that which has riled some other people up the wrong way? But tough… we prefer to do it that way. You can definitely look at Skunk Anansie as a band that are kinda shaking things up quite a bit. We invoke very strong reactions. We're not a band that just plods along selling a few records here and a few records there, always nice and happy and smiley. We definitely aim to shake things up a bit, and we're definitely a band that's gonna be more in your face..."

"Time's up," says Ivan, exploding into the room suddenly. "The other interviews are waiting. I'll bring the Radio Something one down here, then you can do the other two press things upstairs." The room's suddenly full of people, simultaneous conversations and mad shadows. "Radio who?" asks Cass. Mark sings "BBC Radio One" to no-one in particular.

Skin goes: "You'll find out when they sit down." And I go for one more shot. Track ten — Milk Is My Sugar — whatever the Hell is *that* one about ('thy shall convert me / my favourite sin / meat, make it snappy / snap back and thigh / good work for Pellow'!).

"What's it about?" muses Cass agreeably, "it's about breakfast." Then: "Hello darlin'" to a record company girl who's just entered. "Hello Lee, alright?" Lee starts into a "Did you get my fax before you left..."-type spiel and the song-theme gets temporarily lost. Then back to me: "Does that answer your question? About Milk? What did *you* think it was about?" There's a very fine Left Wing poet called Adrian Mitchell who wrote a powerful pacifist poem called Peace Is My Milk.

"And you thought there was a tenuous connection? Naw. Haw haw haw haw." "Way off," guffaws Ace.

"It's filthy," leers Mark. "It's a filthy song that one. Disgusting. Dirty. Sleazy. Filthy." "Why 'disgusting dirty sleazy and filthy'?" protests Cass in mock outrage. "It's about sex. It's about *sex* — I don't see the connection of sex with 'disgusting dirty sleazy and filthy'."

Lee decides to join in the debate. "It's saying things about *him*, though, isn't it?" "Ah, so it's a subconscious thing. *I get it*," nods Cass knowingly. "So what you're saying is that to *you* — sex is disgusting dirty, sleazy and filthy?" "Yes. If you do it properly. Yeah."

The interview fades out in endless loops of manic laughter.

The third Skunk Anansie album, POST ORGASMIC CHILL *(March 1999), as the title suggests, represents something of a cooling off period for the band. After which... splitsville. And Skin (Deborah Anne Dyer) went on to* CD *assignations with both Black Sabbath guitar legend Tony Iommi, and Motorhead's Lemmy!*

© Dogger

RADIO ANNIE NIGHTINGALE AT THE WICKED SPEED OF SOUND

The million radio channels of globalised Earth are roaring open. Bursting out in a vast and expanding sphere of static and gibberish up there beyond the vinyl planet-roll horizon and now out somewhere edging past Sirius. Even now — as I write and as you read — early broadcasts are being downloaded by confused Klingon-esque organisms drifting in hellish gas giants with temperatures of molten lead, provoking stylish pseudopods, claws, fins, or tentacles to twitch and tap rhythmically and irrationally to strange Be-Bop Hip Hop Rockabilly alien backbeats. Joe Meek achieves his ultimate escape velocity as he's translated into intergalactic trash-twitterings, along with all the other records that shaped my life:

Elvis' Girl Of My Best Friend — the first record I ever bought; The Electric Prunes' I Had Too Much To Dream (Last Night) — the greatest 45rpm single of all time; Smokey Robinson & The Miracles' staggering work of heartbreaking beauty, The Love I Saw In You Was Just A Mirage; The Byrds' Eight Miles High; The Ramones' Beat On The Brat; Prodigy's Outter Space; The Kinks' Days; Augustus Pablo's King Tubby Meets The Rockers Uptown; Fleetwood Mac's Green Manalishi; Television's Marquee Moon; The Yardbirds' Happenings Ten Years Time Ago; Flamin' Groovies' Shake Some Action; Jefferson Airplane's White Rabbit; Sex Pistols' Holidays In The Sun; Bo Diddley's You Can't Judge A Book; Jan & Dean's Dead Man's Curve; Bob Dylan's Just Like Tom Thumb Blues (Live); Human League's Being Boiled...

Plus every stupid B-side, cheap guitar lick, and raw sax solo by session players whose names I'll never know, every drum program, brain dead profound-dirtbag lyric and shivering keyboard run that's momentarily illuminated my life... and the DJs who played them. The catalysts. The interface between creator and consumer.

So what makes a DJ? What made **ANNIE NIGHTINGALE** *— Radio One's first and longest surviving female DJ — into a DJ in the first place? And what qualifications do you need to be a DJ? I read the book, sat in on the show, and even found time for an interview...*

HAT MAKES A DJ? Even now, they hang out there in the drizzling darkness outside Broadcasting House. Annie's tribe. Annie's own personal fandom. Multi-racial, street-stylish, effortlessly cool even there, even excluded from Radio One's inner sanctum. In fact there's more people *outside* the studio than there are *in* it. "Exactly" she purrs agreeably. "This is *it*! There's nobody else *here*!" She mimes a sudden dramatic about-face, *"Maybe I shouldn't publicise that fact? There could be terrorists out there listening!?"* Relax, panic's over. "But no. We have Claire, the producer. And we have people who come in to answer the phones. There she is — say Hello to Natasha." Natasha, in short skirt and Doc Martens, turns and waves. "So there's just the three of us here. And you. But I'm not complaining. I love what I do. To have two-and-a-half hours of total radio freedom is *vital* to me." As all around us the white noise billows and Neolithic bass-lines shudder, threatening eardrums and bowels alike.

I'm here to investigate the woman Jo Wiley describes as "the original DJ-bird", on the oc-

casion of the book that celebrates her thirty-year on-air career with One FM. And tonight Annie Nightingale is warm and concerned, fulsome with 'that's-a-good-question'-type encouragements. She looks you in the eye directly and unwaveringly, fixing your attention, only her upthrust cleavage providing distractions on a deeply primal level. Desperately maintaining that eye-contact, I mention I've been reading Mark Radcliffe's *Showbusiness: Diary of a Rock'n'roll Nobody*. It's a fun read, too, even if you don't learn a great deal about the art and craft of being a DJ from it. Whereas that's exactly what you *do* get from *Wicked Speed* — Annie's decade-spanning autobiographical retrospective. "Mark's a lovely bloke, I'm very fond of him, though I haven't read his book yet. And yes, people *do* ask me 'what's it like?' They want to get some idea about what this stuff is all about. Maybe that wasn't Mark's intention? Maybe it was not his brief to do that. But I've done a book before [*Chase The Fade*, Blandford Press 1982], and I thought, well, why not? That's one of the reasons I decided to leave the Diana section in..." Annie was on air when the first garbled reports from Paris began to filter through. There'd been an autowreck. But the 'People's Princess' was okay, she was in hospital. Then — no... the story developed by the minute. How was she to react? What tone to adopt? "It all happened *here*" she stresses now. "And the whole thing kind of focuses exactly what it's like when you have a situation like that. I went back and wrote it there and then, just like a diary, while it was still very fresh in my mind. The immediacy of the occasion, and exactly how it felt. I thought it was important to do that. Then I thought 'we'll see if this still makes sense in six months time'. So I used that, rather than just describing an ordinary day in the life of Radio One. At least it says that was what happened *then*."

WHAT MAKES ANNIE NIGHTINGALE A DJ?
Have you heard, it's in the stars? Or perhaps it's genetic, but it never occurred to her "that being a DJ meant being *A Bloke*. A Bloke with A Very Large Ego". Similarly, it never occurred to her that "DJs were all men because that was the way

they *wanted* it, because they regarded themselves as sex symbols in exactly the way male Pop Stars did". Do. That was true of the 'Personality DJs' of the mass 1970s BBC audiences who saw radio width-band popularity as a necessary first step towards TV celebrity. Just as it's true of the Chris Evans laddish *Loaded* mindset, one which Sara Cox seems to have taken on-board. Annie was always different. And she still is. For her there's no studio 'posse', instead, hers is an intimate one-to-one-with-the-listener radio style, providing what *Trainspotting*'s Irvine Welsh describes as a 'surrogate cool big sister' ambience. "You never know who's listening, you really don't," she confides. "I even had an e-mail from an Astrophysicist in Belgrade saying 'I listen to your show'. I've been desperately trying to find his e-mail address to get back to him! Thing is, we go out on this thing called the Astra satellite. And people listen in some pretty weird countries under all sorts of extraordinary circumstances. So we say 'ring in'. Now obviously with e-mail you reach out across the world to people"... while all around us a phalanx of avant-garde hipsters crank up the beatbox through sequences of Underworld's frenzied full-on attack, through Barry Adamson's pensively ambient interventions, into Electrotheque's brutalist meltdown.

Annie's gene-code for all this is far from obvious. She was, she says, a 'fat untidy-looking child', then an 'ugly teenager' — a self-judgement scarcely borne out by photos in her book. But we'll let that pass. She's also deliberately vague on dates, except to stress that she was 'a proper teenager, rebelling against a society that I really abhorred'. Think early-to-mid 1960s. Instead, she muses on why such "a typical middle-class suburban girl from such a typical middle-class environment" should have "yearned so passionately for adventure and felt so different in my expectations from my contemporaries?"

97-99 FM **B B C** RADIO 1

The answer she predictably provides is 'Rock'n'Roll politics'. Delving deeper, she's a 'product of the North-South divide'; her father's family, based around Richmond Hill, strongly disapproved of the Northern 'lavatorial humour' of her Lancastrian mother's side of the family. While her mother, who trained in chiropody under the *original* Dr Scholl, sacrificed her career ambitions to conformist 1950s gender expectations. Perhaps there are clues there? But yet again, such easy socio-biological clues get messed-up further by the fact that her father, it seems, 'treated his only child as a *person*, both as a girl *and* as a boy'. "He gave me the expectation that I could achieve anything I set my heart on". It was he who bought a 'tiny white Bakerlite radio' and taught little Annie to be 'meticulous about tuning it precisely'. The resulting knob-twiddling led to her discovery of 208 Radio Luxembourg. And from that to Chuck Berry, through

to her bohemian phase of Dave Brubeck, Jean-Paul Sartre and Paul Klee, through — I suppose — to the legendary excesses of her Montpelier Road home in Brighton, where Keith Moon and Primal Scream partied and the Orb DJ-ed in her front room... to here. Now. In the techno-warrens of Radio One's Great Portland Street studios mixing a chemistry set of sounds, from the delirious groove of Red Venom's Let's Dub It On, through the lurid manicured noise of Urban DK's Risk, into the meanest leanest most inscrutable electronics of the Chemical Brothers' Life Is Sweet, and on.

But isn't 'DJ' a weird sort of job description? "I know. I know. It sounds ridiculous really. People used to come in and look and say 'Yes, but what do you actually *do* for a living?'" Coming down to bare essentials, isn't the DJ the interface between the music and the audience? The person who puts the needle to the record, or the laser to the CD... or whatever the Hell it is? "Yes. That's right." But also, over the years she's been doing it, the job-definition has changed and evolved, all the way from Smashey & Nicey — to Arman Van Helden. "It's changed immensely" she concurs. "Now there's much more to it than there was. We don't have engineers to balance the sound any more. And it's all vinyl..."

"We get sent all the newest promo vinyl" adds Claire brightly, "and the levels are all over the place. Technically they're a nightmare. That's why I prefer listening to it direct off the radio rather than through the desk, that way I can better tell what it sounds like."

"Although I do play some CDs, as you can see," says Annie. "So we have to *do* a lot more, and there's a *lot* more to do. But then, that's the way of the world, isn't it? Less people working much harder."

Okay, so you're a rocket scientist. But is it interactive? As Martin Clunes once said, 'do the audience play half the music'? Should radio DJs merely follow the ratings-pull of their listeners' taste, or take the riskier course of trying to create that taste? Does she ever get pissed off with music? There are different answers to fit different decades of her career. And there have been three of them: the *Sound of the Seventies*, the cult eighties *Sunday Request Show*, and now (what I like to call) the Sunday Morning Dance-arama. Along the way there's been much coming and going of her on-air colleagues, such as Janice Long, Liz Kershaw, Mary-Anne Hobbs, and Zoe Ball. But there's always been Annie. Radio One's first, and arguably greatest, female DJ. Some people dance across decades and make a nonsense of categories.

She shrugs an engagingly shucks-who-me? shrug. "I've just got this great enthusiasm about what I do. There are new Fool's Gold mixes around now which are huge club records. And I'm actually reading a book about the Stone Roses as the moment," she adds. "God, you need to know your Manchester for that. But you see, there have always been people like that. People who just manage to jump across genres. And I'm listening to new stuff all the time. Now I've found this label called Whole Nine Yards — a name derived from an American football field, I believe. They just take it on a bit further." Her own Dance compilation — *Annie On One*, issued through Heavenly Deconstruction Records in the mid nineties — took her own hands-on involvement still further. But is this Dance scene possible without performance-enhancing 'Ravers Little Helpers'? Even a polite but perceptive John Peel was moved to ask if Annie had, er, taken E's, as he'd noticed the quantum shift in her programming output. She side-steps, "child-birth gave me my first experience of hard drugs" she explains, quoting the NHS-friendly pethidine as the culprit.

WHAT WILL MAKE YOU INTO A DJ? And I think of Annie's tribe, even now, hanging out there in the vibrating darkness outside Broadcasting House. Annie's own multi-racial, street-stylish, effortlessly cool personal fandom, hanging out waiting for an opportunity to meet the bands, the DJs. That might have been Annie. After all, that's the way she started out. "It was. I really did that. Sometimes they do it 'cos they want to get into broadcasting. And it's a good place to start. It *does* work. It's this whole thing I say about the 'you'll do nipper' syndrome..." *Wicked Speed* explains how Annie began in local journalism, graduated into regional broadcasting, and finally into Radio One through this process of 'being there'. Hanging out. Helping whenever the opportunity arose. Biding her time. Watching and learning. Until, in a crisis situation, she became the only candidate capable of filling in — hence what she defines as the 'you'll do nipper' syndrome. "For example, Natasha's keen to get on at the BBC. And I'm sure she will. She's the kind of person who doesn't mind coming in at ridiculous hours, because you actually learn an awful lot. It ruins your Saturday night. So, you have to be adaptable. But, you want to do it? You want that job? Well, you *work* for it!"

Back to definitions. Getting historical for a moment, around the time of the first House Music explosion the role of DJ split off into two separate disciplines. There's the 'mindless-chatter phone-in traffic-update'-style radio presenter. And there's the club DJ, who plays the decks like musicians play their instruments. "Exactly. And I think it's so fantastic. *These* are the new heroes. I mean, being a club DJ is a completely *different* skill to just being a broadcaster. They don't *speak!* Generally they don't say a word live. That is not their thing. But people like this guy who's on at the moment [Carl Cox], they are megastars..." She inhales with awe at the pugilistic pulse-pounding plethora of beats coming from the speakers. "These people work so brilliantly, using their equipment exactly like an instrument. We had the Scratch Perverts in here some time ago, it was all done live, and it was *terrifying* to watch. They do it with such *incredible* skill. That's why House and Acid House are such important movements. That kind of innovation, that scene, came out of the [US Housing] Projects, out of people who are deprived, as usual. That music is all they had. And I thought by now there'd be lots of Channel 4 documentaries about it. But there hasn't really been any. That's another aspect to it... there's a lot of bits that I didn't manage to fit into this book. There was a piece in *The Independent On Sunday* about a club called Lush in Northern Ireland, where all the Catholics and Protestants are seen dancing together. It seems that these clubbers have done more to sort out the Troubles there than any Peace Process. And I thought, if those people can do that, that's phenomenal. So I'm going there in a couple of weeks, and I might just sort of hang around for the weekend. 'Cos I want to write a film next. I wanna do a film, very much about that aspect of it... But I still love what I do. And I think about it all week. To have two-and-a-half hours of total radio freedom... it's *vital* to me..."

Wicked Speed
by Annie Nightingale
(introduction by Irvine Welsh)
ISBN 0-283-06197-9 / Sidgwick &
Jackson, 1997 / £15.99

Also by Andrew Darlington

Euroshima Mon Amour
Sci-Fi poetry 'from the inner mind to the outer limits'
ISBN 0-905262-27-1 / £3.99 / Hilltop Press, 4 Nowell
Place, Almondbury, Huddersfield, W Yorks, HD5 8PB

Beast of the Coming Darkness
Science Fantasy novel (forthcoming)

thoughts & words
my back pages

To me, it all begins like the introductory sequence from that James Bond movie, *Live And Let Die*. You know the one: the stately dignified funeral procession through the streets of New Orleans. The guy who asks 'Whose funeral is it?' And they say 'yours'. Then, once they've killed him and stowed his corpse in the coffin, the procession erupts into incandescent jazz. And that's how the music of the twentieth-century began. Black marching bands in multi-racial New Orleans, departing from the script into uncharted realms of improvisation around Blues notes and African rhythms. From there to New York and Chicago it spread out to engulf the world, carried on the accelerating momentum of global consumerism, until by the 1940s it intellectualised itself out of Pop altogether and into Bebop, allowing the mainstream to re-immerse itself in those same Deep South USA Blues roots to re-emerge as Rock — which stayed around against all the odds through to the end of the century. And into now.

But think back — erase and rewind — to all the unimaginable wealth of creativity and trash, inspiration and vacuity, beautiful simplicity and magical complexity that grew from those first few euphoric inspirations. And if its permutations have now about run their course, then somewhere in the world there's probably a group of musicians working in isolation and for the pure Hell of it, who are — without realising — laying down the basis for an as-yet unimaginable music-form that will spread out and dominate this new century as Jazz and Blues and Rock did for the last. Perhaps it will be some technologically-driven variant of electronic music growing out of Dance, with 'downloading' eroding the major label market hegemony. Democratising it. But more probably it will arrive in some form we can't yet imagine. A new coded message going around the planet. A new ethnic formulation erupting out of the culture collisions and collusions thrown up by economic migration or mass settlement due to internecine war, environmental degradation — or global warming.

But hey, the future's not ours to see. What will be, will be. I hope I'm still around to see it. And that I stay aware enough to be a part of it. If only as a member of its audience.

It's bound to be a great trip...

Index